Cultural Socio

Series Editors: Jeffrey C. Alexander, R. before ... inglis, and Philip Smith

Cultural sociology is widely acknowledged as one of the most vibrant areas of inquiry in the social sciences across the world today. The Palgrave Macmillan Series in Cultural Sociology is dedicated to the proposition that deep meanings make a profound difference in social life. Culture is not simply the glue that holds society together, a crutch for the weak, or a mystifying ideology that conceals power. Nor is it just practical knowledge, dry schemas, or know-whow. The series demonstrates how shared and circulating patterns of meaning actively and inescapably penetrate the social. Through codes and myths, narratives and icons, rituals and representations, these culture structures drive human action, inspire social movements, direct and build institutions, and so come to shape history. The series takes its lead from the cultural turn in the humanities, but insists on rigorous social science methods and aims at empirical explanations. Contributions engage in thick interpretations but also account for behavioral outcomes. They develop cultural theory but also deploy middle-range tools to challenge reductionist understandings of how the world actually works. In so doing, the books in this series embody the spirit of cultural sociology as an intellectual enterprise.

Jeffrey C. Alexander is the Lillian Chavenson Saden Professor of Sociology and Co-Director of the Center for Cultural Sociology at Yale University. From 1995–2010, he edited (with Steven Seidman) the *Cambridge Series on Cultural Social Studies* and from 2004–2009 (with lia Adams, Ron Eyerman, and Philip Gorsky) *Sociological Theory*. Among his recent books e *The Civil Sphere* and *The Performance of Politics: Obama's Victory and the Democratic ruggle for Power.*

on Eyerman is Professor of Sociology and Co-Director of the Center for Cultural Sociology Yale University. His areas of research include social theory, trauma, and memory, and has taught undergraduate and graduate courses on these topics. He is the author of *The / assination of Theo van Gogh: From Social Drama to Cultural Trauma.*

David Inglis is Professor of Sociology at the University of Aberdeen. He is founding editor of the journal *Cultural Sociology*, published by Sage. His recent books include *The Globalization of Food* and *Cosmopolitanism.*

Philip Smith is Professor and Co-Director of the Yale Center for Cultural Sociology. His recent books include *Why War? Punishment and Culture*, and *Incivility: The Rude Stranger in Everyday Life* (coauthored) among others.

Interpreting Clifford Geertz
Edited by Jeffrey C. Alexander, Philip Smith, and Matthew Norton

The Cultural Sociology of Political Assassination
Ron Eyerman

Constructing Irish National Identity
Anne Kane

Iconic Power
Edited by Jeffrey C. Alexander, Dominik Bartmański, and Bernhard Giesen

Seeking Authenticity in Place, Culture, and the Self
Nicholas Osbaldiston

MEANINGS OF LIFE IN CONTEMPORARY IRELAND

WEBS OF SIGNIFICANCE

TOM INGLIS

Softcover reprint of the hardcover 1st edition 2014 978-1-137-42912-4

First published in 2014 by
PALGRAVE MACMILLAN®
in the United States—a division of St. Martin's Press LLC,
175 Fifth Avenue, New York, NY 10010.

Where this book is distributed in the UK, Europe and the rest of the world,
this is by Palgrave Macmillan, a division of Macmillan Publishers Limited,
registered in England, company number 785998, of Houndmills,
Basingstoke, Hampshire RG21 6XS.

Palgrave Macmillan is the global academic imprint of the above companies
and has companies and representatives throughout the world.

Palgrave® and Macmillan® are registered trademarks in the United States,
the United Kingdom, Europe and other countries.

ISBN 978-1-349-49171-1   ISBN 978-1-137-41372-7 (eBook)
DOI 10.1057/9781137413727

Library of Congress Cataloging-in-Publication Data

Inglis, Tom.
    Meanings of life in contemporary Ireland : webs of significance /
Tom Inglis.
        pages cm.—(Cultural sociology)
    Includes bibliographical references and index.

    1. Values—Ireland. 2. Meaning (Philosophy) I. Title.

BD431.I465 2014
306.09415—dc23   2014019086

A catalogue record of the book is available from the British Library.

Design by Newgen Knowledge Works (P) Ltd., Chennai, India.

First edition: November 2014

10 9 8 7 6 5 4 3 2 1

For Carol

Contents

SERIES EDITOR'S PREFACE

CONTEMPORARY CULTURAL SOCIOLOGY EMERGED THREE DECADES AGO, struggling against macro-sociologies that conceived society in external, objectivist, and deterministic ways. The search for theories and methods to reconstruct the meanings of social life has meant looking on the inside, at the subjective sense of things, at actors' own views of themselves and their worlds. Yet, as the project of creating a cultural sociology advances, it must resist the danger of turning inward, neglecting the external environments of action. The *Meanings of Life in Contemporary Ireland* avoids the Scylla of objectivism and the Charybdis of subjectivity. Tom Inglis shows that open-ended, in-depth interviews, selectively conducted and theoretically informed, can provide data for a historically informed, cultural-sociological account of an entire society. He also demonstrates that phenomenological and semiotic reconstructions of codes, narratives, and symbols, far from displacing accounts of power and stratification, actually allow these disturbing distortions of the human condition to make sociological sense. More than a major theoretical and methodological effort, this work offers a new empirical understanding of contemporary Ireland, a nation subject to unusually intense religious and economic transformation. Inglis brings the human condition alive, and the social environment that constrains and enables it as well.

JEFFREY C. ALEXANDER

PREFACE

MOST OF US IN THE WEST HAVE REALIZED THAT WE NO LONGER LIVE IN an age when we believe that there is only one definitive meaning to life. However, there are fundamentalists who are adamant that they have a total, universal explanation of life and how to live a good one. The rest of us live in a stew of bewilderment, confusion, and doubt as we stumble toward the only certainty, death. And nobody knows what happens when we die. There are those who are convinced that there is life after death. Others believe that there is just this being. There is no God, no heaven, and no hell.

We live in a scientific, secular, postmodern age. Whether we know about God or not, we do know that matter is made of atoms, that we can predict the weather over the next twenty-four hours with increasing certainty, and that smoking increases the risk of cancer. Most of us live in societies in which there is a separation between religious and political rule. And we live as cosmopolitans recognizing and accepting that what is true and meaningful for one person may not be so for another.

We develop a knowledge and understanding about the meaning of life from stories around us. Many of these come to us through the media, through newspapers, literature, songs, films, radio, and television. Others come from personal experience. We learn how to tell stories about ourselves, what to emphasize and what to leave out, and what words to use. These stories become part of our identity and sense of self.

Some stories are apocryphal; they have a deeper meaning and resonance. They reach out across generations and say something meaningful to perhaps millions of people. Nations, families, and communities are built around stories, shared collective memories that bind people together. But most stories that we hear in our everyday lives are transitory, local, and personal.

Most of us live in a cocoon of family, friends, colleagues, and neighbors: we only get to hear a tiny proportion of all the stories that are told each day. Many of the stories people tell have similar themes. They are about who they met, what was said and what was done and by whom, or what was strange, startling, and upsetting. They are stories about happiness and pleasure, sadness, pain, and suffering. They reveal the nature of unfairness and injustice, love and tragedy, success and failure. They are a reminder that life has many different meanings. We hold on to these meanings and truths. They help us communicate and collaborate. They bind us together and prevent us from falling into the abyss of meaninglessness.

It is difficult, at the best of times, even for people who are extremely close to each other to get close to one another's experience and understanding of the meaning of life. We can listen to what people say, but there is always a gap between what they say and what they feel and experience. Language is a medium: there is never an exact correspondence between what is said and what is felt and understood. Much is lost in translation. We often rely on nonverbal signs and gestures to read and understand the moods and motivations of loved ones. We use tried and trusted words, often in the form of aphorisms and catchphrases, to try to name and describe our experiences and understandings of life. "Do you know what I mean?" In this sense, we never develop an exact understanding of the experiences and meanings of others. We only develop an approximate understanding.

In a struggle to discover the meaning of my life, I began to develop an interest in what other people in Ireland considered as the meaning of their lives. My wife, Aileen, died in 2005. Her death turned my taken-for-granted world upside down. All that was solid about my beliefs and values seemed to melt into air. At the same time, I realized that whatever meaning I had developed in my own life was inevitably similar to that into which other Irish people had been socialized. We had used the same cultural ingredients, and we had constructed similar identities and stories about ourselves. To discover the meaning of my own life, I had to try to discover the meanings in their lives. And, so, during the years 2008–9, I interviewed one hundred people in Ireland trying to discover what was important and meaningful for them. During the time of the interviews, I was in the middle of writing a memoir, trying to discover how Aileen and I had come to be the way we were.

On the one hand, there may be some who might feel that having my own intimate concerns meant that I may be prejudiced during the interview process, and that I was far too involved to develop any sense of objectivity or detachment. On the other hand, it is difficult, if not impossible, to have a meaningful conversation with people about the meaning of their life if they do not think that you are genuinely interested in what they have to say. I had to be careful to balance my detached scientific self, which wanted to develop a rich, deep understanding of the meaning of the participants' lives, with my more emotional, caring self, which wanted to connect with them and, as much as possible, "step into their shoes."

The possibility of "stepping into the shoes" of others was made more difficult by the fact that I was, at the time, in my late fifties, an academic, and came from a professional middle-class background. However, what made it easy for me to understand what my participants told me was the meaning of their lives was that I was brought up in the same culture, I knew how to read and adapt to different people, how to respond to what was said and done, and how to interpret gestures and "read between the lines" of what was said in response to my questions.

THE PARTICIPANTS

I tried to interview as many different people as possible. As mentioned elsewhere, my goal was to get a cross-section of men and women, of different ages and from different social backgrounds. (For a more detailed account of the methodology, see the Appendix.) I confined the interviews to five different areas:

Mayfarm, a predominantly working-class, inner city area of Dublin,

Hillbrook, a large county town,

Castlebay, a rural area in the west of Ireland,

Greyrock, one of the satellite villages that developed around Dublin in the last thirty years, and

Falderry, a third-level college in the suburbs of Dublin.

OUTLINE OF THE BOOK

Meaning is both subjective and social. To understand the way people are suspended in webs of meaning that they recreate each day, I begin with a detailed description of the everyday life of Angela Doyle, one of the participants. I then place her within the context of the structural transformations and long-term processes of change in Irish society and culture. In this way, we can see each of the participants as unique, yet somewhat the same and, yet again, in many ways, very similar to each other.

Chapter 2 sets out the theoretical and methodological issues and problems in trying to capture the way meaning operates in everyday cultural life. It uses Angela Doyle as an empirical coat hanger on which these issues and problems can be analyzed. How do we understand what people say and do, and how they are shaped by culture? The chapter begins with a discussion of what social meaning is, and how it is related to subjective meaning. While it is necessary to try to develop some understanding of subjective meaning, it has to be located within the context in which action takes place and, at the same time, within the social structures and long-term processes of change that frame action. In addition to this attempt to link the micro with the macro, it is also necessary to place the attempts to create and sustain meaning within the struggle to attain power.

Chapter 3 examines the importance of place, family, and socialization in the creation and maintenance of people's identity and sense of self. It begins by looking at the influence of place. Many participants were still living in the areas in which they had grown up. The attachment to place is often strong despite poverty and other social problems. Family life is woven into community to create strong webs of bonding and belonging. It can vary between being happy and supportive to being a site of emotional turmoil and conflict. But whatever happens in the family has a lasting affect on people's identity.

Social life in contemporary Irish society is deeply embedded in consumer capitalism. People have to balance their needs and their interests in earning a living with those of bonding and belonging. Chapter 4 explores the differences between webs of meaning that are oriented more toward collaboration and fulfilling more material interests and those oriented toward love and care. It focuses on the cultural repertoires of business people, people in the public sector, and those at the margins of—or those who are excluded from—the labor market. There is, however, a general recognition among the participants that relationships of love and care are more important than money and success.

People's lives are shaped by the political field in which they operate, particularly by the state. The question for an Irish democratic society is how people engage in the political field. Chapter 5 begins by exploring the nature of political engagement in Irish society, giving a brief description of the history and structure of the Irish political field. It then describes the type of engagement in politics among the participants. The motivations and strategies of those who see themselves as political leaders are examined. Party-political people are contrasted with radicals and intellectuals. However, most of the participants saw politics as a game that they watched and followed in the media and did not participate in much, other than by voting at elections.

As in most Western societies, sport has become a major part of contemporary Irish culture. Chapter 6 begins with an analysis of this growth. It examines the role and function of sport in everyday life. I argue that while sport cannot be seen as "the new religion" in Irish society, it fulfills many of the functions that religion has performed in the past. The chapter then goes on to look at the influence of sport in the lives of the participants. It shows how, for many of them, sport is central to their personal identity, and how it develops social bonds and a sense of belonging. However, for some participants sport had no importance at all.

In chapter 7, the religiosity of the participants is put within the context of the changes in Irish Catholic culture and society. The decline of the dominance of the Catholic Church in the religious field is described and analyzed.

The majority of the participants grew up as Catholics. I have divided them into four types: Orthodox, Cultural, Creative, and Disenchanted. Emphasis is given to the spiritual and moral lives of Orthodox Catholics, their beliefs and practices, and their relationship with the institutional church.

One of the main findings of the study is the move away from the definitive explanation for the meaning of life provided by the Catholic Church to more open, fluid, ambiguous, and often contradictory explanations. For the majority of participants, the webs of meaning in their lives are spun from a central hub of meaning built on love and care for others. Chapter 8 outlines the ingredients of love and then describes some of the main love stories encountered during the study.

In the conclusion, I go back to the issues and problems of trying to capture the complexity of the webs of meaning within which Irish people are suspended. To be in any way successful, such an attempt has to try to capture the subjective meanings of the people who spin the webs and, at the same time, place the webs within the context of the structural transformations of Irish society and long-term processes of social change.

ACKNOWLEDGMENTS

THE PEOPLE WHO CONTRIBUTED MOST TO THIS BOOK CANNOT BE mentioned by name. Ethical concerns require that they remain anonymous. Over the past few years, I feel that I have come to know the hundred people who welcomed me into their lives and allowed me to interview them. I have spent hours and days reading the transcripts of their interviews. They came, as the expression goes, from all walks of life. And yet they were all generous, kind, and gracious in giving their time to me. Reaching into the heart of their lives was a strange and exhilarating experience. Any success that the book achieves is a reflection of their willingness and ability to bare their souls to a stranger like me.

The study would, equally, not have been possible without the five gate-keepers who introduced me to all these people. They too have to remain anonymous. But they too were all exceedingly generous with their time and made huge efforts to persuade friends, colleagues, neighbors, and acquaintances to let me interview them. It was because these gatekeepers were so well liked and trusted that most participants decided, in turn, to trust me.

I am very grateful to Susie Donnelly and Paola Carrettoni who helped me with the transcriptions. I have discussed and debated the issues raised in the book with numerous colleagues and friends, but I would particularly like to thank Michael Cussen, Manus Charleton, David Blake-Knox, Hugo Hamilton, Mary O'Callaghan, Mary McDonnell, Christien Brinkgreve, Cas Wouters, Stephen Mennell, Aogán Mulcahy, Sara O'Sullivan, and Siniša Malešević. Jeffrey Alexander was from the outset very encouraging and supportive. His comments on an earlier draft were enormously helpful.

I am lucky. I am suspended in strong webs of love spun around family and many good friends, particularly my partner, Carol, my daughter, Olwen, and son, Arron, my daughter-in-law, Jenni, and my two grand-daughters, Isla and Faye.

CHAPTER 1

WEBS OF SIGNIFICANCE

ANGELA DOYLE LIVES IN GREYROCK,[1] ONE OF THE NEW COMMUTER TOWNS that developed around Dublin during the heydays of the Celtic Tiger economy. She is forty-one. She is married with three children. She is a stay-at-home mother. She grew up in the suburbs of Dublin where her parents still live in the same house. She is the second youngest of five children. She has three sisters and one brother. They were all born fairly close to one another. The eldest sister is forty-eight. Although she does not see much of them, she says they are a close-knit family.

As a child, she went to the local primary school and then on to secondary school. She was a suburban girl with lots of friends. She knew her husband, Martin, as a teenager. He lived around the corner. "We used to hang around together...so we know each other since we were sixteen." Looking back she initially said she had a happy childhood: "It was grand, it was fine." But then, almost immediately, she became emotional, corrected herself, and said. "My father was an alcoholic so...it would...[have been] different."

After she finished school, she went to work in a large factory. She moved to another factory and then she and Martin got married. Their son John was born two years later. It was after her daughter Sarah was born in another two years that they decided that she would give up her job and they would move to Greyrock: "The house price was cheap and so I could give up work and be with the children." Martin works as a service engineer and, like many others in Greyrock, he commutes to Dublin to work.

They had one more child, Frank. He is nine. John and Sarah are teenagers. Angela misses her own family, and sometimes she regrets leaving Dublin. But, she says, the "kids love it down here...so there is no way we would move back [to Dublin] even...if we won the Lotto...It would be a real shock for them to move from here." She loves her house, her garden, the estate, and Greyrock. She thinks it is especially good for the children:

> I think it's just…quiet and…you can let them out and you don't have to be worried about them. And they've good friends. This estate is really nice…they can go out with their friends and, you know, the neighbours will keep an eye on them and everything.

Family is very important to Angela. It gives her the most satisfaction in life. She says it is simple. "Happy family, happy kids, and we're all sitting watching a DVD together and everything is happy." She is still very close to her sisters and brothers and her nieces and nephews. She doesn't see much of them, but they preside in their absence. "If there is anything wrong I could ring them and rely on them." She is closest to her younger sister: she phones her at least once a week. She would be on the phone to her mother every day or every second day. She hears everything about the wider family through her. "My mother is the go-between for everybody."

Angela has learnt to understand and deal with her father. Although he is an alcoholic "he didn't ruin it, he wasn't you know, a bad alcoholic…We went to the beach…we went on family holidays…like my mother was sort of in charge of the money so he didn't have the money." She says that her father was drinking "as far back as I can remember." She remembers the time he gave up drinking for a while. They all went down to the psychiatric hospital to talk with him and the psychologist: "We all did it like, we did it for him like…none of us said no…but you know…it's his fault not our fault…you know…he's his own worst enemy, like you know."

Angela has learnt to be honest and open about her father. "Well I tell everybody my father's an alcoholic…I'm not one to hide, you know what I mean." When her oldest son, John, took the pledge at Confirmation, they told him that his grandfather was an alcoholic. But, she says, John hadn't even noticed. Although she is wary of him, she allows her father to have contact with the children. "I trust my father to mind my kids, you know what I mean like…if the kids go up [to Dublin] he'd bring them down crab fishing and he'd go for a walk and he'd have chats with them and everything like that." She has also developed strategies to deal with her father that she has learned from experience, "he's only allowed down [to Greyrock] if he hasn't been out [drinking]."

None of the family is close to her father. For Angela, "he's there, but he's not there." Most of the time, she says "you could say out of sight out of mind." When she was young, her father went away to work. But her mother was always there. She says that her mother was always helping people out, and that she learnt from her the importance of being helpful and kind.

Angela is chairperson of the local primary school parents' association (PTA). When I asked her why she became involved in this voluntary work, she said "I've always liked helping...I don't see the big deal of going and helping people...I just like doing it." However, she recognizes that it has other benefits. She says that it gives her a chance "to meet people and I have a chat...and its gets me out of the house like, and you know." Her involvement in the PTA followed on from her becoming secretary of the local Gaelic Athletic Association (GAA) club:

> Well the children were in the football...the older one joined when he was ten and they didn't have...help, so I started typing up the names...and doing bits like that, and then they asked me to be the secretary. I did that for two years and that was enough. And then I was at the [school] AGM...I'm always with the parents in the school, even if I wasn't...on the committee as such. But I always volunteered to help if there was anything on. So then I was just elected as chairperson...this year.

Although, as chairperson of the PTA, she holds a position of importance in the community, she has no interest in becoming involved in politics. She votes, but that is about all. And when she votes it is for the candidate rather than the party. "I vote for the people that have...done things for the local community...anybody...once they've come to the door and said things and...I know they've done it." Similarly, although she was secretary of the local football club, she has little or no interest in sport. "I'd follow the Irish team and the rugby and that, but other than that, I wouldn't really be into sport."

Angela's life revolves around her family and her house. It is the hub of her activities and her sense of self. She has developed a large mature garden. She mainly grows flowers, but this year, with the children, she has begun a vegetable plot. She also likes to make her own greeting cards. She used to always make things for her children, like costumes. She used to get the children to make their own cards for their aunts and uncles, and then she started making her own Christmas and birthday cards. Now she doesn't buy them anymore. She handmakes them all.

Like many of the hundred people that I interviewed in 2008–9, Angela was worried about the economic recession that had begun to take hold in the country. Being in the public sector, her husband suffered both a pay cut and an increase in the contribution he had to make to his pension. "We were going going grand and then just to have this big lump [of money] taken out, now you're saying 'oh my God.'" She worries about her husband, because he worries about money. "I'd like to have more money just to have the worry gone and not with the way it is at the moment, you know...with the pensions…I'm not saying loads of money, just enough, you know that just you don't have to worry at the back of your head…'cause I'm quite happy with my life, just a bit more money."

Angela struggles with mental health issues too. After the birth of one of her children, she suffered badly from postnatal depression. She let herself go: "When your brain is messed up…when you feel down and everything, you just you don't care really what you look like." She says she gets stressed too easily: "When I'm having people for dinner I get stressed…I'm trying to be less stressed…When I was a secretary [of the club] I was very stressed…and the kids didn't want me doing it anymore, so [that was] another reason I gave it up."

She thinks she is too emotional. When she saw the questions and topics we would be covering in the interview and, in particular the one about suffering any illness, loss, or tragedy, she said she knew that she would start crying. "I don't cry as much as I used to, I'm better…[it used to be] if I'd see a coffin on the telly I'd start crying." She does not like the idea that, if they saw her crying, people would think: "just, [so] you know, Angela's crying again."

As well as dealing with her father, Angela has had other upsets in her life. Six years ago, she had a miscarriage at twenty weeks. Then she became pregnant again, but there was another tragedy. The baby was born dead, and she herself almost died:

> I had a full term stillbirth, well it was thirty-six weeks and I developed a health syndrome which was kidney and liver failure. My liver…stopped, but they got it going again. I was nearly going to be put onto dialysis and I saw the white lights. I went out on the delivery table twice, so that was the biggest tragedy.

She is stoical about it all: "I'm lucky to be alive, and if it was me that died and the baby survived, there's four kids without a mammy."

Angela is Catholic. She believes in God and she reaches out to him through Catholic prayers and rituals. "I mightn't say nice things to him but I do talk to him." She does not think much about whether Jesus is the son of God: "I'm told he is and…I haven't been interested in whether he was or not, but yeah he is." Similarly, while she believes in the teachings about Our Lady, she really holds that "it is God, or nobody like." She says her prayers every night: "I'd say the Our Father and the Hail Mary and then I'd say bless my mum and dad and my family."

She thinks that God did intervene and save her life that time she nearly died. She believes in miracles. As an example, she says that when she and Martin went to Lourdes, he went through the water and came out dry. She says she is a little superstitious, especially about magpies. "Well if I saw one now I'd have to salute it [to] cancel my bad luck, you know this sort of way...and then, well if we saw two, I'd say that's grand, something good's going to happen. And then under ladders, I wouldn't like to walk under a ladder now."

There is a strong magical element to her religious thinking. If she loses anything, she prays to St. Anthony and promises him a fiver if she finds it. She also has medals and scapulars. "They bless me, they mind me." She does not think of hell. She believes that everyone goes to heaven. "Heaven is up there and it's nice...It's full of clouds and I'm going to meet everybody else that has died."

Although her children go the local Catholic schools and although they have had their First Holy Communions and Confirmations through the school, the church has little importance for her: "I think I can manage without the church." She rarely goes to Mass. She would go at Christmas and sometimes she would go to her own local church: "I'd go in...like you know, if it's the two babies' birthdays [her miscarriage and still born child], or anybody else who has died. I'd go in and light a candle for them." However, she says that when she suffered the miscarriage and stillbirth, it was not the Church or her religion that made her feel better; it was her husband, her children, and her wider family. The Catholic church is still a major institution in her life, not least because she lives in a society in which 85 percent of people are Catholic. She comes from a deeply committed Catholic family and her children attend a Catholic school in which she is the president of the PTA.

She thinks the church is always asking for money when it has plenty of it. She also has little time for priests: "They haven't got as much power as they used to and I think...for older priests like it's very hard." Nevertheless, she thinks that many priests "think they're God, nearly, you know what I mean that they have this almighty power over you and they don't anymore." Martin's uncle is a priest and "he christened all the kids, he married us, he did the funerals, he does everything in the family for us." But she sees him as different: "He's an uncle so we don't see him as a priest or anything like that."

She says that, in comparison to herself, her younger sister is extremely religious: "She'd make up for all of us in the family. She'd had enough prayers [said] for all of us." Angela narrates the story of the time her aunt gave her a medal; she thinks it might have been of St. Theresa, and she took it from her handbag to show her sister and how her sister "blessed herself and kissed it" because she believes you get "extreme power from it." Angela said that when she saw her sister's reaction, she quickly took the medal from her and put it back in her bag as if she found its potential power frightening.

As with money, success is not important to Angela. She sees success in terms of having a happy family: "Success [is] in my family and success [is] in my kids doing ok…and healthy and happy kids that's important to me." The happiness of her life revolves around her husband, her children, and her wider family; "once there's no stresses around me…[and] I just know that the kids…and Martin are happy. That's what makes me happy."

UNDERSTANDING ANGELA

Angela Doyle has a knowledge and understanding of Irish culture.[2] It has shaped the way she sees and understands the world. She uses it to create and sustain the webs of meaning in which she is suspended.[3] But culture is not closed and stationary. It is perhaps best conceived of as a huge complex reservoir of meaning and understanding that permeates every individual and every aspect of social life. It is filled with millions of cultural ingredients, symbols, words, gestures, ways of being, saying, and doing, many of which have been captured in books, songs, radio and television programs, films, and so forth. Some of the stories are local and national. Others have their origins outside Ireland.[4] Angela makes use of a tiny portion of the culture to which she has been exposed to spin her webs of meaning.[5] As we shall see, while there is some similarity to the webs of meaning that people in this study have spun, while they have made use of similar language, incidents, experiences, and anecdotes, while they have similar stories to tell, they are all different. This is what makes the webs of meaning so complicated. People make use of different cultural elements and then spin them differently to create their own unique webs. We can, then, see Angela as having a repertoire of culture, of different ways of being and presenting herself depending on the acts and scenes in which she is participating. She uses symbols, gestures, words, phrases, and anecdotes to create, maintain, and develop an identity and sense of self. These have been gathered together into different frames of thought. She shifts between these frames of thought, some of which are inconsistent and perhaps contradictory, as for example, when she talked about the Catholic Church and its priests. She uses all of these different cultural ingredients, these repertoires, strategies, and frames, to create an overall personal cultural style.[6]

To understand Angela Doyle, we need to understand her within the context of how Irish people use culture to create webs of meaning, to create identities and a sense of self, of what they talk about, the way they talk and present themselves, and of what is important and meaningful to them.[7] We need to develop a feel for what it is to be Irish. But we also need to develop an understanding of how Irish culture has been shaped by changes in social structures and discourses (e.g., the penetration, of consumer capitalist society and liberal-individualism), by shifts in the balances of power between institutions within social fields (e.g., the growth in the power of the media and the state in the religious field and the decline in the Catholic Church's monopoly over morality), and by long-term processes of change such as globalization and informalization.

To understand Angela Doyle we need, then, to understand the culture in which she is immersed and how it has changed. We need a rich, thick description of what it is like to have grown up and lived in Ireland. Most of our understanding of Irish culture comes through forms of high and popular cultural products, from philosophy, art and literature, and from films, radio and television programs, newspapers, music, and so forth. These give us good insights into Irish culture, into the minds and hearts of Irish people, and the meaning of their lives. However, they do not produce a systematic picture. They do not have a framework for gathering pieces of evidence. Producers of these cultural products want to capture the meaning and feeling of what it is to live in Ireland and to be Irish; they are less concerned about the validity and reliability of what they say. Often there is a sense of capturing the truth, of revealing the moods and motivations of people— they, so-to-speak, are deemed to "hit the nail on the head"—but there is no concern to formally or rationally test the truth of what they say or write.

Concerns for systematic arguments and making valid and reliable statements about Irish culture, whose truth can be tested, tend to come from the humanities and human sciences, for example, from literary critics, historians, linguists, and from anthropologists, sociologists, archaeologists, geographers, philosophers, psychologists, and so forth. Although human scientists may have the same interests and concerns about meaning as those who work within the humanities, what makes them different is the methods and theories they use. Historians, tend to look for clues in archives, to concentrate on gathering and assembling facts, and to avoid using abstract general theories in their search.[8] This is what makes general historiography different from, for example, a Marxian approach in which social life is interpreted in terms of social class, a labor theory of value, the means of production, the state, ideology, and so forth.

There are fine differences in the theories and methods that human scientists use in the attempts to capture the meanings of life in Irish culture. Anthropologists tend to avoid abstract general theories and use more focused concepts in their search for meaning. Moreover, they tend to look for clues not within a whole country but in one particular place, perhaps over a number of years.[9] They usually immerse themselves in the culture, learning the language, the beliefs, values, ways of being and seeing, practices, and rituals that comprise everyday life. Many sociologists, on the one hand, will often use abstract general theories to look for and examine any

clues within long-term historical processes of change such as moderniza-
tion, globalization, secularization, individualization, and informalization.
Other sociologists use social surveys, interviewing people using standard-
ized questionnaires, as a means of increasing the validity and reliability of
their findings. This enables them to make accurate statements about the
population as a whole. On the other hand, some sociologists like me, who
have previously conducted large-scale social survey research, realize that,
particularly when it comes to discovering the meanings of people's lives,
there is a need for an in-depth, qualitative method that uses a less-structured
approach and a more flexible and open schedule of questions.

CHANGES IN IRISH CULTURE

People get used to looking at black-and-white grainy photographs when they
want to understand the past. So too, with Ireland in the 1950s, photographs
are a reminder that the past is, indeed, a different place and that people
did things differently then. They reveal not just changes in the standard
of living, the sparseness of homes, and different fashions, tastes, and lifestyles, but also differences in the way people presented themselves. There
is a mixture of humility, shyness, and awkwardness in front of the camera,
combined with more formal, often austere, poses.

Sixty years ago, Ireland was a relatively homogeneous society. They majority of the people were white, English-speaking, and Catholic. They lived in
rural areas and small towns, did not finish secondary school, had access only
to national radio and television, and rarely traveled abroad except for those
who went back and forth to Britain, where they lived and worked. In many
respects, Ireland was neither fully traditional as, for example, were some of
the islands of the West coast, nor fully modern as some of the multicultural
cities of Britain.[10]

Culture revolves around creating and sustaining meaning and, in most
cultures, the bedrock of meaning is religion. Religion provides a model *of*
life—a total explanation of the meaning of life—and a model *for* life, that
is, for how life should be lived.[11] Many anthropological studies carried out
in Ireland during the twentieth century portrayed Irish culture as deeply
Catholic, conservative, hierarchical, and patriarchal in which sex, desire,
and self were repressed.[12] Culture shapes individuals not just through ideas,
values, beliefs, and attitudes but also by instilling desires, moods, and motivations. Irish Catholic culture instilled not just a loyalty and commitment
to the institutional church and its teachings and practices, but also a view
and understanding of what constituted a good life and a good person. People
used Catholic language, metaphors, and symbols to develop and maintain a shared understanding of life. A strong commitment to family and

community was linked to a culture of self-denial. The body became the site of penitential practices of repression and mortification. Expressions of self were limited and controlled through external forms, particularly through strategies of humiliation, belittling, and teasing, which led to and reinforced internalized self-restraint.[13]

From the 1960s onward, the strong Catholic shell that had encased Irish culture began to crack. The main force of change was the gradual shift in employment away from agriculture toward manufacturing and services. The Catholic moral economy that had revolved around family, community, and self-restraint gave way to an economy based on growth, ambition, success and, with it, an increased emphasis on self-realization through taste, lifestyle, and consumer preferences.[14] The protective shield of censorship and the prevention of the expression of non-Catholic thought in the public sphere, particularly the media, began to be penetrated through changes in legislation and increased reception of foreign radio and television stations. Increased penetration of the market and advertising into everyday life led to a moral economy based on the fulfillment of desire and conspicuous consumption. These changes were reflected in family life, particularly in child-rearing practices.[15] Women became less dependent on Catholic culture. They did not have to embody church teachings and rhetoric to attain honor and status. Mothers no longer encouraged their daughters to be like them. More importantly, they did not encourage their children to join the religious life and become priests, nuns, and brothers. This meant that in successive generations the ability of the church to maintain Catholic culture in schools, hospitals, social welfare homes, and in wider society through local and national associations began to decline.[16]

Over the last sixty years, women began to distance themselves from the images and roles into which they had been socialized by the Catholic Church. Instead of marrying at a young age, becoming a mother, and having (in comparison to other Western societies) a large number of children, many women began to stay on in education, enter paid employment, and stay there even after marrying and having children. Nevertheless, despite these changes, many women, like Angela, took on the role of being a housewife and mother with ease. Angela has been shaped within a culture that sees mothers as the primary caregivers and homemakers. It is a way of being that Angela accepted willingly and, it would seem, without question.[17] She grew up in a suburban estate, married a local boy, and moved to live in another suburban estate, and then gave up her job to stay at home and look after her husband and children. There is a structure and routine to her everyday life that reaches beyond her home and brings her out into the local community. She sees herself primarily as a wife, mother, daughter, and sister. The way she sees and understands herself, the middle-class suburban life she lives, her tastes and preferences, the regular, habitual practices that make up her everyday life, have been molded by institutions and discourses into which she was born, socialized, and continues to live. The norms, beliefs, values, and attitudes that she embodies in her everyday life fit into her routine inter-actions with family, friends, and neighbors. She is at home in the way of life she has developed. She is like a fish in water.

The erosion of the influence of the Catholic Church on Irish culture meant that it no longer held a monopoly on the explanation of life, par-ticularly in relation to suffering, death, and salvation. The secularization of Irish society and culture was reflected in the declining influence of the church over the state, the media, the market, and many other institutions. This is linked to a decline in the obedience of the laity to church rules and regulations, which in turn is associated with the increasing privatization and personalization of religiosity.[18] The decline of the church as a major insti-tution in Irish culture means that it does not shape the lives of people like Angela Doyle, and she does not use Catholic culture as much as a means of building her identity and creating webs of meaning. In the heydays of the church's symbolic domination of Irish culture and society, most people lived in Catholic time and space. Being Catholic permeated their everyday lives. Increasingly, being religious moved out of churches into homes and from within homes into the privacy of the bedroom. At the same time, there was a move away from orthodoxy, to people choosing the teachings, practices, rules, and regulations to which they would adhere.[19]

The secularization of Irish society is linked to the globalization of Irish culture. What is different about contemporary Ireland is the volume and variety of messages and ideas coming from myriads of sources all around the world. Compared to what was available to Angela's mother and father through the radio, television, and newspapers, there is now a constant flow of global culture that her parents and she can tap into. Many of these mes-sages and ideas are not just instantly available but also contain teachings antithetical to the Catholic Church's model for how to live a good life. They also led to a questioning of the church's authority. This enabled, first, the media to ask questions about the church, which could not have been asked previously and, then, the state to conduct detailed, meticulous investiga-tions into church affairs and how it was regulated.[20]

The shift from a Catholic culture of self-denial to a culture of self-expression and fulfillment was not always smooth and easy. For the first 50 years after the formation of the new Irish state, certainly up until the early 1970s, Ireland remained a settled society and culture. The Catholic Church increased its monopoly over morality and its symbolic domina-tion of Irish society. This led to a taken-for-granted, often unquestioned conception of the position and role of women in Irish society, particularly among women. From the 1970s, particularly with the struggle for the empowerment and emancipation of women, there were major cultural conflicts around fertility control, abortion, and divorce, all of which challenged the dominant Catholic view of women, marriage, and the family.[21] Issues that were previously beyond the realm of discussion became a matter of public debate that was often bitter and acrimonious. Ideological positions were defined and defended. These changing cultural conditions enabled different strategies of action by women. Things could be said and done that were not possible previously. There were shifts in the balances of power, between girlfriends and boyfriends, husbands and wives, fathers and daughters. These changes are evident in the strategies of action that Angela developed around her father's alcoholism. What was once hidden away and not talked about became discussed, openly and frankly, with children as well as adults.

In the 1990s and 2000s, the cultural strategies of many people like Angela led them to mix and match increasing emancipation with many of the rituals and traditions of Catholicism while distancing themselves from the constraining rules and regulations of the institutional church. For many Irish Catholics, family life still revolves around children being christened in church, going to Catholic schools, making their First Holy Communions, and receiving Confirmation with most of them going on to be married and buried within the rites of the church. In this sense, Angela has moved from being a more traditional orthodox Catholic—as her sister and parents are—to being a cultural Catholic who, although she embraces a Catholic heritage and "chain of memory," does not see the institutional church as relevant or meaningful in her life.[22]

What has changed is the way Angela sees and understands herself, and how that self-understanding is no longer shaped by the Catholic Church. Her daily life is not lived in religious time. She does not engage in Catholic rituals. Her home is not decorated with religious pictures and statues. The church does not have the same physical presence in her home or in the village. Her daily diet of messages and ideas are mostly secular. She does not think religiously. She sees herself as Catholic, but does not see the church and its teachings influencing her life choices or shaping the image she has of herself and what it is to live a good life. And yet, in many respects, she is not very different from her mother. She has three instead of five children, but her life revolves around them, her husband, her parents, her sisters and brother, her nieces and nephews, friends and neighbors. She may not be as involved in the church or make as much use of Catholic culture, but her sense of what it is to be a good person, particularly a good mother, and what it is to live a good life, has been shaped by the same culture as her mother.

What is perhaps most different is that Angela no longer operates in the same Catholic culture of sin, guilt, shame, and self-denial.[23] She does not think of hell, she does not talk about sin, or about going to confession. She is not ashamed of her father's alcoholism: she is able to talk about it openly and honestly. She enjoys the pleasures and comforts of her home and lifestyle but would like just a bit more money.

The process of secularization and globalization is also linked to informalization. This involves a relaxation of strict rules of etiquette and social controls in relation to the protocols of who can meet who, when, and where, the way people dress and the ways in which they address and talk to each other, and what they talk about. At the same time, there are increased expectations and demands for the expression of emotions, but in a controlled way. Informalization is also linked to a decline in traditional authorities and a closing of the social and psychic gaps between men and women, parents and children, and between social classes.[24] While Angela is conscious about her crying so easily, and feels she needs to control it a bit more, she is not ashamed and, in some respects, she recognizes it as a good thing. She is emotionally attuned and attached to her husband— whom she sees as her best friend—and her children. They sit together to watch films and television. She talks openly with them about her father's alcoholism.

The process of individualization is linked to the decline of institutional religion in everyday life in which people lived their lives as part of an all-embracing ideology within which the self and personal choice were negated. This is especially the case in relation to choice of partners, marriage, separation, and divorce. People have become their own moral arbiters, the judges of their own transgressions.[25] Individuals increasingly construct their own identities and sense of self and create and maintain their webs of meaning within the existing cultural packages of family, religion, media, and the market. Individualization also revolves around people seeing, thinking, talking, and critically reflecting about themselves as individuals. The practice of confession has moved out from the box in churches, to the therapist couch and into the media. Radio and television shows, and many popular cultural magazines, are filled with celebrities talking about themselves, revealing their secrets, worries, anxieties, and concerns.

And yet, despite all of the long-term processes of change that have swept through Ireland there is much that remains the same in Angela's life that does not differ significantly from the culture in which she grew up. She may have let go the authority of religion in her life, but she holds on to her extended family. She balances her commitment to and care for others with a strong sense of self: she sees herself as the master of her own destiny. This requires new ways of thinking and talking about herself. And yet despite the penetration of the spirit of consumer capitalist culture, despite the promotion of liberal-individualism—and the imperative to pursue self-fulfillment, pleasure, and happiness—there is little evidence that Angela has become aggressively individualist.[26] In contrast to the type of rugged, frontier land form of individualism, of being continually reflexive, alert, and ready to face the dangers of global, consumer capitalist society, Angela seems to be softly and gently enveloped in the cocoon of family and community.

While it is important to place Angela within these structural transformations and long-term processes of change, we need to focus on the context within which she spins her webs of meaning. If we could trace Angela's weekly movements in and around her house and garden and, from there, in and around the housing estate and neighborhood in which she lives—the shops, the school, the GAA club, and so forth—her way of being may not be significantly different from her mother's. There are the ritual activities of cleaning, washing, shopping, cooking, gardening, listening to the radio, watching television, reading the paper, talking to her husband, looking after her children, and generally, reaching out, collaborating, helping, and caring. If we could enter into Angela's mind and discover the thoughts and ideas she has while she is doing all these things, they too might not be all that different from those that occupy her mother. Angela may have become more secular, informal, and individualist in her way of being, she may see and understand herself differently, the content of ideas, beliefs, and values she encounters in her daily life may have changed, but she is still rooted in family and community. In other words, the cultural ingredients that she uses to spin her webs of meaning may have changed somewhat from those of her mother, but their structure, the patterns of social interaction, and the ways things are said and done may not have changed significantly. The meanings of life that she inherited from her parents, into which she was socialized, became so deeply embodied that, despite the arrival of new, alternative, and often competing meanings and understandings, Angela still uses these inherited cultural ingredients, particularly when it comes to dealing with the vagaries of life: transition, illness, tragedies, loss, and death. Despite the globalization of Irish media and culture, the dramatic increase in contact with other cultures through education and travel has made Angela comfortable, confident, and competent in the way she uses Catholic culture. It forms an overall plausibility structure, a kind of sacred umbrella or web of meaning, that she uses to create and sustain other webs of meaning when they become weak and threatened.[27] But it is not a rigid web of meaning. It is rather, flexible, adaptable, and transposable within different scenes and contexts and is used, in particular, to make sense of events that are arbitrary, unpredictable, and uncontrollable.

ANGELA'S SAMENESS AND DIFFERENCE

In some respects, Angela Doyle is like *every* other Irishwoman. She lives in a liberal, democratic state that is shaped by economic forces outside of it. She lives in a post-Catholic consumer capitalist society that is dominated by the market and the media. She lives in a culture in which, despite changes in legislation and social policy, mothers and women generally do most of the caring and labors of love. She is like *most* other Irishwomen in that she has been socialized into an understanding of what it is to be a woman, daughter, wife, and mother. She knows the demands, expectations, and responsibilities of these roles. She knows, almost intuitively as a form of second nature, what she can and cannot do and say, how these roles are played out always in terms of each other and in terms of the roles other people play in her life.

She is like *some* other Irishwomen in that she is from a particular social class, married, with children, and living in a suburban housing estate in the Greater Dublin area.[28] While she lives in a world of fine differences in which she sees herself, for example, as quite different from her sister, we can say that they were both molded within the same socialization processes at a particular time in Irish history. If we were to look at her through a long-term historical prism, we would see that her beliefs, attitudes, routines, and rituals are similar not just to those of other women in Greyrock, but to those of women in other suburbs of Ireland as well.

She is her mother's daughter. She may not wear the exact same cultural clothes and she may not wear them in the same way, but the way she sees and understands herself and the world in which she lives—what we may call the fundamental principles of life and what it is to live a good life—she inherited from her parents, teachers, priests, and nuns. Over the years, these were filtered and blended with media and marketing messages and with the attitudes, beliefs, and values of her friends and other people she met. In her everyday life, Angela brings this embodied sense of self into contact with other people whom she encounters in different social fields. We can imagine her meeting and greeting neighbors and friends in the village. There is a similarity in the gestures, the body language, the nodding of the head, the hand to the mouth at shock, the hand to the shoulder in support, the laughter, the sighs and, in between, the words flow to recreate the shared meaning, the sense of bonding and belonging.

At another level, Angela is unique. She has a unique life story. No other human being has lived the same life, has had the same experiences, and has developed the same knowledge and understanding of life. Since the day she was born, a unique combination of social institutions, discourses, and long-term processes of change were filtered through the particular prism of her family, school, and neighborhood to produce her character, personality, and identity. She sees, reads, and understands the world in which she lives in a very different way from all those around her, even those to whom she is most attuned and connected. She has a sense of self that has been accumulated through myriads of different experiences, which will die with her when she dies. The accumulated experiences, thoughts, and emotions over her lifetime have produced a unique sense of self, a unique human being. It is this embodied self that sees and recognizes itself in the mirror, washes and dresses in the morning, and presents itself to her husband, children, neighbors, and friends and "re-presents" itself from their reactions. It is this self that operates in and through the various different roles she plays as wife, mother, sister, daughter, neighbor, friend, and voluntary worker. In fulfilling these roles she recreates and develops the various different social identities that she has inherited, including what kind of woman she is, what kind of middle-class person, what kind of Catholic, what kind of Irish person, and so forth. She also recreates and develops personal identities such as being a gardener, card-maker, voluntary worker. And it is in fulfilling her roles, whether as mother, daughter, or gardener, that she is to some extent similar but always different from other mothers, daughters, and gardeners.

CONCLUSION

We all have an interest in the meanings of our lives. It is the stuff of novels, films, and soap operas. It is what makes us stop, talk, and listen to others. We learn about ourselves through the stories, events, and experiences of other people. Human beings are not rational automatons. They do not go through their daily lives as highly rational, calculating actors seeking to maximize their self-interest. Human beings are emotional and reasonable. They want to bond and belong, to feel attached and attuned to each other. They do this by trying to see and understand the world from the point of view of others. A good novelist or filmmaker does this. We can see and understand the world from the perspectives of the different characters that are created. Knowing and understanding how others think, feel, and understand is central to our own self-realization. It is what makes us human.

In this chapter, I have tried to identify and describe how Angela Doyle—who may be seen as a very ordinary woman, living a very ordinary life, in a very ordinary part of contemporary Ireland—sees and understands the world and how she operates in everyday life. I have tried to show how she makes use of the culture of contemporary Ireland in which she is immersed to create and maintain meaning and how, in turn, that culture has been shaped by long-term processes of change and economic, social, and political structures, and by institutions, contexts, and codes over which she has little control.

In the next chapter, I explore the problems in trying to capture the meanings of Angela's life. When it comes to interpreting culture and meaning, nothing is obvious and straightforward. The meanings of Angela's life are not immediately clear: they do not form a decipherable whole in the same way as $1+3+5 = 9$. Any attempt to get close to the subjective meanings of her life are bogged down by issues of translation and interpretation and the reality that our own webs of meaning distort the way we see and understand her. There will always be a gap between the "real" Angela and the way I have presented, described, and interpreted her. In this sense, we can never fully understand Angela; we can only approach her and, through asking her questions, develop an approximate understanding of the meanings of her life.

CHAPTER 2

CULTURE AS MEANING

IN HUNDRED-YEARS TIME, ANGELA DOYLE WILL BE DEAD AND MOSTLY forgotten. She will be a name among all the other names in the graveyard in Greyrock. To die is to enter into meaninglessness. For the moment, however, her life is full of meaning. We can imagine her busy in and around her home, on the phone, organizing meetings, driving down to the village, and meeting with neighbors. We can imagine her actions when she meets and greets those she knows, the smiles, the expression of delight, the inquiring look, the attentive look, the gasps of "ah no," the nod of agreement, the graceful touch, the laughter. We can imagine Angela as a skillful social actor who has played this role many times, a role that she learnt first from her mother. All the time, she weaves in and out of encounters, greetings and conversations, she is creating and sustaining webs of meaning. People know and understand her actions: whatever she says and does is appropriate to the context and to the people involved. As in her interview, she constantly checks to make sure that the meaning is being maintained. She regularly interjects phrases such as "you know like," or "you know what I mean" at the end of sentences. If she says or does something inappropriate, or if people don't understand what she has said, they may often seek clarification: "you don't say," "what," "honestly," "go on," and so forth. These interjections will often be reinforced by grimaces or gestures of puzzlement signaling possible misunderstanding. They are all part and parcel of keeping the meaning going. We never really know what is going on in each other's heads. We never really know how what we say and do have been received and understood.

We know that there are often gaps between what people say and what they do. We know that gestures and body language are often more important than the words that accompany them: "It is not what you say but the way that you say it." People are constantly struggling to interpret the motivations and intentions behind what people say and do—they ask themselves,

"What is really going on here?" To make matters more complicated, we only know and understand ourselves through others. It is through their reactions to what we say and do, by the way they respond and reflect ourselves back to us, that we know and understand ourselves. Other people are the mirrors of self-understanding.[1] What people talk about to others—their ideas, interests, worries, and concerns, what they have done and experienced, what they have felt—and to whom they talk—loved ones, neighbors, colleagues, and strangers—become the basis of creating and sustaining webs of meaning. In their everyday lives, people make use of culture to recount events, to tell stories about themselves, to reveal what is of interest, what is relevant and meaningful to them, and to listen and respond to other people's stories and experiences. It is the stories that we tell each other that make us human.[2] It is this daily interactive communicative process that reaffirms people's sense of themselves and gives meaning to their lives.[3]

All of this is important, for although we often take it for granted that we are able to say meaningful things and to communicate and create meaning with other people, it is often not quite as simple or straightforward. When, for example, Angela says or does something that is not understood or seems contradictory, it is not that she lied or was being deliberately misleading, but rather that the meaning was not picked up the way she intended. It fell through the webs. Action, then, is meaningful when what is said and done has logic and meaning for the actor and for the particular people involved in the relationship. If Angela blows her husband Martin a kiss when he is going out the door, the gesture has meaning for her, for him, and the children who see it. We can also see it as having meaning for millions of other people in Western society.[4] However, if Angela scratches her ear when she gets stressed, it may not make much sense to anyone outside her family or friends. It may, however, make sense to an outside observer such as a clinical psychologist who sees it as a subconscious nervous reaction to stress. When she makes reference to a religious experience, such as feeling that God or a saint has intervened in her life, or when she lights a candle for her dead babies, we can see it as religiously meaningful action. This is what adherents to different religions do. It is recognizable as meaningful, even for those who are not religious or belong to another religion.

In studying meaning, we are, then, really only interested in shared meaning—action that is oriented toward others.[5] But what constitutes shared meaning varies. The meaning of some statements and actions is more ambiguous than others. If Angela says "I like making cards more than soup," the meaning is more ambiguous than when she says "2 x 2 = 4." We realize that the second statement is more rational and scientific. It is accurate, reliable, and verifiable. It has the exact same meaning in every context and can be proven to be true. The problem is that Angela does not talk about herself and the meaning of her life in such precise, rational, unemotional language. Moreover, we recognize that some actions are more meaningful than others. While the scratching of her ear may not have much meaning to many others, when Angela talks about love, God, and miracles, they are meaningful because they are central to being religious, to the search for the meanings of life, and to establishing shared beliefs and values about the meaning of life and how it should be lived.[6]

Much of Angela's everyday social behavior is meaningful to herself and others because it is rational: when she turns the knob of the door to open it, when she cuts the flowers to fit in the vase, when she licks the glue of an envelope before sealing it. All of these actions are within the realm of purposive, rational, goal-oriented behavior. To understand some of her other behavior, such as lighting candles for her dead babies, where the meaning is less clear, we need to know the motives, goals, or rationale behind them.[7] But sometimes action falls between explanatory stools. We may observe that Angela is crying. We could read it as a distress signal, a cry for help, or it could be a signal that she is a warm, loving woman. But whatever other people decipher as the reason for her crying, it could be that she may not understand the reasons or motives herself. She may not be able to put them in words.[8]

There are, then, many aspects of Angela Doyle's behavior that are instinctual and emotional, that arise spontaneously often from biological human needs of bonding and belonging. These become blended with the type of social meaning that characterizes rational action. Instinctual and affective behaviors do not have any meaning until they are integrated into rational meaningful actions.

DO YOU KNOW WHAT I MEAN?

The problem in trying to say something sensible about meaning in everyday life is that meaning seems so obvious and taken for granted. Angela was socialized into a world in which she learnt to identify and classify the world in the same way as everyone else. When she says "dog" we know exactly what she is talking about—that it belongs to a particular genre of animals, and that it is not a "cat" or a "cow." Even among dogs, Angela may be able to distinguish an Irish Setter from an Irish Wolfhound.[9]

However, Angela did not make up these terms. The language, terms, and concepts, she uses to describe her world have all been inherited over generations and are continually being reinterpreted. We assume that Angela sees the world in the same way as everyone else, but as a middle-aged, middle-class woman from Greyrock she sees the world differently. This brings us back to the notion that Angela is similar, yet different and unique. She reads and understands the social space in which she operates, but she does so in a biographically determined way, with ideas and concepts not of her own choosing.[10]

This notion that we read and understand the world in the same way is central to bonding, belonging, and communication. The people with whom Angela lives and interacts assume that the outside world exists independent of them. Those who engage deeply with her in everyday life are often able to "read her mind."[11] As members of the same culture—local, national or global—there is an assumption that the outside world is the same for everyone, that how Angela sees and understands the world is how members of her family, her local community and, to a lesser extent, all of us see and understand it. If we didn't, then we would not be able to communicate with her. We would not be able to "put ourselves in her shoes." We would not be able to understand her.[12]

We can say, then, that the meaning of any action in which Angela engages is different (a) for her, (b) for her husband, children, and those who know her intimately, and (c) for outside observers such as myself who are not involved in these intimate relations. Moreover, the meanings that Angela creates with her family are constantly being modified from the very moment that they are created. Webs of meaning are often spun in a fast, free-flowing choreography. As an outside observer, I am not attuned or attached to Angela in the same way as those who have intimate relations with her. I can only develop an approximate understanding of what it is to live in her world.[13]

The sociologist is a detached observer. When I briefly entered Angela's world and tried to discover how she read and interpreted it, to capture her attitude to life, her hopes, fears and concerns, I had another intention beyond trying to become attuned to her. I wanted to try and place her in a wider picture and to do so in an objective, detached manner. In order to capture some of the meaning of her life, I was interested in going beyond the taken-for-granted ways in which she sees the world. Working within the rules, theories, and concepts of sociology, I wanted to tell a different truth about her life. In the same way that Angela has a stock of knowledge to read and understand her world, I have a stock of sociological knowledge. My interest is to identify, describe, and explain Angela's life by classifying and categorizing it.[14]

The problem then is that what I am trying to produce is a meaning of meanings. Angela has a way of making her life meaningful and, through sociology, I am trying to develop a way of explaining or making meaning of her meanings. She classifies the world and I develop theories and concepts to classify her classifications. This is the difference between natural and social sciences. When a natural scientist uses terms such as molecules, atoms, and electrons to analyze the natural world, their meaning is only in terms of how the scientist defines them: molecules have no definition or meaning for themselves. However, when I use the term "Catholic" to describe Angela, this has meaning for her. I am trying to find out what it means to her to be a Catholic woman. There is nothing close to an agreed social scientific definition of what it is to be a Catholic, so my understanding of what it is to be Catholic may be very different from Angela's.[15]

Moreover, whatever terms I use to describe Angela, whether it is "neo-liberal Catholic" or "middle-age" they are typifications that are removed from the face-to-face reality of the woman that Martin and her children encounter in their everyday lives. I cannot know Angela in her unique-ness, in the same way that those who are emotionally and physically close to her do. The more I use abstract general concepts such as "middle-aged," "middle-class" the more I move away from her uniqueness. Despite my best efforts, the picture I have painted of Angela is generalized. She becomes a "generalized other."[16] Like the different types of dogs to which I referred earlier, she becomes a type of person that is understood in terms of other, different types. She is what she is not.

However, and this is the twist that occurs by adopting a detached, sci-entific perspective, the more we understand the culture within which she lives, the more we can develop an objective perspective, the more likely that we can understand her uniqueness and sameness. The task, then, is to try and enter the taken-for-granted world in which Angela lives, get a feel for what it is like to experience and understand its logic while, at the same, standing outside it. But the more unique and atypical her actions are, the more difficult it is to understand and explain them. And this is difficult not just because of the lack of correspondence between scientific concepts and theories and Angela's taken-for-granted world, but because what constitutes typical actions varies over time even within the same culture. It may be easier for some detached observers to understand the logic of Angela sitting down with her family to watch a DVD than to understand, for example, how she looks to St. Anthony to help her find things that are lost.

The way we know Angela is through her responses to my questions and the way I have put these together to create a generalized image. The questions I asked and the ways in which I read, interpret, and present her responses are an attempt to provide an objective perspective on the subjective meaning of her life. The success of this endeavor depends on the clarity and consis-tency of the theoretical framework that I construct. It also depends on the extent to which the objective explanation that I develop is understandable to Angela, her immediate group, other Irish people and, more generally, all human beings.[17] The danger in trying to develop a logically consistent, objective, detached, scientific understanding of Angela is that the more we use abstract general theories and concepts, the more we move away from her and lose an understanding and appreciation of the logic of her practice and worldview. In doing so, Angela comes to be seen and understood as a puppet who is manipulated and controlled by structures and processes that she does not understand.[18] We need to accept, then, that whatever construction I make of Angela's life through sociological theory is just a construction and does not necessarily correspond to her construction, let alone to any objective social reality, and that this sociological construction does not have any greater validity than her reading of her own world.

CULTURE AND MEANING

Life is meaningless, but humans wrap it up in webs of meaning. We are born as animals and we die as animals, but in the period between life and death, our lives are soaked in meaning. From our earliest moments of perception we become exposed to signs and symbols, particularly language, through which life becomes shared and understood. It is this ability to create and sustain meaning that makes humans different from other animals.[19] The development of symbols and language enabled humans to communicate with each other, to create shared systems of knowledge, understanding and meaning which, in turn, enabled them to master and control their environment and other species, and to create enormous complex webs of social interdependence. It is this shared sense of meaning that is as important to our lives as the air we breathe and the food we eat, and that creates an understanding of who we are and of the world in which we live. Meaning is the canvas of human life on which all economic, political, and social activity is written.

As children grow up, they become enmeshed in cultures, in ways of being and seeing, in symbols and practices that have been handed down through generations. These develop into dense webs of meaning that are often "taken for granted" and unquestioned.[20] They become second nature to them. Culture shapes people's knowledge and understanding of the world in which they live but, at the same time, people actively and creatively use culture to realize themselves as individuals, to enhance their opportunities in life, and to pursue pleasure and happiness.[21] But culture is not a homogeneous, unified system. There are, for example, as many ways of being Irish as there are people who see and identify themselves as Irish. Moreover, the way Irish culture shapes people, and the way Irish people use culture, varies between gender, age, class, religion, ethnicity, race, nationality, and so forth. Indeed, these divisions and the boundaries between them often become second nature to people.

Culture, then, provides a map or a blueprint through which people can read and interpret the world in which they live and, at the same time and as part of the same process, people use culture to create and sustain meaning with each other. Children are socialized into webs of meaning by parents, teachers, friends, neighbors, within families, schools, churches, communities and, increasingly, via the media. Children develop an ongoing, ontological sense of self —knowledge of who they are —through their daily interaction with others, through having positions and playing roles. They learn what it is to engage in meaningful interaction, to say and do things that make sense to others. This expands from specific others, such as their mother and father, into a "generalized other."[22] It is this ongoing sense of self and the ability to engage in meaningful interaction with other people that become the basis of social behavior.

WHAT DOES CULTURE DO?

Culture is made up of all the symbols, language, and gestures through which people create and sustain meaning.[23] These symbols have been developed and refined throughout history. They come together as a systematic way of seeing, understanding, and communicating a knowledge, an understanding of, and an attitude to, life. Culture is what makes us human and what makes social life possible.[24] The core of culture in almost all societies is generally expressed in religion. It provides both an explanation *of* life, and the guidelines *for* living it. It provides a cognitive map for making sense of the world and enables people to develop the necessary and appropriate attitudes, feelings, and ways of being to live in it.[25] In this way, the culture into which Angela Doyle was socialized enables her to interpret, make sense of, and give meaning to her life. She is able to communicate and share this understanding with others. At the same time, by creating within her appropriate desires, feelings, moods, and motivations, culture enables her to be part of the society in which she lives.[26] Her desires are shaped by the culture in which she lives. While there is a logical coherence to the symbols that create meaning, culture is continually changing. In settled times, the change can be smooth. In unsettled times, the change can be contentious giving rise to cultural wars and ideological conflicts. This is especially the case during social revolutions.[27]

We can, then, see culture as shaping lives through providing ideas about what life is about and how it should be lived. Like everyone else, Angela Doyle has an interest in living a good life, being a free woman, knowing the truth, creating beauty, and so forth. The Catholic culture in which she grew up has shaped the way she fulfills these interests. It shapes her goals in life and the means by which she can fulfill these goals. However, throughout her life, Angela has encountered new ideas, new ways of thinking, that have switched the way she fulfills these interests down a different track.[28]

Apart from logical, rational ideas, culture also generates feelings and moods that are not necessarily rationally articulated but are part of a shared ethos.[29] Angela Doyle does not have a systematic, ideologically coherent view of God or salvation. But when it comes to understanding the arbitrariness and unfairness of life and remembering her dead babies, she knows to go to her local church and light a candle. This reveals the link between the Catholic Church as a cultural institution that shapes and constrains Angela's ideas and goals, and her ability as a cultural actor to adapt the practices, rules, and regulations of the church to her own needs and interests. She may not go to Mass and she may be distant from the church, but there are some rules and regulations that she has to obey in sending her children to the local Catholic school, and protocols to follow when she goes go to church. However, she is also able to develop her own ways of being Catholic in terms of her relationship with God, saying prayers and lighting candles.[30] The Catholic culture into which Angela Doyle was socialized may have provided her with a general map of her life and what she should do, that is her general orientation, but it did not dictate what particular path she took or her responses to the events and experiences she had along the way.

Culture is a bit like a vocabulary: there is a vast range of meanings that are available to people, so vast that most are not generally used. Angela could explore bookstores, the local library, the Internet, or other sources to find out more about the meaning of her life, but she is content with what she has. She has not felt the need to explore culture to find new meanings and personal identities. When she felt she almost died, she did not go in search of a scientific explanation of what had happened. On an ongoing basis, she uses traditional cultural concepts such as "family," "happiness," "God," "Saint Anthony," and her belief that magpies can portend good or bad luck to explain her life. She uses phrases such as "that's how I view it," "I think my life is good," "I'm quite happy with my life." She says, you know what is right and wrong "from your own experiences in life." She does not feel the need to elaborate.[31] She may suffer from depression but she has little doubt about what life is about. She seems to assume that everybody sees and understands the world the way she does. Like many other people I interviewed, Angela has not developed an ideologically coherent and consistent view of life. She mixes and matches bits and pieces from her cultural heritage to develop an ongoing, sustaining, and comfortable meaning to her life.[32] As we shall see, there are other people that I interviewed, many of whom had a similar class and educational background as Angela Doyle but who, in comparison, used culture much more actively to develop an understanding of their life experiences and to create and maintain their webs of meaning.

People, then, use culture to develop a personal identity and sense of self. They adapt and blend different cultural elements to create a unique way of being in the world. Angela Doyle only uses only some elements of her Irish Catholic culture— but very differently from others, particularly her sister who is much more committed—in order to develop her own personal Catholic identity. These ideas and beliefs about life are mixed with different moods and emotions that are revealed and expressed depending on the context and who is present. She can be emotional, depressed, happy, pragmatic, and stoical. The way she presents herself may vary according to the roles she plays. There may be subtle differences in the way she greets and speaks, and what she talks about, depending on whether she is with her mother, or her father, husband, children, friends, neighbors, teachers, club members, and so forth.

Through her socialization and education, Angela developed a variety of cultural skills, habits, and styles of being and presentation that she has made her own and that have made her who she is. She learnt the basic skills of politeness, of smiling, listening and being interested in other people, of being reliable and trustworthy. She learnt to read and assess the character of other people, their strengths and weaknesses. She knows how to gossip, to talk about others, what can be said about others to whom. These are important skills in maintaining group boundaries, in distinguishing insiders from outsiders, and within the groups, identifying the relative position of each member with regard to one another. From her mother, she learnt the importance of helping out and caring for others. This was probably central to her becoming the secretary of the club and president of the PTA. All of these habits, skills, moods, and motivations are bound together by an overall worldview that enables her to read and understand with confidence the world in which she lives.[33]

When we think of culture, it is often in terms of a system of inherited beliefs, values, and practices that shape the lives of people within it, steering their actions by providing them with motivations and goals. People have ideas about what to do and say that come from within the culture and which they then put into practice. Another way of looking at culture is to think of it as a kind of reservoir of language, symbols, gestures, aphorisms, ways of being, talking, and doing, which some people use more than others, which everyone uses differently, to create meanings and identities. If Angela Doyle was shaped by Catholic culture then we might expect her to have the same values and beliefs as her mother. She does have Catholic values, but they are more personal, more informal, and less institutional. When it comes to understanding her life, to creating the moods and motivations that sustain her, she draws from the Catholic cultural reservoir into which she was socialized. She uses Catholic ideas, beliefs, and practices on different occasions for different purposes. She has the ability to use them in a flexible, dynamic way. She uses Catholic culture for a variety of objectives—to attain comfort and consolation when she thinks of her dead babies, to communicate with her mother and sister, to raise her children, and to have herself and her family accepted into the community. It is, then, the particular cultural ingredients that Angela uses, the strategies of action, ways of being, saying, and doing that she has become good at, which she has developed and perfected over the years that shape the webs of meaning she constructs and direct her toward different goals and objectives. It is this way of using culture that provides a sense of agency, creativity, dynamism, difference, and unpredictability in social life.[34]

This, then, leads to a subtle difference in the way we understand culture. We are used to thinking of ideas shaping beliefs and values, and these values, in turn, shaping action. However, when action becomes habitual, ritualized, and deeply embodied, the ideas, beliefs, and values that sustain that action tend to be filtered in. Such ideas, beliefs, and values are, so-to-speak, cultural ingredients that are well-known, tried, and tested and good for creating and sustaining meaning and explaining actions. On the other hand, ideas, values, and beliefs that do not keep the meaning going, that weaken, threaten, or undermine the webs of meaning get filtered out. The more the action becomes unreflective and habitual, and the more people feel good and gain pleasure, comfort, and security, the more likely it is that they will develop rationales for continuing their behavior. But these rationales emerge from the body, from a sense of emotional well-being, pleasure, comfort, and happiness. However, much of the interpretation of social action is still located not just within the Cartesian dualism of mind and body but, as well, within the notion that the body is directed by ideas formed in the mind.[35]

Angela, then, has developed habitual ways of being, creating, and maintaining bonds with her husband and children, her parents, her siblings, friends, and neighbors. These webs of meaning, their structure, and the ingredients she uses to spin them have been shaped by institutions, particularly the Catholic Church, the market, and the media. Even though she has become distant from the Catholic Church—"I can manage without it"—it still plays a major role in her life. But, at the same time, she has been socialized into the habitus of being Catholic, and she knows how to present her Catholic identity. She has moved away from the habitual practices that reinforce awe, respect, and fear of the church. She is no longer concerned with being a good Catholic. She is more concerned with living a pleasurable life, being a good mother, and engaging in rituals that make her husband and her children happy. So, when toward the end of the interview, I asked Angela, what was the meaning of her life, she talked about the pleasure of habitual ways of being: "No stresses around me...that the kids...and Martin are happy and there's...nothing stressing them out, that's my life. That's what makes me happy." And, as she mentioned earlier, she is happiest and least stressed when the family are gathered together to watch a DVD. In this sense, the pleasures and rewards of the market and the media have taken over from the Catholic Church as the dominant institutions in her life.[36] It would seem that for Angela it is a family that watches DVDs together, as opposed to praying together, that stays together.

As well as operating within institutions such as family, religion, the market, and the media, Angela has learnt to deal with cultural codes and practices in which she is constrained to partake often for the sake of honor and respect. In her positions as secretary of the club and president of the PTA, she knows when and how to return favors, visits, phone calls, and text messages. These are all part of the general cultural skill of gift giving. She will have learnt to whom she should give a gift, when it is appropriate to do so, what kind of gift to give, how to measure the value and message of a gift, and how to make it not look like a commercial exchange. This is what she has done in designing and making her own greeting cards.[37] There are other cultural codes within which Angela operates that are central to her creating and maintaining dignity and respect such as the appropriate behavior for a woman, how to be civil and polite and not cause offense and, more generally, and how to be seen as a rational, predictable, reliable cultural actor.[38]

The strategy of Angela's action in moving away from the church and toward the pleasure and comfort of her family was part and parcel of the shift from the culture of self-denial into which most Irish Catholics had been socialized for generations. Angela became good at being a wife and mother, in caring and looking out for her husband and children, in playing her part in the community, in sending out her homemade cards, in maintaining a beautiful home and garden. It became central to her identity. It is not so much that Angela has specific goals and objectives but rather that she has developed a number of cultural skills. She knows what she is good at, and this leads her to take on tasks and have aims and objectives. Her strategies seem to have extended to making people feel good about themselves, talking up their achievements and successes, encouraging them to be ambitious, praising people for enjoying themselves, and making them feel that they are worthy of self-indulgence. Angela, then, has developed ways of being and doing that lead to specific lines of action that are based on who she thinks she is. She chooses lines of action that she thinks are promising and that will succeed and will be rewarding. She learnt to do this, to build this sense of identity from a young age, to distinguish herself from her siblings, parents, and friends.

CULTURE AND POWER

People like Angela Doyle use culture not just to create meaning, but as a means toward an end, that is toward maintaining and increasing their social position, power, and influence. She uses culture to maintain her overall social class, her position in the various social fields in which she operates —family, education, sport, religion, and so forth and, through these, her honor and respect.[39] In this perspective, creating and maintaining meaning is not a separate end in itself, it is inextricably bound up with fulfilling material interests. What makes her strategies difficult to describe and analyze is that the motivations and goals of maintaining meaning are closely interwoven with those of attaining more material rewards and benefits. In this sense, everything that Angela does comes from interests that are, at one and the same time, oriented toward creating and maintaining meaning and seeking material gain. Her actions are motivated both by creating bonds of meaning and by gaining power.[40] The problem is that it is often difficult, if not impossible, for Angela, let alone a detached observer, to identify which interests are being fulfilled as often not only are they fulfilled simultaneously, they are at times in conflict with one another. Again, it comes back to the notion of Angela Doyle being immersed in a habitus and in playing a game in which her moves and strategies are not based on some rational calculation but rather a feel for what is appropriate.[41]

We can see Angela as a wife, mother, friend, and neighbor creating and sustaining love, care, and meaning in her everyday life but, at the same time, she is enveloped in a struggle to maintain the status, honor, and respect that comes from fulfilling these roles and, more generally, the middle-class position that comes from her husband's occupation, her education, her voluntary activities, and her social status achieved through her housekeeping, childcare, gardening, and artistic activities. All of these can be seen as forms of capital. Her wealth and income have been accumulated and are reproduced through her cultural capital (her educational background and her sporting, artistic, religious practices), her social capital in terms of the social networks in which she is involved and the favors she is able to bestow and receive, and her symbolic capital, from the honor and respect she has accumulated from creating and maintaining meaning and attaining these capitals.

Her symbolic capital comes from the embodiment of the dominant attitudes, beliefs, and values of the middle-class community in which she is enmeshed, the shared way of reading and interpreting the world, of enacting family and community life. This not only blesses and legitimates and reproduces her class position, it bestows honor and respect on her and her family. When we read how Angela responded to my inquiries about what was important and meaningful in her life, it is important to realize that her responses, while they describe her bonds of belonging and the way she spins her webs of meaning, also reveal the cultural strategies she uses to fulfill her material interests in reproducing her power in the form of the different capitals that she has accumulated.

From a utilitarian, materialistic perspective, then, we can see Angela's thoughtfulness, care, and concern as strategies she has developed to be seen and recognized as a kind, loving woman and all the honor and respect that comes from being so. Being seen as a "lovely" woman enables her to accumulate other forms of capital, particularly social capital. She uses culture to build a charismatic image of herself based on individual personal qualities.[42] While this symbolic capital legitimates her other capital, particularly her class position, it is also an independent form in itself that can be traded for social, economic, and political favors. Her interest in attaining honor and respect, in being liked, and in being seen as a good wife, mother, daughter, neighbor, friend, and so forth, involves her in a form of gift economy that often necessitates economic sacrifices.[43] In moving to Greyrock, Angela made the decision to forgo her interest in accumulating economic capital by giving up her employment and career. Her strategic decision to invest in symbolic capital was tied to her depending on her husband's earnings which, in turn, tied her more to making her marriage work.

Her accumulation of symbolic capital is in some respects built on a denial or hiding of interest in attaining economic capital or, more generally, being self-interested. She is immersed in an economy of reciprocity and gifts in which monetary values and material interests have to be concealed or, rather, deliberately misrecognized. Angela, then, hides her interest in money. She uses the phrase "as long as I have enough." One can imagine that Angela did not get to be the president of the local PTA simply through her wealth, education, religious, and other forms of cultural capital. Her ability to develop and maintain bonds and build bridges between people depend on her being caring and kindhearted —cultural strategies she learnt from her mother. The strategies Angela uses to attain symbolic capital are different from those used to attain economic or political capital. She does not have many direct employable skills, resources, or power of command. Similarly, she has little or no interest in accumulating cultural capital through education or being interested or involved in music, art, or literature. The strategies she uses may be closest to those used to accumulate social capital. Her ability to develop and maintain bonds between family, neighbors, club, and committee members and to reach out and make new friends and contacts —to build bridges —depends not so much on her economic and cultural capital, but on her being liked and appreciated.[44] It may seem, then, that Angela is relatively powerless, that she is dependent on her husband, and on fulfilling supportive roles in the community. And, yet, akin to any high-flying professional or businessperson, she seems to have made positive choices and taken charge of her own destiny.

STRONG AND WEAK WEBS

When social life is disrupted, when there is a strong conflict of interest, an emotional upheaval, a tragedy, illness, death, or injustice, the meaning that was once shared and solid can melt into thin air: all that was once taken for granted becomes questioned. The normative social order that was seen as obvious and legitimate comes to be in danger of being seen as arbitrary and illegitimate.[45] While breakdowns in meaning can be social and large scale, most breakdowns in meaning in everyday life tend to be more private and personal; they tend to take place in homes. The breaking of strong personal bonds through loss, trauma, or tragedy can throw the normal, taken-for-granted order of everyday life into chaos. This often happens with the death of a parent or child, or the loss of, or separation from, a loved one. There may be public ceremonies such as a funeral, but the breakdown in meaning is generally lived out in backstage regions.[46] These are where strong webs of meaning are spun. It is where the "slings and arrows of outrageous fortune," the traumas and tragedies of life, are teased out and unraveled. There is a struggle to create meaning out of events and experiences that appear unfair, arbitrary, and meaningless. There is an attempt to renew shared belief and practice, and to recreate the shared sense of identity, bonding, and belonging. This is what happened when Angela suffered the trauma of losing her baby and almost dying during childbirth.

What makes the family or group different is that the meanings that are created derive less from rational, calculated, bureaucratic interests and more from emotional and reasonable interests in bonding and belonging. It is within families and small groups of intimate friends that people are less concerned with success, mastery, control, and domination, and more concerned with love, care, concern, feelings, and emotions. This is the realm of practical reason rather than instrumental, calculated, efficient, and productive action.[47] It is in this way that families and informal groups act as therapeutic centers. They become cocoons, safe havens in a heartless, rational, scientific, organizational world in which people become more directed by means toward ends rather than ends in themselves.[48]

The division between strong and weak webs of meaning is, of course, an analytic device and does not correspond to all the realities of everyday life. For example, many religious gatherings could be seen as comprising both strong and weak webs. Strong believers may go to Mass to participate with others in a sacrament that will help them go to heaven. But they may also become involved in dressing for the occasion and chit-chatting with fellow attenders who they do not know very well. However, it is only in strong webs that the idea of a personal, loving God and the notion of salvation and life after death might be questioned and debated. What makes strong webs of meaning different is that they often revolve, as much if not more, around what is done rather than what is said—around ritual and ceremonial activities that create a sense of emotional connectedness. Conversations are less oriented to the development of rational arguments leading to agreed positions, and are more about taking turns in talk, enabling people to talk, listening, being attentive, and caring.

What is of interest, then, is the relationship between strong and weak webs of meaning. Most social interactions are suspended in weak webs of meaning. There is a continual attempt to identify and reaffirm the temporary social contract as to "what is happening here": there is generally little or no reference to beliefs about the meaning of life. The checkout assistant is generally not directly interested or concerned if the customer has suffered a major trauma, is dying, or no longer believes in God or life after death. In other words, the meaning of life in everyday activities is pragmatic, superficial, and taken for granted. It is not open for debate and discussion. You cannot ask, what is going on here? However, when a loved one dies, it may be understandable and acceptable to do so. There is, then, a time and place for everything, including when, where, how, and with whom to discuss the meaning of life.

One of the fundamental questions in sociology revolves around the extent to which fundamental beliefs shape what happens in everyday life, not just in families, but also in politics, economics, science, media, the arts, and so forth. From one perspective, there is the notion that shared beliefs about, for example, when life begins, how it is created, and what happens when one dies shape people's values, ethics, and conception of what it is to live a good life. Religions have traditionally provided the basic beliefs that enable individuals to integrate and cooperate on the basis of a mutual, voluntary commitment to shared values. In this view, even though Irish people may no longer be formally Catholic or Christian, they have been shaped by Christian values and beliefs. Over time these have become secularized and, in some instances, blended with values and beliefs from other religions.[49] These core beliefs and values about the meaning of life and how to live a good life shape the laws that are made, the politicians that get elected, and the direction of economic activity. However, rather than thinking of values as directors of specific behavior, it is better to think of values and beliefs about what is important in life as cultural resources that people use in their everyday life as guides to behavior.[50]

It is also important to remember that often what appears in everyday social life as calm and untroubled may hide confusion and doubt beneath the surface. Even when Irish culture was settled, Catholic, relatively homogeneous, closed, and isolated, there was never a complete shared consensus about the meaning of life. What, for example, was said and done in religious ceremonies might suggest shared beliefs and values, but may hide some deep doubts for many of the participants. There is often a tacit agreement in onstage behavior not to declare any skepticism that may be voiced in more backstage regions. [51]

CONTEXTS

If we were to develop a more complete understanding of Angela Doyle's webs of meaning, we would need to understand the structures, discourses, institutions, and codes of behavior in which she is suspended, the cultural ingredients she has at her disposal, and then, how she uses these ingredients in specific contexts. The webs of meaning are as fine and different as they are dense. As a sophisticated cultural actor, Angela is able to create and maintain meaning by reading, decoding, and anticipating what people say and do to each other. She is able to distinguish between the meaning of a nod, a wink, and a joke. She knows that they vary depending on the context and the participants.[52] She would know that shared meaning can and does break down, sometimes regularly, even with loved ones, and even during a pattern of interaction when the shared meaning seems strong. People misread and misunderstand what is said and done; they may be uncertain or suspicious of each other's intentions and motivations. When this happens, Angela has learnt how to repair the situation and reestablish a shared sense of meaning and of what is happening.

People read what is said and done in terms of "what is really being said or done" and "what is it that's going on here."[53] Some of this is strategic. We can imagine Angela, like everyone else, manipulating meanings to her advantage by employing various strategies such as masking her intentions, concealing her interests, putting a positive or negative spin on stories about people or events, and so forth.[54] And yet, at the same time, there is an overall moral contract or obligation within each social interaction to create and maintain a shared sense of meaning.[55] People may present positive images of themselves; they may deliberately misrepresent, conceal, and play things up or down, but they are also anxious not to be seen as liars, cheats, and con artists.[56] Social interaction is based on a shared understanding or moral consensus: people may use a variety of strategies to shape and manipulate each interaction with others to their own benefit, needs, and interests but, nevertheless, there is a base level of plausibility, an agreement about what can be said and done.[57]

While the overall context and meaning of most of these public encounters are taken for granted, each encounter is different and is negotiated afresh. There is a normative order, a social contract about what can be said and done, and individuals have a moral right to expect that the shared meaning of the normative order is maintained and, at the same time, have a responsibility to help recreate this meaning. This meaning and normative order derives from people being recognized and accepted for who they are, as legitimate participants who have status positions and who are entitled to be creative in how they present themselves to others. While there is a freedom to be creative, there are also recognized rights, duties, and responsibilities pertaining to each participant in each social interaction.

For example, as noted above, there is a consensus about what customers can say and do and how they interact with staff at the checkout in a supermarket. There are normative expectations about queuing and everyone being treated in a fair and orderly manner. Through words and gestures, greetings, questions, and answers, customers and staff share courtesies and compliments, and reassure each other about the mutual fulfillment of the social contract in which they are engaged.[58] Part of this contract is that while the customer can ask the staff member about the price of something, she cannot ask her if she thinks she should get her toe-nails clipped, let alone what is the meaning of her life, at least not in all seriousness. It is in the realm of the unthinkable. It is breaking the accepted code of manners and politeness. It could be emotionally disturbing. It could weaken and undermine the fragile webs of meaning.[59] However, as we shall see with Mark O'Neill in chapter 4, such questions can be asked if they are seen as part of a joking interaction, of the banter and repartee that can take place between customers and sales assistants.

The codes and conventions that operate in social interactions and that enable shared meaning to be negotiated and represented are derived from the deeply internalized culture that operates through language, common beliefs, and values. They enable meaningful communication: they are the mechanisms through which people can recognize and accept difference, and convey sentiments of honor, dignity, and respect. The codes and internalized culture of shared meanings that form the base of the normative order of public life are often only revealed or questioned in a crisis. Webs of shared meaning create a normative order that enables greater interdependency. They stretch from domestic to organizational life, they enable people to love and care for each other, as much as for mutual objectives to be achieved among strangers. They enable cooperation and collaboration and business to be accomplished.

In all cultures, there is, then, a basic way of being, of seeing, understanding, and reading the world, which is taken for granted, that is, generally, beyond question. It is the way things are, the ways things are done. It is a shared meaning not just of what is going on in a particular interaction setting, but what is going on generally, of what life is about. And within this there is a shared understanding of how life is to be lived. Obviously, this is closer among tight-knit groups, such as members of the same religious cult or sect.[60] However, it also pertains to all members of the culture. It is a shared understanding of cultural codes and protocols, of how men and women relate, about courting, marriage, family, children, and so forth. While we associate habitus, or the shared way of seeing and understanding the world, with social class and the various social fields in which people operate, we can also think of a habitus that exists across all social fields and classes. This is the realm of shared predispositions and beliefs about the meaning of life and how it should be lived. There may be a shared understanding of basic human rights and about what is immoral and evil. But it would be wrong to think that there is some strong fundamental consensus about what is right and wrong in everyday life. It would be better to think of this realm of shared meaning as a series of overlapping complex webs that are woven by individuals in their everyday lives from the cultural materials available to them that may often be contradictory and sometimes irreconcilable.[61]

We can see, now, how the specific contexts in which Angela operates can themselves be placed within a wider cultural context. This wider cultural context could be characterized as an Irish habitus that generates understandings of the way things are said and done. They are inherited predispositions, shared ways of talking and presenting oneself that generate moods and senses of bonding and belonging. This habitus has then, of course, to be placed within the context of an increasing global culture, of changes in the structure of capitalism, the media and the market and, finally, within long-term processes of social change. If we were to develop a more comprehensive understanding of Angela Doyle and the other participants in the study, we would need to understand how these contexts blend together. It is within these different contexts and the multitude and variety of cultural ingredients that Angela's webs of meaning are spun. However, it is impossible to unravel all the webs and distinguish the different ingredients with which they have been spun. All we can do is develop an approximate understanding.

INTERVIEWING ANGELA

Having set out some of the theoretical difficulties in trying to understand and interpret the meanings of Angela Doyle's life, it is now necessary to outline briefly some of the more methodological challenges (I deal with some of these challenges in more detail in the appendix). I wanted, as much as possible, to enter into Angela's world and to understand the way she saw and understood herself and the world in which she lived. Trying to achieve a detailed and accurate understanding of Angela, or any of the other participants, during a short interview is, of course, impossible. On the other hand, I felt that if I developed a good rapport with the participants, if I developed a sense of trust and became attuned to them as quickly as I could, it would be possible to gain some insight into the meanings of their lives. It is perhaps best to consider the interview with Angela, and with all the others, as an attempt to take a photograph with a cheap camera and a lens that moves in and out of focus so that some images are clearer than others.

The problem with interviews is that they are artificial forms of social relations. I tried to make the interview into a light, informal conversation of the type that Angela might have seen on television or heard on the radio. My primary intention from the outset was to get Angela to talk about herself, about her background, the people with whom she had grown up, and the major events and experiences of her life to date. However, any attempt to reduce the artificiality of the engagement was negated by the formal requirement (made as part of my being given ethical clearance by my university to conduct the study) of having to explain the terms and conditions of the interview and then getting the participants to sign a consent form. It was further constrained by the palaver of me setting up my tape machine to record the interview.

There were other structural constraints too. No matter what my intentions, no matter what strategies I employed to make Angela feel at ease, it was an inherently unequal, potentially exploitative relation. I may have tried to make it seem relaxed and informal, but it was generally me and not Angela who asked the questions: I directed the conversation and the relationship. My task throughout, then, was to recognize the structural inequalities in the relationship and to try to overcome the symbolic domination that was inherent in the situation. The strategy was to make Angela loosen up so that she would talk freely and honestly about herself. In some respects, then, my symbolic domination forced Angela to live the lie that the interview was not a formal exercise being conducted by an academic.

To overcome the structural constraints, and to enable and encourage Angela and the other participants to talk openly and to enter into the meanings of their lives, I had to be responsive and flexible to what I saw as their concerns, anxieties, needs, and interests.[62] This was achieved by being caring, polite, and sensitive to their needs, interests, and concerns. It involved adopting a body disposition that was humble, combined with eye-contact that was warm and sympathetic rather than distant and detached. The task was to communicate this to Angela, to make her feel that I was genuinely interested, committed, and sympathetic to understanding the meanings of her life and how she had come to see, understand, and live in the world as she did.

It is at this moment that all strategies of making a positive self-presentation, of using masks and cues, come down to a moral interaction: despite the structural inequalities and forms of domination, Angela somehow recognized and accepted that I wanted to try and discover the meaning of her life. To keep this moral contract alive, I had to achieve a difficult balance of directing and controlling the interview and, at the same time, ensuring that Angela felt that she was in control of what she said. The main strategy that I employed was "active and methodological listening." This required surrendering myself as much as possible to Angela. Instead of an attempt to be detached and objective, I tried to immerse myself in her worldview. This involved adopting her language, feelings, thoughts, and ideas. I tried to pick up and interpret the wide range of "non-verbal signs, co-ordinated with verbal ones" that indicate how an utterance or response should be interpreted. These are feedback signs such as "yes," "right," "you know what I mean," as well as laughs, sighs, nods of the head, and other nonverbal signs of attention and communication. Of course, as I have argued, these play a crucial role in everyday life interactions to capture, identify, and describe the intention, emotional content, and meaning of what is being said.[63]

The danger in adopting this approach to interviewing, which demphasizes concerns about being detached and objective, is that the interviewer may ask leading questions and and put words into participants' mouths and create thoughts about themselves that they never had. These dangers are well known and recognized. In a semistructured, free-flowing interview, it was easy for me to make assumptions about Angela, that she conformed to the image that I had of her before the interview began—on the basis of her home, her dress, and her general style of self—and that was added to as the interview progressed. The more I believed the image to be true, the greater the danger of missing vital clues and misreading and misunderstanding what she said.[64] And, of course, to make matters even more complicated, there was the danger that Angela was all the time reading and responding to the image of her that I was projecting.

The problem, then, is that meaning can never be studied in a completely detached, objective, scientific manner. Meaning cannot be understood in a laboratory through rational scientific methods. Moreover, attempts to identify, describe, and understand meaning are always distorted by the context in which the investigation takes place and the intentions, interests, and preconceived meanings of the researcher. As a researcher, I may have tried to be detached and objective in my attempts to capture the meanings of life of the people I interviewed, but I was hampered by who I was. I could not overcome the influence of my life history, my own meanings and beliefs, my social class and religious background, and my academic interests in conducting the study.

The problem is that whatever sympathy and concern I had for my participants, my interest was always primarily scientific, and the questions I asked always had the objective of eliciting knowledge about them. This involved steering the participants into areas of their lives they might not have previously or otherwise explored. All similar sociological investigations thus find themselves situated between two limits (doubtlessly never completely attained): total coincidence between the investigator and the respondent, where nothing could or needed to be said, because nothing could be subject to question, and everything would go without saying; or total divergence, where culture and language differences and difficulties and a complete lack of trust make any communication impossible.[65]

CONCLUSION

In trying to understand the webs of meaning in contemporary Ireland, I have moved from a more structural, analytical realist reading of culture and what it does —how it shapes people's lives and how it is used by people to shape their lives —to the microworld of everyday life, to the view from below and to looking at how people create meaning, communicate, and relate to each other. While it is difficult to make connections between the micro and the macro, between the subjective and the objective, because they are two different lenses that provide two different views, it is possible to develop some interpretive links by thinking of people's lives as stories that they tell about themselves and thinking of sociology as a more abstract, general, theoretically and empirically informed interpretation of these stories. As we shall see, while all the participants seemed to strive to be honest, coherent, and consistent in what they said, the number who sought to develop a logically systematic, scientific explanation of their lives was very small.

Meaning is often created and maintained through the stories people tell each other, the descriptions and interpretations they make of other people, and the encounters, events, and experiences of their everyday life. The short descriptive accounts and the longer stories that people tell about themselves and others become the bedrock for creating and maintaining understanding, meaning, and communication.[66] The ongoing recounting of what we have done, where we have been, whom we have met, or what we have experienced, has the function of creating an ongoing sense of self that goes beyond the experiential "I," transcends particular situations, and creates a historical self that others come to know and to whom they can relate. Talking about ourselves makes it easier for others to know and understand us. Telling stories and relating experiences to others enable us to develop an ongoing coherent sense of self that transcends the succession of particular events that we experience. They also enable other people to read and understand us, and for us to interpret their reading, to reflect on our sense of self, and to represent ourselves alternatively.

The people in this study have been socialized into a way of talking about themselves.[67] The words they chose, the concepts they use, have evolved over generations, becoming increasingly more differentiated and sophisticated. We can see this as part and parcel of individualization. Moreover, it is not just that people talk more about themselves, it is also how they talk. The ways of talking have increased in variety and become more informal. Talking has always been encased within rules of listening, turn-taking, and displaying emotions. Increased individualization and informalization means that people are willing and able to talk about issues, experiences, and meanings in their lives in ways that previous generations were unable to. This provides sociologists an opportunity to access areas, such as the meanings of people's lives, which was previously not possible. It also necessitates new approaches and methods and new theories and concepts that can help reveal the complexity of the webs of meaning that people spin. The problem is that, for a long time, in the process of becoming more sophisticated, the language and theories of sociology had become increasingly detached from the meanings of everyday life.[68]

This brings us back to the use of concepts and abstract general theory in providing sociological interpretations of meaning. This book, the way I write about Angela Doyle and the other people that I interviewed, can be seen as a series of readings. If we see Angela Doyle's life as a series of accumulated events and experiences, we can then see and understand the interview as her reading and interpretation of these for me. This becomes a first-order reading. We can see my sociological interpretation of her readings as a form of second-order reading. The problem, as mentioned above, is to find a balance between the two readings. If we rely on first-order readings, of just reading transcripts of my interview with Angela Doyle, of letting her speak in her own words, there is a danger of not being able to understand, let alone explain, the wider context in which her meanings have been produced. However, if the second-order readings become too detached and analytical—if the reality of Angela Doyle's is life is to be explained only by social structures and long-term processes of change that are "beyond'" her, and if nothing that she says about her life will ever help understand how she has come to be the way she is—there is the danger of explaining her away, of seeing her as some kind of puppet that is pulled by unknown and unseen forces. More importantly, it denies the importance of her agency in creating social and cultural change, that the way she uses culture changes culture.

The ongoing daily activity of creating meaning, of creating and maintaining the "plausibility structures" that enable ongoing interaction and communication, depends on people using culture to identify and describe themselves. What they talk about and how they talk about themselves is conditioned by the culture in which they live. But they still have considerable choice: there are as many cultural ingredients available to construct an identity and sense of self as there are words in a dictionary. Most people, in talking about themselves, in putting themselves in context, particularly to strangers, talk about where they come from, their upbringing, where they live now, who they live with, what they do for a living, what they like to do in their spare time, and perhaps what worries, anxieties, illnesses, and ailments they suffer from. These descriptions and stories are mirrored in the media through novels, films, television soap operas and serials, and celebrity magazines. It is through capturing the stories of others and telling our own stories that we capture the meanings of life.

And yet, while specific contextual descriptions may be missing, the ways in which the participants talked about themselves and what they talked about still reveal the language, symbols, and cultural material with which they clothe their lives in meaning. In reading their descriptions and stories we gain an insight not just into their lives but also into the wider culture in which they operate. Many of the meanings they create are derivations or adaptations of the ways of being and believing that they inherited from their parents. These meanings enable them to enter into a shared collective consciousness, an agreement of what life is all about. These meanings create within them the necessary moods and motivations that are essential to being part of the same meaning system, the same culture.[69] By entering into their stories, their descriptions of themselves, and the way they speak, we can imagine what it is like to live their lives, to have experienced the same things that they have.[70]

CHAPTER 3

PLACE, FAMILY, AND IDENTITY

IN AND OF THEMSELVES, PLACES LIKE CASTLEBAY, MAYFARM, AND THE other localities in which I interviewed people, have no meaning. They are simply geographical areas. For outsiders, like myself, the roads, houses, shops, pubs, and churches do not generate the same emotions as for those live in the area. I did not grow up in the same webs of meaning. There are no personal experiences, no collective memories. I have no understanding of the different people who live in the community, their characters and personalities. I have no feeling for the sights, sounds, and smells in which the memories are embedded. I am not part of the stories that are told and shared.

It is in this way that communities and homes become sacred. The webs of meaning that are spun afresh each day, create and recreate patterns of interaction, ways of being, saying, and doing that become part of everyday life. People are suspended in spaces, objects, and rituals. Spaces become places when they are invested with practices, beliefs, and meaning. Houses become homes when people invest them with furniture, goods, decorations, pictures, photographs, and mementos. In homes, there are spaces, practices, and things that belong to adults or children, women or men, humans or pets. There are things that belong to individuals, that are part of their personal identity and sense of self, that set them apart. And, in this world of identities and differences, there is a shared sense of meaning about place and everything and everyone being in its proper time and place.[1]

Adults, then, become attached to objects and places in the same way a child becomes attached to a teddy bear. A chair has a structured meaning in relation to the other furniture in a room. It takes on a permanency. It belongs beside the fire, facing the television, with the red cushion and the small table beside it. And often it tends to belong to someone, and other people take positions in the room in relation to it. The chair becomes an embodiment of social relations and positions.[2] We tend to think of place of neighborhoods, homes, rooms, and objects within them as having more meaning in traditional societies made up of relatively detached, enclosed communities dominated by face-to-face relations. In Ireland, the importance of place has been captured by authors like McGahern and his lyrical, poetic descriptions of life in Leitrim in the middle of the twentieth century. He brought intense emotional meaning to the nooks and crannies of the house in which he lived, its rooms and furniture, the garden and the lanes and roads that led into the local village and its peculiar array of houses, police station, post office, and shops.[3]

It is perhaps because so many people live increasingly mobile lives that we are inclined to associate the importance of place with settled rural society in which families lived for generations in the same houses, villages, and small towns. In these homogeneous places, there were important but fine distinctions between families and the neighborhoods in which people lived. The sense of place extended beyond homes into the wider community and into the surrounding towns and villages. As much as there was a time and place for things in family homes—and ritual movements in and around these—there were proper times and places for what people did and said in each others' homes, in schools, churches, clubs, pubs, and cafes. Individuals knew and understood themselves in relation to others. They presented themselves to each other and recognized their similarities and differences.[4]

There is plenty of evidence to show that Irish people are on the move, living and working in different places around the world. This involves reaching out to and connecting with family, friends, and loved ones who are living in different places in different time zones.[5] This might suggest that in a highly mobile, globalized society and culture, place, whether local or national, no longer has the same significance for people when compared to previous generations.[6] Research findings from other countries indicate a divide between those who live global, mobile lives and those who live locally. People who are embedded in the local who see and understand themselves as belonging to a particular place, are more likely to be elderly, less educated, living in rural areas or small towns, are less open to others, and less willing to travel, and participate less in transnational, more cosmopolitan cultures.[7] However, while there is some evidence from the current study to support these findings, there is enormous complexity in the way the local and the global interrelate in contemporary Ireland. In many respects, it is not just that the attachment to the local is an equal and opposite reaction to increased mobility and globalization, it is also that people are deeply attached to the places in which they live, even though some of these places are socially marginalized and deprived.

There is an old saying in Ireland that "you can take the man out of the bog, but you cannot take the bog out of the man." It is an aphorism that captures the effect that socialization into local webs of meaning has on the individual, shaping not just his or her identity, but also his or her interests, desires, hopes, and expectations. There were many other people that I interviewed who left the community in which they had grown up, and the webs of meaning in which they had been suspended and who traveled and lived abroad. And yet the overwhelming impression is that most of the participants—those who never left and those that went away and came back—are deeply attached to the families and places in which they grew up. Indeed in the case of Castlebay and Mayfarm—the rural area in the west of Ireland and the working-class, inner-city area of Dublin where I conducted interviews—not only were the majority of the participants living close to the place in which they had grown up, but also were living in close proximity to brothers, sisters, and other family members.[8]

There is a view of Ireland that suggests people are constantly on the move, in and out of the country. This comes from a long history of emigration. Since the Great Famine in the middle of the nineteenth century, Ireland has always had some of the highest levels of emigration in the Western world. During the end of the twentieth century and the beginning of this century, emigration declined and, instead, there was a rapid growth in immigration. This image of global flows of people in and out of the country is often linked to images of people commuting and traveling, and living fast, complex, mobile lives. But the picture that emerges from my study is different. Most of the people I interviewed were not just embedded in but also were deeply attached to the families and communities in which they lived. Of the hundred people I interviewed, fifty-eight lived in the area in which they had grown up. The proportions varied. The figures were highest in more rural areas such Castlebay (seventeen out of twenty) and Hillbrook (fifteen out of twenty). The image of these people is one of going and coming, of living and working abroad for periods of their lives, and then returning back to Ireland and, often, to their local community. But even among those who had not grown up in the neighborhood, sometimes referred to as "blow-ins," there was still a strong attachment to the place in which they are now living.[9] Among those who did not grow up in the neighborhood, twenty-four had grown up in another part of Ireland, fourteen had grown up abroad, and four worked in the neighborhood in which I did the interviews, but lived elsewhere.[10]

Webs of meaning are, then, always spun at a particular time in a particular place. Social relations, identities, and memories are always enmeshed in place. In this way, many of the participants belonged to different places, where they lived before and where they are living now. But the strongest sense of belonging seemed to be toward the place in which they grew up.

THE STABILITY OF FAMILY

The Irish family may have undergone radical transformation through long-term processes of change, but there is plenty of evidence to suggest that it is one of the key institutions in Irish society. The Census of Population in 2011 showed that the majority of Irish people still marry and have children—although no longer necessarily in that order. Seven in ten people lived in family households.[11] Half of all family households were couples living together with children. Whatever else happens in their lives, it would seem that the majority of Irish people take it as second nature that they will marry and have children. Although there is no longer the same religious or moral imperative for couples to marry in order to live together, people seem to want to marry. In the 2011 Census, only 12 percent of families comprised cohabiting couples and the majority of these (six in ten) did not have children. And there is evidence to show that when cohabiting couples do have children, most of them get married.[12]

What is remarkable, then, is that when it comes to spinning webs of meaning, most Irish people do it within families and, as we have seen, these families are embedded in webs of local neighborhood meanings. One might expect the nuclear family to be under greater threat with the decline of institutional religion and close-knit communities revolving around extended families and, at the same time, increasing globalization, mobility, and individualization. Though there has been significant increases in the number of couples that have separated and divorced, the actual numbers are relatively low and there is little evidence to suggest that people separating and becoming divorced has undermined the institution of marriage and family.[13]

There have, then, been some changes in the structure and culture of family life in Ireland. Nevertheless, there is a picture of overall stability; most people still marry and have children, and most children grow up with their natural parents. A national study of nine-year-old children found that eight in ten lived with both of their natural parents who were married to each other and had been living together since the child was born.[14]

For almost all of the people in this study, the most important webs of meaning in their lives are spun in and around family. It is the core from which other webs of meaning are spun. It is the linchpin that binds each new generation into the existing social and cultural webs of wider life. Children become suspended in meanings of life passed on to them by their parents. These webs and the different ways in which they are spun have a lasting effect on their orientations, tastes, preferences, identities, and personalities.

These webs can create emotional upheavals and engulf some children in fear, self-doubt, and uncertainty as much as they can cocoon them in love and care.

The family has been long regarded as one of the key institutions of Irish society. Its special position is reflected in the Irish Constitution. Families, like individuals, are never independent entities. They are always enmeshed in relations of power. What is said and done within families are shaped by institutions, discourses, and long-term processes of change, by the state and its educational, health, and social welfare services, by the Catholic Church and its teachings in relation to marriage, divorce, sex, and fertility control, and by the market and the media and their messages of consumption and entertainment and the fulfillment of pleasures and desires. Irish families are shaped within these institutions and discourses.

The problem in developing an understanding of family is that it has become such a common feature of society that it is taken for granted.[15] The image of family as comprising husband, wife, and children living together at home becomes an ideal that has to be achieved.[16] The realization of this ideal with each new generation is not left to chance. The family is constituted as something set apart from the rest of society and, therefore, as sacred. Unless people are loved, looked after, cared for within families and become suspended in family webs of meaning, they will have to be looked after and cared for by the state or the church. It is within the family that children learn the meaning of life and what it is to live a good life. The problem is that although the family is both taken for granted and sacred, and although it is shaped by similar institutions and discourses, it is never realized in the same way. There are as many different families in Ireland as there are individuals who make them. And yet the notion of "the" family is invoked as if it meant the same thing to everybody. The task, then, is to try to capture the nuances, differences, and complexity of family life in Ireland. We have to try to understand the variety in the forms of families and the ways in which they operate and create and maintain structures of meaning. What are the strategies of action, the rituals of conversation, caring, visiting, sharing, doing favors, giving and receiving gifts, participating in family reunions, the telling of stories, and the recording of events in photographs, through which the webs of meaning become and remain strong? These practices generate a sense of bonding and belonging, a feeling of cohesion that transforms the family into a reality that exists for itself.

Families transcend relations in particular spaces. Family members can preside in their absence. Even when family members are apart, they are often imagining, thinking, and talking about each other. When members are attached and attuned to each other, they create a sense of ontological security. Individuals' life histories, their memories, their knowledge and understanding of who they are, are embodied in family relations. Even when these relations are full of conflict, they are at the center of an individual's meaning and understanding of life.

Where Webs Are Spun

Jim Lennon is in his late forties. He lives in a farmhouse in Castlebay, a remote rural area in the West of Ireland. He grew up there with his parents and his two sisters. His father died fifteen years ago and Jim now lives on the farm with his mother and his younger sister. His older sister and her husband had lived in England for thirty years. They returned home recently and built a house nearby. Jim is a professional guitarist. He lived and worked in New York for many years, trying to build a career, but he did not succeed. He never married. When I asked him how he would describe his childhood, he said:

> I had a freedom that was unreal. I mean I grew up on the farm. Fine. But what my memories of it were, let's say pre-working on the farm, at the age where you're just around your parents and not working and just doing stuff. I just remember like [an] endless amount of days of just travelling through the fields with the dog and friends, going fishing, hanging out, setting up a camp in the field as if you were living in some other part of the world, y'know what I mean, like little soldiers. Continuous long, long, long warm summers of just spending time with friends and girlfriends. I mean like friends of a certain age. Hanging out together just in the fields. Sitting around talking, totally free... so my childhood was that, growing up and living inside my own head in terms of being a child and imagination and all of that.

Ian Sheridan is in his early sixties. He too lives in Castlebay. He grew up in a family of three sisters and two brothers: there were three infant deaths as well. His father was a carpenter and had a small amount of land, enough for a couple of cows. His mother was a housewife. Ian left school when he was about fifteen. He stayed at home until he was about seventeen—doing "whatever was needing doing around the house, working bits and pieces"— before he went to work in England. He married a local girl. They had their first child in 1972, and he decided to come back to Ireland. He has seven children now, but he has separated from his wife. He looks back on his childhood with fond memories:

> I'd a fantastic childhood. My parents were... my father was a carpenter. They never had feck all money, but my mother was a brilliant cook and she was a very resourceful lady... But great freedom. We went down this river over here on summer days, autumn times down picking hazelnuts. And some of

my mother's family just live down the road here, or they did, that's where she came from and there used to be loads of blackcurrants... my aunt, great-aunt... used to make lovely blackcurrant jam. Old Pat used to go down fishing... but I had a very fantastic childhood, yeah. Great freedom, great support, great love. Very little criticism of any sort, y'know. I realize it was probably pretty close to an ideal set-up. Feck all material stuff, but we had great support.

Our identities and sense of self are formed during childhood and adolescence. These inherited social identities change and develop over time, mainly by becoming interwoven in other webs of meaning and the development of more personal identities, and also by the way we look back and remember the past. Identity is built on memory. It may well be that Jim Lennon and Ian Sheridan have rose-tinted glasses when they look back on their childhood. It may be that talking fondly of their childhood reaffirms their identity and gives them a stronger sense of belonging to their families and neighborhood. It may be that they have come to believe in their own rhetoric about life in the West of Ireland being idyllic: they gloss over the fact that they both grew up in poor times in a relatively deprived area of the country in which, for many people, unemployment and emigration were the main facts of life. Maybe they have learnt to tell the stories of their childhood in a certain way, with a certain spin, that makes a virtue out of poverty. It is part and parcel of the sense of bonding and belonging. It suggests that people did not worry about material things, about having enough money to rear large families. These stories have helped them become so enmeshed in webs of meaning, in ways of being and seeing, that they have become embodied in their identity and sense of self, and legitimates them living in Castlebay, making it difficult and perhaps impossible for them to live elsewhere. Telling good stories about childhood are central to maintaining family memories as well as strong webs of meaning.[17]

Family and place combine to create a strong sense of identity: people become wedded to the webs of meaning in which they were brought up. Consider Carol Flynn. She is twenty-three years old and lives at home in Castlebay with her parents and her younger sister. Her brother and older sister live away. Carol is a country girl. She went to study in Dublin but did not like it. "I was so looking forward to finally coming back here and living here. So just being here is just hugely important to me." She got a degree in graphic design but came back home to set up her own business. She hated the city. She hated the idea of everyone living on top of one another and there being no sense of community:

Like they talk about being isolated and afraid in the countryside and yet if you're living in a housing estate. Like one of the first nights I moved to

Dublin I was going asleep...and I heard the person coughing in the next house. And immediately I woke up and "feck." Like this person's head is like 3 foot away from mine, 'cos their bed must have been right beside mine. And I'm thinking, all there is between me and this person is a piece of concrete and I've never met them. I don't know who their mother is. I don't know when their birthday is.

She firmly believes that she got ill from living in Dublin. "My body was always sore, somehow, when I lived in Dublin." She admits that she has suffered from sciatica since she was a teenager, but insists that it was exacerbated in Dublin. Again, this could be a classic case of homesickness but what is noticeable is the way Carol uses the cultural code of the rural-urban divide to suggest that it was not just her: anyone who was brought up in the countryside with a sense of space and community would feel the same.

Sarah Gilsenan is sixty-eight years old. She never married. She lives in the same apartment complex in Mayfarm into which she moved with her parents and two brothers in 1957. It is the same complex that became ravaged with drugs in the 1980s. Sarah grew up in a small enclave of cottages in the city center until she was sixteen. She says that living in her neighborhood "was more like country living than city living because there were so many cows in barns beside us. There were pig yards. There was a donkey in our own yard, and a goat." And yet they were only a short walk from St. Stephen's Green in the center of the city.

During those years as a child, she learned the importance of helpfulness among neighbors. It was a very close community: "If you were doing something wrong a neighbor wouldn't think anything of it to give you a smack because they knew your grandmother before your mother. Everyone knew if someone was going away, or if someone was home from England. They said of the community that 'it was seed, breed and generation.' They knew everything about you, your parents, your grandparents." She learnt about hardship. Money was not that plentiful. Her mother had to go out and work. She had to keep house from the age of ten, cooking and cleaning, looking after her brothers, as well as going to school. Many of her friends today are her former workmates.

During her childhood, her father was away most of the time working in England. She was the eldest. She left school at fourteen in 1955 and went to work in a factory. She moved to another factory after seven years and worked there until she retired. She worked for forty-two years, "non-stop." She lived with her mother until her mother died seven years ago. Her two brothers are married. Both live in the greater Dublin area. She sees them every week, "and we talk every day." One brother has four children and the other two.

The most important people in her life are her family and friends. She used to meet her friends two or three times a week, now it is maybe once. They play pitch and putt, but the club they all belonged to closed down, and now they are in different clubs. She usually plays on a Friday. She used to play twice a week in the old club, but she now prefers to go on weekend trips with her friends. As well as pitch and putt, she does her art, she plays bowls, and she reads. She always wanted to try art, and so, when she retired, she joined an art class: she mainly paints in oils, pastels, and acrylics. The living room has many of her pictures. She did a portrait of her mother. She finds painting relaxing. She likes sport. She used to play a lot of table tennis and, now, she likes pitch and putt because it helps her to be out in the fresh air. She does not watch much sport unless Ireland is playing.

Simon Walsh also used to live in one of the flat complexes in Mayfarm, but he moved out when he was sixteen, after his brother was murdered because of his involvement in drugs. Now he lives in a local housing estate, but it seems the webs of meaning, the sense of bonding and belonging, are not as strong as when he lived in the flat complex:

> Like when you're living in a community, people in flats like, you get close and you know like you can walk out your door and you know there's somebody there you can talk to. But when you're living in a house it's totally different like. You walk out your door and say hello to someone and that's it, you're just gone. You're out for the day, you're out doing your job. You go home then and then you're back in your house again. But in the flats it's not like that. Like if you went to work, you'd come out and there's your mates there. You 're having a laugh with them and stuff... [E]ven when new people come into the place you engage with them all, like if they have a young fella you'll engage with the young fella and stuff and become mates with them like. But up here, up in [the houses where he now lives] like, is totally different like. You'd have to really go to a pub... to actually meet someone... You'd see your next door neighbour, right, and she'd say hello to you and stuff but the thing is she wouldn't stop and have a conversation with you.

Simon is still deeply attached to the flats, even though it was where his older brother Eddie died of a drug overdose. Eddie and his cousin had started smoking cannabis and then taking cocaine and soon become involved "with the wrong" people selling drugs. Eddie had gotten into debt. He then started taking heroin. The people for whom he was selling the drugs came after him, telling him that if he didn't come up with the money, they were going to kill him.

Then one day, Eddie was over at his aunt's flat across the block. Simon shouted across for him to come home for his dinner. But as Eddie was coming back home, the gang that was looking for him chased him. That night

Eddie snuck out of the flat, got some heroin, mixed it with the methadone he was taking, and overdosed in his bedroom.

It was Simon's other brother, Billy, who found Eddie. Simon ran into the bedroom. He tried to wake him up, to walk him around the room, but he wouldn't respond. "I looked at him and like his eyes were closed. There was green stuff coming out his nose and I couldn't believe it, do y'know that kind of way?" Eddie died in hospital that night.

LIVING ALONE IN WEBS OF MEANING

Kitty Healy is a spinster who lives on her own in the house on the main street in Greyrock. She was born in that very house sixty-eight years ago. Like Sarah Gilsenan she is still suspended in the webs of meaning into which she was born and within which she was reared. And, like Sarah Gilsenan, she is specially devoted to her mother.

Her father died when she was seven, and her mother raised Kitty and her three brothers and four sisters. Kitty qualified as a teacher and went to teach in the local primary school. She taught there until she retired. In the beginning, her mother looked after her and, then, later in life, Kitty looked after her mother, until her mother died some years ago. Kitty talks animatedly and passionately about her mother; she says her mother "was a great woman." Kitty loves the family home and the village. She is full of stories about her mother and the house. In its heyday, it was full of sounds with the comings and goings of herself, her parents, her sisters and brothers. She was the youngest. Kitty is proud of her house. When she was a teacher she used to remind her pupils of the importance of their home. "No matter what, Our Lord came out of a stable, your home should be your castle really and . . . be proud of it." Her house has always been a focal point in the village. People came for miles around to get the bus to Dublin and waited at the stop opposite the house. She remembers how, once, the local parish priest refused to change the clocks back to summer time. People would arrive in the village and have to wait an extra hour for the bus. Her mother took pity on them and told Kitty to go over and invite them in for a cup of tea. She remembers the house being full of villagers, particularly at the weekend. On Sunday mornings, children often fainted at Mass because, in those days, if they were receiving Holy Communion, they had to fast from midnight. If they did faint, they were always brought to Kitty's house. Caring and sharing was a central tenet in the honor code taught to her by her mother, and by which Kitty has lived all her life:

> "Owe no man anything, you pay your lawful debts and you give everyone their own" that was definitely preached big time and if you had anything to

spare, you share it. That was general through the village you know, there was no such thing as hoarding or anything else.

After her father's death, she began to sleep with her mother. She remembers her crying at night. Looking back, she can see how she and her mother became mutually dependent on each other. She says that her mother was almost psychic when it came to reading and understanding her. She said they had their rows, but they also laughed a lot.

Kitty is terrified of dying suddenly, "that I'll go like my mother, suddenly you know, I'd hate that." But when I asked her what happens when you die, she was effusive and told the story of her mother's death. The story was told with great ease and fluidity. It was as if she had told it many times before. It is a story not only about death but also about Kitty's life:

I was with my mother... I was the one who told the nurse that she was dying. That was extraordinary,... my mother's brother was buried on... the Sunday she died. I'd gone into her [in hospital] the Friday morning—I'd go into her before school in the morning and when I'd come home in the evening—but on the Friday morning when I went in she asked me the date and I told her and she said "that is near Christmas" and I say "yeah" and she gave me a strange look and she said "I think I will go home for Christmas, if you don't mind" and I knew, I literally knew what she meant and I said "I don't mind Mammy". And then the... Friday night I was in the hospital when the phone call came to say Uncle Frank had died. I couldn't tell her because you didn't know how she would react, but anyway, Saturday when I went in, she was on about if could I stay. We were going down to the removal down in Wexford and I was saying "I can't stay now Mammy, but I'll stay tomorrow night", "I want you to stay the night" she said to me and I said "Mam, I can't". And then she looked away from me for a while and she came back and she said "that will be time enough"

...So anyway, Mam went off asleep, but I did something I wouldn't have done since childhood... as I said when I used to sleep with her after Dad died, she often said to me "Will you sing a hymn for me now and we'll fall asleep?" And that night I sang "Be not afraid". Now I had no choice...And I sang into her ear, you know that was all, for that it was half nine until...about half ten and then it was "Here I am Lord" and that went on until ten past eleven and I had to change to "I am the bread of life."

And I knew my mother was dying. I went out to the nurses and I said "Mammy is dying" and they came back, three of them came in and said "Kitty, she is asleep she's fine." "No," I said, "she's going." And I'm phoning my sisters and brothers and I'm telling them. So I rang each of them in turn and I said "I'm telling you Mammy is dying, [even though] the nurses say she's ok." I'd finished the last phone call and they came running and said "come quickly." So we started the rosary, the glorious mysteries, it was a Sunday evening so it was the glorious mysteries and the third glorious mystery, the coming of the spirit and I've never experienced anything like it.... There is great joy [to be] had to it and that's from somebody who absolutely lived in her mother, dying.

We can see how Kitty's identity is closely enmeshed with her mother, the house, and the village. In many ways, when she was talking about her mother and telling me stories about her and the house, it seemed as if there was very little difference between them.

Kitty has not always lived on her own. After he mother died, she had a cousin who lived with her for twenty-one years. He had come back from America after his parents died. He was an alcoholic and died of cancer. Kitty felt it was her duty to care for him, even though she hardly knew him when he first arrived, and even though he seems to have made little or no contribution to the house.

She maintains contact with all her family. She is particularly close to two of her sisters: "every single solitary day after six (o'clock) they ring. They've never missed."

Brian Doheny is a parish priest near Hillbrook. He is sixty-seven years old and lives on his own. He has a couple of fields attached to his house. He has three ponies and two dogs. Besides being bachelors, many Catholic priests live on their own, and Brian is one such priest. But again, these priests' main attachments, identity, and sense of self are rooted in other family members. Brian says he feels lonely at times:

> At times of great celebration, maybe within my own family or maybe in general, people celebrating Christmas or Easter, and you go back when the whole hype is over, to a lonely empty house and only the dogs appreciate you... kind of you know. A sense of deep loneliness and isolation... but thankfully it's only a transient thing and tomorrow morning there's another celebration of some kind, that you have to be in form for, and that's it.

He has four brothers and a sister. He is particularly close to his brother and his wife who live in the family home. He visits them regularly. They have eight children, all of whom are grown up and married, and so there are often lots of grandchildren around when Brian visits. He says it is "like Heuston (train) station on a Friday evening, they all converge with their little ones."

When we think of family, then, it is also important to think of the varieties of connections. Gordon Cleary is gay. He is in a transient relationship: at the time of the interview, his present partner was about to leave and return home to Europe. But his identity and sense of self is strongly rooted in his family of origin:

> I've a few friends but I wouldn't have any that I would absolutely consider to be on the same level as family. I think because I've been relatively transient, both in terms of moving from job to job and, from you know say ten or fifteen years ago, country to country, that I'm not really kind of keeping those links. So I've always had this core, three sisters, father and a dog, that have always been kind of there and will continue to be there.

Brian Mason is a fifty-two-year-old successful businessman, involved in local politics, who lives in Castlebay, where he grew up. Brian is different when it comes to family. It seemed to me that the majority of people whom I interviewed, while living in a wide variety of family relationships, were deeply attached and attuned to other family members. However, there were examples of those for whom the webs of meaning were weak and tenuous. If family is what family does, then it would seem that it does very little for Brian. He is divorced from his wife and, mostly, lives alone. But, as he said, "It's kind of an unusual separation, we get on perfectly well, she was here earlier today for tea and to water the stuff in the greenhouse. She worked for me for three or four years after the divorce."

He has five children, whom he hardly ever sees. His father had died four months earlier. He was never close to him or his mother who is still alive. He rarely visits her. He said his childhood was "fast and furious" and that it was "over before it actually began." He was born on a farm, "without light, without water, without this bathroom system. We didn't even have a road. We walked across a number of fields to find a road and...it was perfectly normal, lots of people lived exactly the same way." He grew up with his sister and two brothers. He says his parents "were excellent people but not very professional as parents." He left school when he was eleven and went to work installing and fixing domestic appliances.

After his divorce, he got to know a local woman who had broken up with her partner. "And then one evening she took a bus, she walked up that wee road from where the bus left her to here, and she stayed here for ten years." But he never became attached to her. He is a loner. He said there is nobody that he would feel lost without. He has never gotten close to anyone, so he has never felt lost without them. He has a saying. "I've never met anybody who disappointed me. I never figured they'd make it, and I was right."

Brian Mason comes across as odd and indifferent. He is not part of the normative order that we expect from people, of wanting to live in a family and be disappointed when they cannot. We may feel Brian is cold and calculating in the way he relates to other people. But his difference reveals the power of the family as an institution and how it is taken for granted. It is a bit like the way we have become accustomed to the state. We tend to believe that if there was no family life there would be anarchy. But, as we shall see, as much as there were participants who were attached and attuned to family members even though they lived apart, there were some who lived, or grew up with, no such attachments to members of their families.

The influence of family reaches on and beyond the nuclear family. Families seem to preside in their absence. They are like overcoats that can never be taken off. This web of meaning often reaches out to members of the extended family, to aunts, uncles, and cousins. And for many people, like Sarah Gilsenan and Kitty Healy, the webs of meaning of family extend from the past into the present. Their mothers are still vital to how they see and understand themselves, to how they spin their webs of meaning.

EMOTIONAL WEBS

Families revolve around highly complex ritual interactions of members moving in and around each other in confined spaces. Much of what families do, involves engagement in a complicated choreography of everyday life, interpreting the significance of what is said and done in relation to how it is said and done, and what is not said or done. What makes family life highly complex is the way members express and control their emotions.[18] For the majority of the participants in this study, family life was the backstage of social life in which they recuperated from their engagement in the outside world. It was the place of bonding and belonging, for giving and receiving love, care, and concern, where there was a controlled decontrolling of emotions.

One of the things that many of the families that I encountered were able to do was stay together, and perhaps even tighten the bonds of care and belonging, during times of upheaval, illness, tragedy, or death. Paddy Long had a daughter with his girlfriend. When they separated, he won custody of his daughter. He then began a relationship with his current partner, and they have two children together. However his partner, now divorced, had three children from her earlier marriage. So there are six children in his new family. What was unusual was that his partner's former husband came and lived with them for more than a year:

> He's an alcoholic. He's not able to help himself, y'know what I mean? I had him on my couch for a year believe it or not, because he'd nowhere else to go. He just drank himself into oblivion. He wasn't very good with the kids but what do you do? My friends think I was mad and mental but I just couldn't

push him out, 'cos if I'd pushed him out he'd have died somewhere. He would
have ended up on the road dead and I just couldn't do it.

There were other examples not just of the slings and arrows that families
have dealt with but of the wide range of family types, of who was living with
whom. In this sense, instead of trying to say what the family is, it is better to
capture the complexity of families and what people do within them.

The problem, however, is that besides being a site for love and care, the
family can also be a place of conflict, violence, and sexual abuse.[19] Mary
Finnerty grew up in Mayfarm with her mother and brother. She has no
idea if her father is alive. She knows nothing about him. The three of them
lived with her granny until she was eleven. Then her mother was allocated
a maisonette. Mary says she was a disaster at school. She went, as she says,
"AWOL" in her first year in secondary school. She missed half of the year:

> My Ma had enough of me and then I was living in my aunty's during that
> stage and I got kicked out of her's for going on the hop [AWOL] and that
> [was] like...the final straw, with the school. They [her family] were trying to
> get me back in, and promising me like money and buying me anything. My
> aunty says she'll buy me a pair of runners if I go in. I went on the hop and got
> caught. I got no runners and I got fucked out.

When she was about fourteen or fifteen she started "drinking and
smoking hash and all to beat the band." She became violent. She began
to wreck the house. "I just didn't care about anything or anyone." While
she thinks that she did not have the best childhood, she says: "I wasn't
always unhappy, or I wasn't neglected. I was always looked after sort of."
She struggled on until she was about eighteen or nineteen years old. She
managed to stay attached to her mother, brother, and aunt, and they are
now, along with a woman in the youth project who has counselled her,
the most important people in her life.

Mary is adamant that she would not have survived without the support
worker in the youth project. This young woman enabled Mary to switch
from the culture of drink and drugs and see and understand herself in a new
light. Mary became dependent on her. She began to go to the project first
thing in the morning and last thing at night. "I was just there constantly and
then I started a one-to-one with the youth worker...and she's been my rock
like right through to now." She says they are good friends now. "I'm learning
to deal with things on my own because I would have depended on [her] a
lot throughout the years so I would give her a break. But I know like, that
if anything like [happened], that she is the first person that I would be near
like. She would do anything for me."

The project revolves around trying to get young people like Mary, to move from a culture of drink, drugs, and self-annihilation to a culture of self-fulfillment. She herself has become adept at using this language to talk about herself:

> I keep telling myself because...I get my good and bad days...What I do is live one day at a time. Just like to think that the lesson I have learnt...is that I am important, in life. This is my life and not let everyone else affect [me] or things they have done let you down. Like be stronger than all that, and carry on like.

For Mary, this is a new language, a new way of seeing and talking about herself, a way of understanding the world that is being taught in similar projects in inner-city areas in Dublin. It is a form of education and learning that is a route to engagement in traditional, formal education programs that lead to third-level education and degrees.

We can see here how Mary was born into and shaped by a local culture not of her choosing. She was born into a working-class culture in which learning to opt out of the culture of the educational system and to opt into drugs was a common cultural strategy. It becomes easy for people to become addicts, troublemakers, and misfits. Mary used the culture of drugs to develop her own style of dropping out. It is the dominance of drugs as a cultural repertoire that makes Mayfarm different.

The webs of meaning Mary developed as an addict, while perhaps strong among fellow addicts, were weak with others to whom she was attached. Like many other addicts, if she was to recover, she had to develop a new repertoire. What she had taken for granted about how to see, understand, and operate in the world, what she thought was common sense, had to be challenged and resisted. Mary now works part-time in the youth project with four groups. There is one for fifteen- and sixteen-year-old boys and girls that focuses on sexual health, another for teenage women and mothers that focuses on safe sex. One more group deals with drug awareness and, finally, there is a group that helps people learn how to swim. The general ethos of the groups is one of adult learning wherein participants feel in control of the learning situation. "It is really about what they want to do. They come to you and the first lesson they have is planning, they bring to the table what they want to see happen for the next so many weeks." Again, to learn a different culture, a new way of seeing and understanding oneself, it is necessary to change existing structures and practices. It is part and parcel of the struggle to rebuild existing webs of meaning and spin new ones.

Mary's life now revolves around her family, her aunt, her guide, and the work she does. Caring for other people has been enormously rewarding for her. She is also seeing a psychiatrist: she suffers from anxiety and is on anti-depressants. She says that her head can race with thoughts, and that it is worst early in the morning and late at night. Sometimes when she is feeling low she thinks of the groups of young people with whom she works and she gets an uplift. She loves her work but the problem is that her mother and aunt do not see it as a real job. Like herself, the young people in the youth project are learning about what is important in their lives, about taking ownership of themselves and the community. She is proud of herself because recently she finished a course which she hopes will lead to her eventually becoming a qualified youth worker. It was difficult, but she stuck with it until the end.

The meaning and importance of place, the sense of community in Mayfarm is, then, different in some respects, yet, just as strong as in other areas. People are shaped and learn to live in the community in which they have grown up, into the culture of the place, and the ways of doing things. Maisie Finnerty grew up in a family of fourteen children. Three died, but she has nine sisters and two brothers still alive. None of them emigrated. With one exception, who lives in Galway, they all live in and around Dublin, and there is a good few still living in Mayfarm. Maisie still keeps in close contact with them all:

> Every Friday is our meet-up time. Now I mean like I could go down now...to my mothers, go down to my sisters. But on Friday the others girls would come down. It's mainly all the girls kind of keeping together because the two older boys, they would be the eldest, you wouldn't see much of them compared to the girls. But we have a great ball....There would be...the children and all...They're kind of not babies as much now. There would be...probably fifteen or more, it depends. But it's great fun. We'd have great craic. We'd kind of slag each other...yeah.

But there is a twist in Maisie's tale. Mary Finnerty, whom we just met, is Maisie's daughter. Mary was sexually abused as a child. Back then, within the community and Irish society generally, there was no language to announce let alone describe and explain what was happening. Child sexual abuse was beyond thought. It belonged to the realm of the unsaid, the unmentionable. It is only in recent times, partly to do with the demise of the symbolic domination of the Catholic Church and the emergence of new discourses through the media and the global flow of culture, that people like Maisie have been able to talk about what happened, to put words on their experiences. We can see this in Maisie's use of "ok" in the quote below. We can imagine her saying this to other members of her family and close friends. She tells me about this in order to put me in the picture. But, at the same time, in doing so, she wants to reassure me quickly, that she is "ok" about doing this and that she is, in herself, "ok" now for having done so:

> There was abuse in our house growing up, ok. And it's only in the last few years it's come to light and kind of...with me I'm ok, I'm fine and all. I kind of put it into the back of my head and the whole lot. It wasn't kind of too traumatic for me. I've learned to cope with it and just get on with it. No counselling, nothing. But when...as you've met [mention's Mary's name], and I don't know whether she talked about it or not like, but I can't ask either, so it happened to her as well. So I've gone through the mills with her. I've gone through an awful time with her. Like what she has been through and what she has done and has not done. Like, I don't know how I'm still standing. I don't know how I haven't touched drugs myself or drink, which I don't do anything like that at all anyway. But I still have happy memories as well and sometimes that's why I think I do have a mental block as well. I can only remember certain things 'cos there's a block I think there, that I don't go there.

Although the block is beginning to dissolve and Maisie was able to talk about it, there are parts of the story that she was not willing or able to go into, particularly the identity of her daughter Mary's abuser. She was not able to say how the story got told, but it emerged through Maisie's sisters. It was one sister in particular whom Maisie had not seen for a long time, who was perhaps outside the culture of the family, who broke the ice: "It was between us all y'know what I mean. It wasn't just one person it happened to: it was all. So it was this girl...one of my sisters, that had kind of brought it out and then she was the one, I hadn't seen her for years." The abuse seems to have spread over two generations. She insists that coming out about what happened has heightened the bond between them: "If anything it's after bringing us closer...it's great now because we have that bond again." However, she recognizes that Mary suffered badly from the abuse:

> But I think with [mentions Mary] now it was the hardest for me because she really took it bad. It just kind of came on her all of a sudden like around school...she just wouldn't go home...I went through the mills with her, really now. But we're fine now. We have a lovely place here now and everything is good. She is doing a good job.

Like many other inner-city areas of Dublin, Mayfarm was affected, and still is, with drug addiction. Heroin added to the problems caused by alcohol. Six of the participants I interviewed came from families with a history of overcrowding, violence, crime, abuse, alcoholism, or drug addiction. This was related to the fact that my gatekeeper was a local community activist. While the number of participants from Mayfarm who had personal or indirect contact with drugs and alcohol may not be representative, they do give an insight into how families and the community live and deal with these problems.

TROUBLED WATERS

Family life can be rich, rewarding, and fulfilling. It can also be the source of major upset and conflict. As the interviews progressed and as people told me the stories of their lives, I began to realize how for many of them (twenty to be exact), their life stories were woven in and around alcohol. In five cases the participants themselves had been alcoholics, but in all other cases it was a family member. Three of the five former alcoholics had also been addicted to drugs.

But as we saw with Angela Doyle, the main role of alcohol in the meanings of the participants' lives was how it interfered with, and in some cases, undermined family life. Bridie McPhearson is a seventy-three-year-old woman who lives in Hillbrook with her seventy-six-year-old friend Orla Feeney. They both had alcoholic fathers. Bridie was brought up by her grandmother. She hardly ever saw her father while she was growing up, even though he only lived ten miles away. Orla Feeney grew up in the United States. Her father was Irish. He started drinking when he lost his job and he took to going to the pub every day. As her mother was a long-term patient in hospital, Orla had to look after the house and her sisters. She continued to do this even after her mother came home. Her father began to control his drinking, but then when her mother died, he began again, so heavily that eventually Orla had to ask him to leave the family home. He went to a cousin's house for a while and eventually he had to go into a nursing home. Orla married when she was nineteen. Her husband was in sales. It was a job that involved a lot of entertaining and drinking. He was also a smoker. He died of a massive heart attack when he was forty-eight.

There is plenty of evidence to show that alcohol has become a central part of Irish culture, and there are plenty of statistics to show that the Irish drink considerable amounts of alcohol, usually tending to drink large amounts at one time. Drinking is interwoven into many aspects of social life, particularly celebrations and funerals. Miley Nolan is fifty-nine. He has a successful engineering business. He lives with his wife. His son Jim, who recently returned home from Europe with his wife and child, is building a house behind the family home. Miley's younger son died of cancer some years ago.

Drinking does not seem to be a major factor in Miley Nolan's life, but it was very much a part of his culture. He told me about his grandfather who was involved in local politics for thirty years, and how it led to a lot of drinking: "and all the bad habits of politics go with it I suppose and that he was fond of the gargle you know and would go on a skite of drink as they say every now and again. I heard somebody saying (that)...his take-away...when he'd be going home, was a bottle of whiskey and three dozen Guinness you know."

Miley says he usually likes to relax with a glass of wine and read a book or watch television. However, it was a different matter when it came to organizing his son's funeral. His son had stipulated that there was to be a party in the local rugby club. Miley tells the story, not I suspect for the first time:

> This is a peculiar kind of a brag I suppose in that there was almost ten grand's worth of drink drank the night of his funeral in the rugby club. They had to go up town four or five times to replenish their stocks through the night. They had never seen anything like it, you know what I mean.

Alcohol and tragedy may be part of Irish culture, but they do not necessarily lead to unsettled families. On the one hand, among most of the people who, like Miley, lived in settled families, the sense of attunement and attachment was almost palpable. The responses to my questions demonstrated a consistent sense of general happiness and well-being, despite any loss, tragedy, or bad luck. On the other hand, those living in unsettled families often had a sense of despondency. Geraldine Barnstable is sixty-one. She lives with her husband, whom she met as a teenager. They have three children, all in their twenties. The youngest still lives at home. But Geraldine is estranged from her husband. "We are together but we are not together...And I have learnt to live and not rock the boat and that has been the last 7 or 8 years. People say why stay with him? It's not economically viable for me to walk out." She says she married "another control freak"; the first was her mother. She is estranged from her: she has not seen her in two years. She grew up with three brothers and two sisters, one of whom died. Her brothers have banned Geraldine and her remaining sister from seeing or making contact with their mother. "It's bitter on my brothers' side, it's a mystery to myself and my sister as to why we were excluded...we've been told by various people that there were financial reasons." However, Geraldine is not sure. There was a history of sexual abuse in the family. Her older sister revealed to her recently that both she and the sister who died had been raped by a family friend. However, when they told their mother about it, she did not believe them.

Families are a complex web of emotional relations that are spun on a daily basis and involve intricate reading, responses, and reactions to what members say and do. In settled families, there seems to be a collective consciousness that binds members together that is in turn linked to a collective conscience about what is right and wrong, and what it is to live a good life. Unsettled families tend to be unable to deal with or negotiate difficulties in relationships. Take Sarah Burton, for example. She is fifty-two. She has a successful professional career. She is gay and lives with her partner in Falderry. She grew up in the West of Ireland and had a reasonably happy childhood. But everything changed when she eventually told her father she was gay. He was, she says, a very traditional Catholic who could not accept her homosexuality: "He is one of the old-fashioned men who sees a man as being really important and how could he produce somebody like this." She has since lost all contact with him. Her mother died before she came out as gay: "In a way it was lucky my mother died because I'd say it [her homosexuality] would've killed her off." She has little contact with her brother. "We don't speak, because we don't get on, but he keeps in touch, we just meet once a year. There is fisty cuffs otherwise...mentally and emotionally."

I interviewed about twenty people who could be described as having grown up in an unsettled family environment, probably due to circumstances such as the death of a parent or sibling at a young age, or the respondent being abused, or a parent being an alcoholic.

Lar Cummins had a difficult childhood. His mother seems to have been quite neglectful. He grew up mostly with his grandparents, in the suburbs of Dublin. His parents eventually separated when he was twelve: "[M]y grandmother, she basically reared me like you know. I wasn't in the family home that much, even though I was only five doors away,...we went between the two houses, you know." His mother was an alcoholic. He was told that when he was ten months old, "she was out on the drink one night and had me wherever in a ditch overnight, and they were out looking for me, so you know." His grandmother had died a month before the interview. She was ninety-seven years old. He was very close to her, as he still is to his father. He says about his father that "whenever he's not working, he's drinking." Just before his parents separated, he witnessed his father attack his mother with a knife. He has one brother, but they don't get along, and he rarely sees him. His brother grew up with his mother. When Lar was twenty, he was in a relationship with a girl. She had twins: "They're fifteen now, haven't seen them in fourteen years." He eventually separated from her and is now married. It was his wife who persuaded him to undergo counseling, to try and unravel the trauma of his childhood. He says: "She's a great girl." They have a newborn baby girl and a nine-year-old boy. So despite all the traumas he experienced as a child, Lar has been able to find love and happiness: "I have my family you know, I'm happy."

CONCLUSION

Family life in Ireland has both changed and remained the same. Family formations are of various kinds, yet many traditional familial patterns, ways of being, and ways of creating webs of meanings persist. The material conditions in which families live have changed, particularly in terms of the size and quality of housing, the level of technology, or the general standard of living. There have also been changes in the nature of households: who lives with whom, what families do, and the way husbands and wives relate to each other and their children. Family life has also been influenced by increased mobility and the penetration of the media and the market. However, the results of the 2011 Census show that the family is still a major institution in Irish social life. The majority of adults still live as couples, get married, and have children. Understanding what goes on in families is the best way of understanding what goes on in everyday social life. Not only do families provide an explanation and understanding of what life is about; they also provide a model for how life should be led.

Families are the basis for many aspects of life, but they are the primary institution in terms of creating meaning and understanding of life, of developing identities and a sense of self, and of maintaining bonds of affection and belonging. However, as we have seen, families are deeply emotional entities and the nature and strength of the bonds of belonging vary between families and within families over time.

Family life is the major social hub for individuals, around which they lead their lives. Individuals are constituted as selves primarily within a familial set of relations and the practices of intimacy, giving, caring, and sharing. Family is an embodied space in which people are constituted and reconstituted as individuals and from which they emerge into the network of social fields in which they operate. It is a space in which members create and sustain meaning and where the emotional controls of public life are more readily and easily decontrolled. However, the construction of family is an ongoing and fragile process that moves back and forth between settled and unsettled times. Unless emotions are expressed and controlled in mutually fulfilling ways, the sense of bonding and belonging can quickly diminish and feelings of attachment and attunement to other family members can dissipate.

We, then, can think of families as spinning core webs of meaning, which, when intertwined with place, become hubs from which other webs of meaning are spun. Individuals move in and out of myriads of different webs of meaning in their daily life. But when it comes to core meanings, most are generated and maintained within families. And this is true for both settled and unsettled families, for those that are deeply attuned and attached to one another, and for those that are indifferent or at loggerheads with each other.

CHAPTER 4

MONEY AND SUCCESS

THE WEBS OF MEANING IN WHICH PEOPLE ARE SUSPENDED EXTEND THROUGH
the various groups, organizations, associations, and institutions in which
they operate.[1] In their everyday lives, people move in and through family relations embedded in neighborhoods, into fields of work, the state, the
market, the media, politics, sport, religion, and many more. Each of these
fields is shaped by institutions and discourses that structure the existing
codes, conventions, the ways of thinking, talking, and being. These codes,
conventions, and so forth are enacted in specific contexts and interactions.
We can see each context, whenever humans interact with one another, as
the spinning of a new web of meaning, albeit that for most people there are
only a few, very fine differences from the last web that was spun, whether
among family members, neighbors, or colleagues. And yet while all of these
fields and contexts have particular webs of meaning, they are embedded in
an overall culture of meaning.[2] When people go into a local shop to buy
some groceries, the meaning that is created is shaped not just by the specific
cultural codes of what can be said and done in the context of the exchange
of goods and money but, as part of a wider culture; it is also shaped by language, codes of civility, and state laws. Buying groceries is a common event
across the world, but the specific web of meaning that is spun in the interaction between the shopkeeper and the customer each time, in each place, is
slightly different.

People are also embedded in an overall field of power.[3] A shopkeeper
may have his own style and way doing his job, but he belongs to a particular
social class position, which is determined by the volume of his economic
and cultural capital. The webs of meaning he weaves vary depending on
whom he is relating to—whether it is the shop assistants he employs, his
suppliers, or the customers with whom he deals. As we saw in chapter 2, all
of these relations are relations of power, particularly those of social class.

The local doctor or politician will often be accorded a different form of treatment than the local road sweeper. These class differences are mixed in with gender and status divisions. Women and men are shown different types of treatment, as are older people and younger people, and so forth. The meanings that are woven in everyday life into particular contexts and interactions are, then, shaped not just by the wider culture, but by the field of power relations.

So, like everyone else in the Western world, the people who took part in this study are suspended in the webs of meaning and power that are part of a consumer capitalist society. They are embedded in lives of working and consuming. As well as weaving webs of meaning with family, friends, and neighbors, most create and maintain webs of meaning within the workplace and within their occupations. In pursuing their careers, in attaining knowledge, education, and qualifications, in earning money and accumulating wealth, they also struggle to attain and reproduce their social class position. This necessitates spinning and operating within webs of meaning that are different from those based on love, care, bonding, and belonging. However, attaining and maintaining economic and cultural capital and a position in the field of power is always a cultural activity.

The struggle to attain economic capital is always mixed with the struggle to attain and maintain cultural capital, which, in turn, revolves around creating and maintaining meaning, embodying the particular habitus or shared ways of seeing and understanding the world that characterize the field.[4] Fishermen are different from architects, but they both have ways of talking about fish and buildings, respectively, that create and maintain meaning and enable communication and cooperation as well as competition. The ways in which investor bankers, property developers, doctors, and judges see and understand the world, the webs of meaning they create inside and outside work, are different from those created by bus drivers, farmers, and shop assistants. The webs of meaning that people create and maintain are, therefore, particular to their occupation and class position. Indeed success within any occupational field depends on embodying the habitus, on weaving and maintaining webs of meaning that are particular to the occupation and social class position. The more an investor banker walks, talks, and presents himself as an investor banker, and more he acts the part, the more likely he is to be successful. It is no different for the fisherman, the architect, or the bus driver.

However, besides fulfilling their occupational and class positions, people, as we have seen, are also suspended in webs of meaning that they weave with family, friends, and neighbors, those with whom they have close and intimate relations. These are often not just different webs, but they they can lead to conflicting demands and emotional upheavals. Of course, for some, there is no sharp dividing line between the world of work and the world of home, family, and friends. However, for most people, there is a need to balance the meanings of life that they create with loved ones with those they create through their work. They have to balance the struggle to attain money and power with the struggle to be loved. They also have to balance attaining money and power with their overall conception of the meaning of life and how to live a good one. For most people, throughout the world today and throughout history, the struggle to earn a living and make money has been closely interwoven with, if not dominated by, the interest in living a good life. And, despite increasing secularization, for most people today, the struggle to live a good life has been shaped by religion.[5] However, as we shall see, there is little evidence that religion, and in particular Catholic beliefs and values, shapes the economic actions of the people in this study. Rather, it is that people use various beliefs, attitudes, and values to create and maintain the meaning necessary to keep the action going and, at the same time, to interpret and explain the motivations of their actions and the relation between work, money, and the meaning of life.[6] In this sense, culture establishes not just explanations of life and models of how to live a good life, it also creates the moods and motivations that shape action.[7]

The results of a recent study suggest that when it comes to balancing work with family and leisure, Irish people may be slightly less oriented to work. A study conducted by the Organisation for Economic Co-operation and Development (OECD) found that people in Ireland work on an average 1,543 hours a year, which is 233 hours less than the OECD average. And when it comes to working very long hours, only 4 percent of Irish employees do so compared to an OECD average of 9 percent. But there is a gender gap: while 7 percent of Irish male employees work very long hours, only 1 percent of female employees do so. This imbalance in work life is reflected in domestic life. Irish men spend only 129 minutes per day doing domestic work compared to 296 minutes for women. But in this respect, Irish men are very close to the OECD average for men—131 minutes.[8]

However, most Irish people appear to be happy, no matter how they balance their work lives with family and leisure. The same OECD study found that when it came to life-satisfaction or subjective well-being, Irish people had a grade of 7.0 compared to the overall OECD average of 6.6. In Ireland, 84 percent of people reported having more positive experiences on an average day (feelings of rest, pride in accomplishment, enjoyment, and so forth), compared to negative ones (pain, worry, sadness, boredom, and so forth).

But while these figures give a quick instantaneous overview of Irish people's well-being and the relationship between work and domestic life, they do not capture the complex nuances in the way people work, their pursuit of ambition and material success, and how they balance these interests with maintaining bonds of belonging, of loving and caring for others, and of being loved and cared for in return.

THE SHOPKEEPER

Mark O'Neill has developed a cultural style. It is a no-nonsense, fast-talking, form of self-presentation. There is a strong, continuous flow of words. There is little pause for thought. It is as if he wants to convince you that he is straightforward, that he says what he thinks. If is as if he thinks that if he paused for thought, it might be seen was an attempt to deceive, that he was not delivering "what it says on the tin," that the promise of his product will not be fulfilled. It is his way of being a shopkeeper. His manner is as easy to put on as the white coat that he wears. And yet it is his identity, a way of being in the world that permeates his whole life.[9]

Mark works in the world of retail in which customers have to trust him. He owns a busy shop in Mayfarm. I interviewed Mark in the backroom of his shop. We were interrupted regularly by assistants coming in to ask questions about what they should do and by him answering calls that came through on his mobile phone. He talked to the callers as he talked to me, in a series of quick-fire rapid questions and answers. The approach seemed to be one of direct, decisive, no-nonsense responses: time is money and there is a need to "cut to the chase" as quickly as possible. It is his way of doing business.[10] He was having his lunch while we talked. He was extremely generous and offered to share his sandwiches with me.

Mark is forty-two. He grew up in the world of commerce and retail sales. His father owned a shop when he was growing up. He left school when he was fourteen years and went to work in his father's shop. He has had his ups and downs in the retail world. When he was only twenty-two, he lost his first business. "I went down for a quarter of a million. That was a lot of money." It was a tough learning curve:

> I had a small supermarket. I lost hugely…I paid everyone off…it took me years and that may be a reason I sometimes…buy Margaret [his wife] so many things 'cos for several years, like my mortgage and all at home in Churchmill was frozen for a couple of years like, I was broke, broke…Like the bread men would come into me that I owed money to and I used to give them meat, do you know what I mean, I'd pay them all off. I did deals with the banks in the end and…the biggest wholesalers, but all the small suppliers were paid off.

Again, we can see here how Mark presents himself. He emphasizes that in his world of small businessmen, he is an honest broker and that he paid all his debts. I asked him if he was going to develop his present shop:

No, get busier yes, expand no. I don't believe you can expand in the type of business I do for the simple reason the personal touch is not there... Like if I had a business partner, I'd have no problem doing it if he was the same as me... y'know... chatty on the counter... you have to be able to look after your customers. I believe... you give people personalized service, like I'm more expensive than a supermarket but I think I give a different product.

He explained to me that the retail sector is about keeping old customers, creating new ones, and constantly searching for new products they might buy:

Making sure the customers are alright, making sure the product is right... I'm always trying to think of new things to put in the shop... I've got artisan pizza bases coming in... that was that phone call there. I'm always trying to get new things in.

He likes the interaction with his customers:

The old dears love double meanings, love all that and I would go along like... just... the banter... but Dublin people... like you tell the old dears, "your hair is lovely, oh god your legs look great in those shoes". Whatever, but y'know what I mean... but like that's what I think people like in the shop. Like a woman who works for me... like she's 60 odd and I always say things to her like... I have customers that come in to me that call her the wrinkled old woman and they'll say "ah no, we'll wait on the wrinkled old woman", 'cos I tell them to say that to her. It's just banter in the day. It's better... if you go into a local supermarket now they don't even say hello to you... And I think that's wrong.

Mark's life revolves around his family and his work. He is devoted to his wife and his two teenage children. He says he does not have any friends as such, they are more business acquaintances. He was over in Canada recently and he only went out once socially, "and the only reason I did that was because I owed the guy a favour so I took him for a meal and that was it." Holidays do not interest him that much. He prefers his days off: "like last Wednesday I was off, Margaret and I drove down to Avoca in Kilmacanogue, had lunch, picked up the kids, came home. Kids did their homework, walked the dog, we all watched a DVD together. Good day." He had the following day (after the interview) off and he was planning to do some Do It Yourself (DIY). He could easily afford to get someone in to do it, but he was looking forward to doing it himself:

> I'll do it for the craic because we had a wardrobe taken out of our bedroom and there was a bit of wooden flooring [missing] and I'm actually doing it for the fun of it more than anything else because it's only a tiny little piece. But now, there's wallpaper going up and I would rather go to work and pay someone to do it . . . so the wallpaper man is coming, But . . . I'm hiring one of these air gun things, y'know these nail things . . . never used one before but I'm going to try it tomorrow.

When I asked him what he would feel lost without, he hesitated slightly before saying "I suppose Margaret. I suppose the kids afterwards" and when I probed him he responded: "If I say money does it make me sound shallow?" He says he is always thinking about the business. He is most calm and relaxed either when he is at home or when he is busy at work. "Hate being quiet. Hate business to be quiet, despise it. Not good."

He makes a clear distinction between the world of work and the world of home and family. In work, he can be ruthless. "I once fired a guy on his birthday. Had to be done. I didn't know it was his birthday at the time but, do y'know what I mean." However, he hates having a row with Margaret, which, he says, doesn't happen very often. It upsets him. "I'm no good for rows in my personal life. But [in] business life, [it] means nothing to me to have a row, nothing."

The major disappointments in his life were losing his first business and not buying more property in the 1990s: he had the "private number of a very big bank manager." Mark is concerned about his image. He likes to look and feel good. "I usually always feel good. I have very little mood swings. I wake up this way, I go to bed this way. My kids call me a bit of a robot. I like to look clean, respectable, but I wouldn't stand in [front of] the mirror." He does not exercise or go to the gym. "Eat what I want. Eat cream cakes all the day long. Don't have a weight problem. 30 inch waist."

Mark likes to consume as much as he produces. "I don't have any savings . . . I like earning but I like spending it . . . I have no desire to accumulate it [money]. I want to be comfortable, but I've no desire to accumulate it . . . Don't drink, don't smoke but spend like bee-jaysus . . . I love to shop."

He says that he would spend more on Margaret than himself. He recently bought her a good laptop. She drives a nice car: "I drive a banger," he says. He likes to buy nice things for the house. "I would always try and buy good stuff . . . if she [Margaret] buys something she usually puts up the price when she's telling me . . . most wives put down the price, she puts up the price . . . I'm a bit like that." But he also likes to buy things for himself. He likes watches and shirts: "If I was buying a watch it would be a good watch." He has a strategy about buying: "Most of my shirts are Pink. So I've no problem spending money on myself. But I would still, if I went into an expensive shop and bought two shirts, I'd buy Margaret something as well."

Mark does not believe in God. When I asked if he ever had, he replied:

> Not really…No, I don't…my kids go to Mass. My kids go to a Catholic school. My daughter sings in the choir…At first Holy Communion and all that…I have several priests I know really well. But y'know…I'm not overly religious…like I believe when you're dead, you're dead, that's it…when the chips are down I don't pray. I don't believe in that. That's hypocritical to me.

Mark can be seen as a cultural Catholic.[11] Catholicism is part of his cultural repertoire. He makes use of it not so much for providing an explanation of his life or how to live a good life, but more in terms of it being part of his family heritage. His father is very religious; he goes to Mass several times a week. He does not think the church has had a positive or negative influence on his life. When I asked him if he was spiritual, he asked me to define what I meant by spiritual. I said I had hoped he would but that for me it meant going beyond the material world. He replied: "No, no. The deeper meaning of life? No, I'm not into that…What you see is what you get with me. There is no deeper than me, this is it…I don't have to find myself or anything like that."

He detests any form of fundamentalism and is critical of some of his Catholic customers: "like I've got old dears that come in and they'd go to Mass every day and five minutes later they'd be back biting their next door neighbor…I don't think that's good. I don't think they're religious people, y'know what I mean. That's not religion to me."

For him to live a good life means following the golden rule, "do unto others as you would them do unto you." "I'd be old-fashioned in certain ways. I'd be very old-fashioned in the marriage, like, I believe you're married, you're married. There's no two ways about it. You open a door for a woman. You give a lady…in church, or in a bus, or tram, if someone gets on…you give them your seat. Simple things like that."

We can see, then, how Mark O'Neill is deeply embedded in the cultural life of consumer capitalist society. The webs of meaning that he spins in his shop do not overlap with those of his family: and yet they sustain one another. There is a symbiotic relationship between them. He has a limited or restricted cultural repertoire. He has developed a cultural style. He has his strategies for doing business and for living a good family life. He seems to have little or no interest in the deeper meanings of life, and yet he is suspended in very strong webs of meaning.

BUSINESS PEOPLE

Very few, if any, of the people I interviewed could be classed as very wealthy, certainly not in terms of their occupations, possessions, or the type of houses in which they lived. However, there were many who could be classed as very well off. Terry Barry is a fifty-seven-year-old reformed alcoholic who made his money mainly through property development. His goal in life was success, but he recognizes that success is about luck. He thinks successful people are more lucky than gifted: "Life is very much follow the ball, right place right time, know the right people and be civil and courteous and if you're a bit lucky, you get what you [want]." He worked hard to make his money but he enjoyed it. "Most of all because I enjoyed what I was doing and I was making money which is the main ingredient for...working hard." He works very little at the moment. He likes to play golf and poker (only for the excitement). He likes to keep any eye for opportunities to speculate and the satisfaction of "wiping out whatever money would be borrowed and coming into credit."

Miley Nolan is another successful businessman. He is fifty-nine. He owns a own small company. He enjoys his work. Whenever he went on a holiday, he was always itching to get back to work. He thinks he is successful. But when it comes to money, he thinks he is like his father who set up the company. "He had no regard for money, none. If he had enough tobacco that's nearly all he needed, [if] he had enough money for tobacco he was fine you know what I mean and never any regard for money really...and I don't have any regard for money either." He is happy living in his "very modest house" and knowing that he and his family have enough to eat and drink.

Mick Furlong is sixty. He worked for thirty-two years before taking an early retirement. As well as building up his small farm, he worked for a number of different companies. Last year he bought a small company. He always had an ambition to have his own business. He likes to earn money. He would like to have more:

> Well money is important, there's no doubt about that...Money is necessary, number one, you can't survive without it...but you need money, yeah and I would like to have more money to be honest with you. I would see a lot of benefits in having more money than I have.

He thinks that people who do not have money are a burden. "If you have no money...you're not much good to yourself or anybody else." He says his main worry is money. He is anxious about the recession and is worried if his new company will survive.

Simon Corboy is thirty-two. He is the manager of a shop that he has leased. His work is extremely important to him. When I asked him what

did he get out of it, he said: "I get this house. I get my car. I get my lifestyle."
Simon has a passion for cars, a passion he inherited from his father who
owned a garage that used to sponsor cars in rallies. When I asked him what
he would feel lost without, he mentioned his car. "I got a Christmas present
from my sisters to go to Mondello to do like the race there, which was just
brilliant." He would like to attend more rallies and become more involved
but the demands of work are too much. And yet, like Mark O'Neill, he really
enjoys his work. He likes the people who come into his shop, particularly the
elderly and local country people: "I just find them entertaining." He thinks
the shop is a "crazy place" with a lot of "crazy people" coming and going.

Nan McCormack is fifty-eight. She and her husband own a small shop
in a small village. The shop is to one side of their home. They have five children, one of whom died shortly after birth. Two of the boys have married
two local girls from the same road. Like many other shopkeepers, she and
her husband work a long day, from eight o'clock in the morning until ten
o'clock at night. "I'd spend every day out there all day nearly, and have been
for the last thirty-five years." She depends on regular customers. But unlike
Mark O'Neill she does not seem to have the same banter and repartee with
them. But they know her: they would sometimes ask what was wrong with
her and, she says, "I'd have the usual smile and it might be a forced one."

It was expensive putting the two boys through college, and with the
recession she is worried about money. She hopes that it won't hit her too
hard. She is worried about the forthcoming budget, "I think they're going
to drown us." She says that she has already lost half her pension. Her relief
from the shop is to go out on a Saturday night with her lady friends for a few
drinks and go with them on holiday or to a concert in Dublin. They wanted
to go to the last Tina Turner concert, but it was too expensive. She does not
dress up when she is working in the shop but she likes to dress up when she
goes out. "I love dressing up when I'm away on holidays and that...just
makes me feel good I suppose...I try and make the best with what I have,
shall I put it that way." When I asked her what the meaning of a good life
was she was hesitant: "I don't know. I honestly don't know. Meaning of a
good life would have been plenty of money, would've been flying here there
and everywhere." She did not go abroad much because her husband never
liked flying.

THE CIVIL SERVANT

We can see, then, that for the people mentioned in the previous section,
making meaning in the workplace was more of a means toward an end, of
keeping the meaning going in order to keep the business going. Most of
the participants seemed to demarcate the webs of meaning of loved ones

from the webs of meaning of work. But for most, also, the webs of meaning of work were not only a central part of their identity but also were part of their self-fulfillment. There was pleasure and satisfaction from doing their job. However, there were those who had good jobs but no longer got much satisfaction from them.

Consider, for example, Eamon O'Loughlin. He is a fifty-year-old civil servant. He grew up in a small town in the East of Ireland with his parents and three brothers and two sisters. His father also worked in the public service. Eamon did reasonably well in his Leaving Certificate examination and could have gone to university. Instead he applied for junior clerical officer posts in the state and semistate sectors. He got a number of job offers. He ended up taking the first one offered to him, which was with the government department in which he still works.

He started working when he was eighteen and, as he says, "that was that." Looking back, he thinks he was probably pushed into the civil service. "I was very careful to take advice, or very easily led by my parents... my father would've been a public servant... and you know he would've extolled the virtues of a steady job and pension." There was also the reality that he was the third eldest boy and that his father could not afford to have another son at university. Earning good money at eighteen put him in a different social class:

> So of course you get money in your pocket then and you sort of live that lifestyle of the young single lad around Dublin... you know. It was... quite a social world. There was good craic as they say... Like you know you are better off than a student and you're better off than, you know, an apprentice. It's a nice little job... you get a nice, you know, pay packet and if you have no children and no responsibilities at that age. I certainly hadn't then, you know. It's a nice life... and I got comfortable in there and... about six years into it, which seems like a blink of an eye now... I was getting married and then of course I needed to stay and, you know, I needed the money. It stood the test of time well, you know, the civil and public service... it keeps people in it that need to stay in it and then as a consequence of staying in it you give it the loyalty it expects and all. So there is no place for revolutionaries in there and so in actual fact it was a bad fit for me. I never really examined that though until about... seven or eight years ago.

After ten years in the department, he became interested in the trade union movement and local trade union politics and did a part-time degree in industrial relations and human resource management. He later completed an MBA and, more recently, he completed a course in psychotherapy. In between this, he got married and had two daughters (both now in their twenties). He has separated from his wife and is now in a new relationship.

He and his former wife had been "growing apart and not really communicating" for many years. He was taking sleeping pills and "psycho active medicine," and while he did sleep, he still felt "a small bit drugged all the time." He felt that he had become a different person. He became unreliable at work, and he eventually noticed that it was not just his wife who was giving him a wide berth. It was this experience that led him into psychotherapy:

> I had become quite a strange person in some ways, slightly disconnected from reality, you know, in the sense of I was drugged all the time, you know, mildly or maybe not even very mildly in some cases...it's very hard to explain, it's like a veil, it's like looking at the world through, through a thin scarf, you know that sort of image, that you are removed one little degree from everything, you know.

He has some very close relationships with his work colleagues, some of whom would be close confidants. He knows some of them from the time he started working thirty-two years ago: "They almost fill the role of a brother or sister...I know their wives, I know their children, I know their houses, you know, much more so than I know my own family actually."

Throughout his working life, he has always had "a second thing that I do as well as work." It used to be the trade union, but since his mental health problems, he has taken to exercising, mainly cycling and walking, and spending more time with nature. He likes the arts, particularly music, theater, and cinema. He reads a lot: he feels "quite nervous" if he doesn't have books to read. He has become disenchanted with his work and the public service generally. Although he works full time, he sees his new part-time work as a counselor as more in the role of being a public servant:

> Well my work as a public servant is probably not all that important to me anymore. I used to think it was very important and gradually as time went by I kind of stood back from it a good bit and said well actually it's a bit of a rat-race you know and a not very well paid one either...why not be in the bank or something like that...So there was [once] a sense about the public service...that you were helping people, or that it was as it says, a *public* service. But in actual fact it just turned out as I reflected on it...just as much of a rat race as anything else...So I thought well actually...where you can really help somebody is outside of the organization, in one to one, you know and that's what the counselling thing is about.
>
> So I thought...the bigger the organization, the more bureaucratic it is, and even though the trade union movement is founded on very egalitarian and very helpful principles, it actually is very power seeking as well...Like the taxpayers money is supposed to go for the good of the public, but in actual fact you observe after a while a lot of people on the make wanting a

piece for themselves, wondering how they can get to the top of the tree, you know, and I am sure it's the same in any organization, you know, so.

When he was young he was very interested in Marxism. He viewed Irish society as being "deeply flawed, deeply unfair, the wealthy remained wealthy, the poor stayed poor and the middle classes were where the action was." He recognizes that he himself is deeply middle class and that he was well-drilled in the "rules of engagement," which meant "keeping your head down and your nose clean and not giving back cheek and not saying too much, you know, and not revealing your hand." He is reasonably happy with his circumstances. Like many other people in this study, he would like not a lot but just a bit more money. If he had an extra ten grand a year he might be driving a newer car. But he reflects and says: "I have a house and I have my children reared and, you know, myself and my partner are quite happy."

He believes in the motto that the unexamined life is not worth living. He thinks it is important to reflect on the motives for doing things. But there is also a need to do something that helps other people. He is conscious that the world is divided into the "haves" and the "have-nots." He thinks there are some people who are very greedy, and he does not want to be seen as one of them. His daughter has done voluntary work in India, and she reminds him when he is worried about money that, where she goes, 50 euro would feed a village for a month. He feels privileged that he has been able to take really good holidays and that, particularly as part of his involvement in the trade union movement, he has traveled the world and been to all the major capital cities of Europe.

He contrasts his life with that of his younger brother who opted out of "this kind of life." His brother lives in the same area in which he grew up. His children go the same school as he did. "He has a job...he goes into work and no sooner is work over than he's gone home and he spends all his time with animals and out on his bit of land." His brother is wrapped up in the extended family. He thinks that for all his study of psychotherapy, his brother is probably more in tune with himself. He concludes that "the trade-off for being cosmopolitan and being well travelled and having lived in different places is that you don't have the other."

BEING WITHOUT MONEY

In its report on *Better Life*, the OECD noted that while money may not buy happiness, it is an important means to achieving higher living standards and thus greater well-being. Higher economic wealth is also generally linked to better quality education, health care, and housing.[12] But, as we have seen, the relationship between money and happiness is complicated. Even though these interviews took place at the beginning of one of the worst recessions in Irish history, and even though many people expressed fears and concerns about the future, most of the participants talked down the importance of money. This was not confined to any social class: some of those who said money was not important to them were relatively poor or disadvantaged. Consider, for example, Jane O'Reilly. She is a thirty-two-year-old mother who was about to have her second child. She is a former drug addict and now works in community care. She captures the contradiction of wanting to have more money, yet trying to be happy with what she has, and not yearning for more. When I asked her how important money was, she said:

> Well I'd love to say it's not really. It's not something that I'd have high on my list of priorities. Money…we need it to live y'know but it's not that important to me, money, y'know. Y'know like to have nice things and to be able to buy my child [her 12-year-old son] nice clothes and take him out but eh, y'know, I wouldn't be obsessed with winning the lotto or anything like that way y'know. It's not that important to me y'know.

When I asked her about success, she was equally phlegmatic:

> Y'know success to me isn't about having the right car and the fancy house and the great job y'know. Success to me is y'know, I suppose from the journey I've been through, is to be able to get up in the morning and y'know be there for my son, y'know and having another baby and keeping down a job and that's success to me, being in a loving relationship and being happy with myself I suppose, y'know. That's success to me.

People use culture for many things. They use it to attain and maintain incomes and wealth as well as meaning, happiness and well-being. There were many people like Jane O'Reilly who lived with the weight of low-income jobs with little prospects of great wealth, and who used culture to explain the conditions of their existence and how to make a good life out of what they have.

Maisie Finnerty is the forty-four-year-old woman we met in the last chapter. She went to work in a bakery when she finished her Leaving Certificate. She loved it. She was not well paid, but she had great fun with the other girls with whom she worked. She says they were like a family. Maisie continued to work until four years ago when she was diagnosed with cancer, and she has been dealing with that ever since. She depends on social welfare. She recently moved into a small house and is in a new relationship. She misses work and would love to work at something unusual. She had to look after her niece a few days previously when she went into labor prematurely. Maisie loved it, "it was one of the most fantastic things to see a child born, I have to say. I was on a high after that." She thinks she would like to be a midwife. She says that money is not important to her: "Money is nothing to me. I'm not into having big things." She continued: "Once my bills are paid and, as my mother says, 'if you've a roof over your head and running water that's the main thing,' and she's right."

What we are seeing here is how people make use of culture to understand and explain to themselves, and others, not only material inequalities but also how striving to have more money should not be seen as a good model for life: it is not the source of health, happiness, and well-being. It may well be that these aphorisms are a way of coping with living in poverty or on the edge of it. They are within the same category as many of the parables from the New Testament and such catchphrases as "it is as difficult for a rich man to get into heaven as it is for a camel to get through the eye of the needle."

It is noticeable that such aphorisms tend to be used more by the less well-off. It may be that they have a greater need for them. Consider, for example, Danielle Burton. She is forty-two. She is one of those Dubliners who made the move to Greyrock but, unlike Angela Doyle, things have not gone well for her. She says she had a great childhood. She is still devoted to her parents. She gets up to Dublin to see them at least once a week. Her father is her closest confidant. She got married when she was twenty-four. She had two children, and then her marriage collapsed. It was after she separated from her husband that she moved to Greyrock. She thought it would be a better life for her children. She entered into a new relationship and had another child, but that relationship too ended four years ago. She is now unemployed and dependent on social welfare. She would like to be in a relationship, but her youngest son suffers from a severe form of attention deficit hyperactivity disorder (ADHD). He has started school, but he is not fully toilet trained. She regularly has to collect him from school. When he is at home, he demands constant attention. He is often up until ten o'clock and even when he goes to bed he wakes up when he has night tremors. Danielle feels she could not cope with his demands and that of a partner. The only time she gets to herself is when her son is at school. She is very involved in a local voluntary ADHD support group. She has been trying to find part-time work, but there is nothing in the area. She misses not working. "I'd love to be working. I always loved working." Her last job was working with African immigrants. She liked getting to know them and their culture. She is struggling on social welfare:

> If I have enough to pay my bills and dress the kids and…I don't have the worries…that's where I would be happy. Just not having debts. When I worked everything was always perfect like, you'd have everything on time and I was happy…I really need to go back to work, but I find that it can actually stress

me out... It's not that I want to be rich. I don't go out spending. I don't go off out drinking. I don't go out and buy things, you know that way. I buy what I need to buy for them and they're number one, so they get what they need, you know. It's the same as when I'm out shopping. I'm shopping for all the foods that they eat. I'm actually not stopping... and thinking what I might eat, because I'm making sure that they have what they need, you know.

It is no coincidence that people who end up with little economic and cultural capital and who have a low social class position, use a cultural repertoire of making do and surviving to develop explanations and motivations for their lives. It is also no coincidence that many of them end up as carers, sacrificing themselves through looking after the needs and interests of others.[13]

SUCCESS

When it comes to exploring the meanings of life, there are some areas that are more difficult to explore than others. I wanted to explore to what extent success is viewed in terms of material achievements and gains, particularly in relation to people's work, education, or wealth. Or to what extent did people see success in terms of more nonmaterial interests such as family, intimacy, relationships, leisure, sport, and so forth?

I also wanted to see if there were any patterns, particularly male/female differences, between those who defined success in terms of work and career and those who defined it more in terms of relationships. Furthermore, I wanted to understand the way culture is embedded in class reproduction.[14] As much as working-class children are structurally excluded from availing of educational opportunities and becoming successful, they also, at the same time and as part of their position in society, exclude themselves from occupational and educational success. In other words, in the same way that working-class people might exclude themselves from going to the opera and say "it is not my thing," they might also say the same about going to university, or about being ambitious and trying to be successful at their work.[15] I wanted to see to what extent this mind-set was operating among my participants. Was there a tendency for working-class participants to be more oriented to relationships and family? Was this orientation to family and relationships more prevalent among women, the elderly, and those living in rural areas?

When I asked participants about success, many immediately responded by asking me what I meant by success. Consider, for example, Collette Phillips. She is fifty-five. Her husband is a farmer. All her children did well in education and have developed successful careers. She works part-time in a local veterinary clinic. Her response to my question about the importance of success was: "Depends on what kind of success. What is success? Like, is it success in achieving something in your job, or success in doing the right thing, you know it depends on what you mean by success." When I said that this was why "I throw it out there." She replied:

> To me success is...to be able to interact with people, you know make friends, not be antagonistic, accept people's different points of views...Success in work...I'd like to do my job and...I would like to learn more about my job because I don't have any formal education. But I'm not sure what you call success, not really, you know.

When I responded by saying that I was interested in whether or not people had ambitions to make more money or develop a career, or whether they questioned this dominant definition of success and saw it as something else, Collette said that it was hard to quantify but that for her "success is probably rearing your family."

One pattern to emerge was an almost equal division among the participants between those who, like Collette, saw success more in terms of family, friends, and relationships and those who saw it more in terms of work, education, and wealth. There was also a definite gender divide. Many of the male particiapants related success to work, career, and making money rather than to relationships.

However, among those who emphasized the importance of relationships, men were more likely to refer to sport and camaraderie: women were more likely to mention the family relations. We saw that for Angela Doyle success meant a good family life and having happy healthy kids. There were eleven other women who specifically mentioned their family in relation to success, but only one man. Most of the women who measured success in terms of their family were mothers who were not working. They embraced the traditional dominant culture of seeing success for a woman in terms being a good mother. But, again, there were important differences in the overall pattern. Take, for example, Rosemary McManus. She is a busy, successful woman who is the manager of a small supermarket. Initially she said that success did not mean anything to her. She then clarified this by being phlegmatic about any quest for success, even in terms of raising a family:

> I don't know, because sure, success when you get there you want something else...My whole life...I've reared the children to be able to rear their own, to live their own life, and when we're gone, that's it. That they'd be content and that they won't miss me. But sure I can't help that.

Some people, like Jack Nulty, see success in terms of family. He works for a women's community organization. Again, he was one of those participants who, when I asked him about the importance of success, questioned the meaning of success. "It depends on how you define it I suppose and the fact that I've a successful relationship with the wife and with the daughter, to me that's astonishing." He then went on to say that although his job is not "terribly well paid and I wouldn't be particularly senior...I enjoy it and I know professionally I'm well regarded for what I do."

Many of the people I interviewed related success to being in intimate relationships. Paddy Timmons is a student who has very close intimate relations with his parents and with his friends. He was very reflective about balancing the nonmaterial with the material:

> I suppose yeah success...how do you measure success? And yeah I see myself...taking a couple of years break from studies...and wanting to do it right and get the grade that I think I merit. I see other people...I went to school with who kind of went straight into courses and they were finished by twenty-one and they're buying houses and they're getting mortgages and things like that because they see this as the step...almost that this is what you do next. You go to school, then you go to college, then you get married and you buy a house, you get a car. And I don't see...my life going out that way. I don't measure my success in those ways. I like [being] happy with what I'm doing every day and I have enough. I have a roof overhead. I am not living the life of a pauper. Well that for me is success. If I have friends and family around me then I'm happy. That is how I kind of measure success.

These critical reflections about success can be seen as part of a greater use of culture to explore and explain the meanings of life, and how, for some, relationships and lifestyle are more significant than material well-being. It may well be that those, particularly women, who enter the field of family, love, care, and mutual support have to live the *illusio*—they have to embody the cultural repertoire, the belief and the language of the field—that love and happiness are more important in life than a career and making money. As much as many of those involved in the field of work have to live the *illusio* of the importance of ambition and success, they have to live the *illusio* of love, care, and self-sacrifice.

Ian Sheridan, whom we met in in the previous chapter, is the sixty-three-year-old retired carpenter with seven children, who is separated from his wife. When I asked him how important success was to him, he was yet another one of those who queried what I meant: "Oh like material sort of success?" When I responded by saying that I was interested in how he would define it, he told me that a colleague at work had given him a definition of success with which he agreed:

> If you can make a living, living the way you want to live, that's success...I thought it was brilliant, that would sum it up for me. I have no ambitions to be a millionaire or to have loads of material stuff. I have plenty. To me success, I suppose is [that] I raised a family and they're all reasonably normal [laughs]. Probably more so than myself, but that's successful...the family reared. When the kids were smaller, I was awful concerned if the family [his marriage] died, it'd be a major problem y'know. But nowadays that wouldn't bother me because the family are reared. They're all flying solo, so y'know. I've done my sort of, natural function of rearing the kids, fed them, get them going, that's it. So the rest of my life is either a bonus or a burden, I'm not sure which [laughs].

As I mentioned, about half of the participants responded to my question in terms of their work, education, or being successful financially. Again, it is important to realize that even within this general classification there was enormous variation. There were some like Donal Murphy, a forty-year-old media executive, for whom material success was extremely important:

> I'm driven by it [success] I'm afraid, just utterly, utterly driven by it yeah. But it's a funny, I mean it's like I'm not obsessed by it, but it's just like...right now at the moment...I'm reinventing myself again, cause it's like I want to go higher and higher and higher...I set an agenda and I hit it. And as soon as you've got there, it's like ok, right well that's a bit dull, I'm sort of bored again and off you go. So I suppose in that sense I'm consumed by it. But...the other form of success would just be inner peace and happiness.

We saw earlier the nuanced way in which Eamon O'Loughlin, the civil servant, viewed success. His view of success could be related to the stage of his career within the public sector. However, it would be wrong to think that those in the public sector are somehow less ambitious. Consider, for example, Gordon Cleary. He is a forty-one-year-old lecturer. He had worked in the private sector and had transferred to the public sector to be secure in his employment. When I asked him if this had quelled his ambition or desire for success, he reacted immediately: "No, no...the opposite if any-thing...My goal would be, you know, in say five years time to be known as the best engineer in the country. I realize I'm not a national candidate for self-employment. I know I'm not a national candidate to work in the typical engineering corporate environment. I like to do my own thing."

It is important to remember that what we are looking at here are those participants who when responding to the question about success referred to their work, education, careers, and so forth. But there were participants like Hannah Thompson, a thirty-year-old lecturer, who sees success in terms of work, but no longer strives to be successful:

> I don't feel a need to be a manager. I'm pretty much as high on the management chain as I want to be, which is looking after a programme. I do want to be good at what I do...I have worked in a fast food outlet, but I don't want to be that person again, you know...I don't want to have a job where I wake up in the morning, I come in, I do stuff, I leave and it means nothing.

As well as gender and occupation, there is also the question of age. How did the younger participants see and understand the importance of success? We saw earlier how the student Paddy Timmons talked about success in terms of the quality of relationships. Mai Timmons is the young schoolteacher we met when we were looking at the meanings of families. She lives at home with her parents. She is at the beginning of her career as a schoolteacher and, again, was one of those participants who thought that success was hard to define. She said that when she was in college she was surrounded by very ambitious people. She used to think of success in terms of making "a difference in the world, in a huge way." She thought she might become a politician or work overseas in foreign aid, or become a war correspondent. She would not have thought of becoming a primary schoolteacher as being successful. But she now thinks that the people who make a success of their lives are the ones who make small differences.

Sharon Smyth is a twenty-three-year-old trainee accountant who was busy studying for her exams when I interviewed her. She lives and works in Dublin during the week and comes home at weekends. She is coming toward the end of what she describes as a seven-year journey. She says working, studying, and going to college two or three times a week is tough: "It's hard to keep your motivation up...you have to have a balance with your life too and know when to...have time out for yourself or time out for your friends or your family, you know." When I asked her about success she, like many others, referred to her wish to balance work with nonmaterial rewards:

> Success is important all right, but I think there's a limit to success, you know. If I was to get married and have children, my job wouldn't matter. I don't...I'd rather be at home with children like my mother was. To be at home with my children, when they're growing up and then I could go back to work and then be successful after they have grown up, or you know whatever it may be. But then if I didn't get married, you know, my career probably would be a top three of my priorities.

While the opportunity to make more money and the excitement of making investments and taking risks may be part of the culture of people in
business, it would be wrong to think that these were the only or indeed
primary interests in working. The excitement and pleasure that people like
Mark O'Neill, Mick Furlong, Miley Nolan, and Simon Corboy get from
new ventures and from introducing new products are balanced with the
pleasure they get from the people they meet running their business. It is this
pleasure, as well as, of course, earning more money, that is denied to people
like Danielle Burton. She is not able to indulge in her pleasures. She operates
within a culture of self-sacrifice and making do. Unlike Mark O'Neill who
fulfills his pleasures, and Simon Corboy who has longings and desires, she
does not allow herself to entertain thoughts of self-indulgence.

In some ways, then, we can see that the way people talk about money and
work is part and parcel of their life situation. The have become habituated to
a way of being, and they use culture, whether it is to talk the importance of
money up or down, as a means of understanding themselves and the world
in which they live and operate. They have developed a cultural repertoire,
a series of cultural strategies for being in the world, and they use culture to
explain and legitimate themselves, to live the *illusio* of the field, and to be
successful within it. People, then, inherit and adapt to life conditions and
use culture to explain their live circumstances and help sustain themselves.
However, another important finding was that the notion of a work-life
balance—of people balancing their needs and interests in work with other
interests, particularly domestic and leisure, and of then critically reflecting
about the extent to which they achieve this—was mainly evident among
men, particularly those in professional and managerial occupations.

CONCLUSION

People are shaped by culture, and they use culture in many different ways.
Like almost everyone else in Ireland, the people in this study were socialized through an education system whose hidden agenda revolved around
being competitive and struggling to become successful. The hidden message
within school and college life, the dominant explanation of life that is passed
on from one generation to the next, is that there are those who are successful
in what they do, and there are those who are less successful. This meaning of
life, instilled through a meticulous system of assessments, ratings, rewards
and punishments, permeates every social field in which they operate: people
compete to be successful and to attain and maintain what forms of capital
that are available. The meaning of being successful, and the means to be
successful, will vary depending on the social field. The meaning of being
successful in the field of art is different from being successful in the field

of religion, which, in turn, is different from success in sport, politics, and so forth. For most people in a consumer capitalist society, being successful revolves around attaining economic and cultural capital. For some people, success is about making money and becoming wealthy. For others, success is about attaining cultural capital, being knowledgeable, artistic, religious, caring, and loving. People who are not successful in one field, for example, education, may opt out and seek success in other fields. People who are not good at making money may opt out and seek success in the field of family and in loving and being loved. But it may well be that those who are not successful in attaining wealth or in a career or occupation are forced or directed into the field of caring and of living the *illusio* that money is not important.

CHAPTER 5

POLITICS

ECONOMIC AND POLITICAL FORCES HAVE PROBABLY THE GREATEST influence on people's lives. Whatever meaning people create, whatever they do each day, they are all subject to the state, to its legislations—particularly in relation to taxation—and to the ways in which it provides for education, social welfare, health, housing, and so forth. Consequently, what political parties propose, what politicians get elected, what trade unions struggle for, and what interest groups lobby for, shape what people do and say and how they live their lives. The webs of meaning that people spin and maintain in families and communities are enmeshed in overwhelmingly powerful webs of economics and politics structured by world capitalism. Whatever bonds of belonging they develop, whatever webs of meaning of love and care they maintain, what people do and say is structured by institutional discourses propagated by the state, the European Commission, international agreements, pacts and policies, transnational corporations, global markets, media corporations, and so forth.

In some respects, living in world capitalist societies has become second nature to most of us. There may be political revolutions but there are few social revolutions in which the existing social, political, and economic order—the state, patriarchy, social elites, and traditional hierarchies—are overthrown.[1] And yet, people in Ireland, as elsewhere, could choose to live differently. But they live in a democracy that is based on the rule of the people. The question, then, is how and to what extent do people become involved in politics. To what extent to they take part in civil society? Do they vote? Are they involved in trade unions, local associations, and social movements? Do they actively participate in public debates and discussion about politics? Are they concerned about what constitutes a good society? Or, are they more concerned about their own power and self-interest? To what extent are they wound up in their own lives, in concerns about their families, and remain relatively unconcerned about inequality, injustice, and and trying to transform the existing social order?[2]

As we have seen, most of the participants in this study are caught up in webs of family that reach across generations and into the communities in which they live. At the same time, they are caught up in many different social fields, struggling for different forms of capital, trying to earn a living, and trying to maintain a sense of distinction, honor and respect, thereby reproducing their social class position. But their struggles to attain economic and cultural capital are dependent on the policies of the state that limit and control their ability to keep the money they earn, obtain a good education, have access to health and social welfare services, and so forth. The state is like no other institution as it legitimates and dominates what happens in other social fields. It provides the legal framework for activities in these fields; it structures and limits what people can say and do, and, if need be, punishes and imprisons those who do not comply. The state maintains a monopoly not just over legitimate means of physical violence through the police and army, but also over symbolic violence through what it constitutes as fair, equal, and legitimate. The participants in this study have been affected by the way the state, for example, supported and condoned the practices of banks, big business, and property developers during the Celtic Tiger and enabled the market to operate with greater freedom.[3]

In any social field, change comes about through the activities of institutions, organizations, and groups that operate within the field as well as through the activities of individuals. Within the field of politics, change comes about through people's engagement in the civil sphere and their participation in political parties, trade unions, interest groups, social movements, churches, religious groups, the media, and so forth. It also comes about through the political activity of citizens in terms of their engagement in the public sphere: their ability to listen to and read reports in the media; debate and discuss policies among family, friends, neighbors, and colleagues; and lobby, canvas and, in particular, vote. When it comes to the social and political transformation of Irish society, much depends on the interests and commitments of the citizens.

Most of the participants in this study were born into a mature, democratic, civil society in which change takes place through different policies and legislation being enacted following debate and discussion. What needs to be examined, and what we will look at in this chapter, is the extent to which the participants feel they can change the social, political, and economic conditions of their existence. To what extent are they interested and involved in trying to create a new social order based on feelings of solidarity, of moral responsibility and care for fellow citizens and, for the creation of a good society?[4]. To what extent are people politically motivated? To what extent do they hold strong ideological beliefs? There have been many studies that have examined the role of the public sphere in civil society, but what is missing from these more macro, structural studies, is an analysis of the interests, moods, and motivations of ordinary people, members of the electorate, who participate in the public sphere and the political field generally.[5]

There have been times of political and social upheaval in modern Ireland, particularly during the 1916–1922 period with the rebellion against the English state, followed by the civil war and its aftermath. Unsettled periods of history are associated with strong, deep-rooted ideological beliefs that often lead to armed conflict.[6] The two main political parties, Fianna Fáil and Fine Gael, who have dominated the political field since the creation of the state in 1922, were founded—and for a long time were divided—on the position they took during the civil war. The most recent unsettled period in Irish political history was the conflict in Northern Ireland. However, although it dominated the media, its impact on the political field in the Republic, particularly during elections, was very limited.

It should be remembered that the interviews for this study took place from November 2008 to May 2009 in the early stages of the long economic recession that followed the collapse of the Celtic Tiger. Many interviewees made a reference to the recession and their fears for the future. They were concerned about their jobs, incomes, and mortgages. While the general election in 2011 led to a complete collapse of the Fianna Fáil, the main party in government at the start of the recession, there has been little evidence to show that the very unsettling economic times has led to any major political upheaval. This raises questions about the nature of political debate and the level of interest in and engagement with political organizations and institutions.

There is plenty of survey evidence to show that across numerous advanced industrial societies, citizens, including those from Ireland, have become dissatisfied and disillusioned with the central institutions of representative democracy.[7] A cross-European study in 1999 found that Irish people had a low level of confidence (32 percent) in parliament, and the lowest level of interest in politics (45 percent). However, 80 percent of respondents said that they would vote in the next election and 64 percent said they were satisfied with the way democracy was developing in Ireland.[8] The level of political interest and activity among the interviewees, how they are immersed in political culture and, in general, the extent to which being political is important to them, can shed some light on the extent to which politics matters to people. By revealing the ways in which politics is woven into the meanings of people's lives, we can see the gaps between the electorate and the state and the political parties and the media that dominate the political field.

One reading of the interviews would suggest that the participants I interviewed were good citizens: about 90 of them indicated that they voted in elections. This is slightly more than the 80 percent of Irish respondents in the 1999 European Values Study who said that they would vote in the next election. However, intentions are not the same as actions. Analysis of voter turnout shows that voting in the recent general elections has varied from 63 percent in 2002, to 67 percent in 2007 and 70 percent in 2011.[9]

The problem in analyzing election results and opinion polls is that the results do not capture the complexity of the attitudes, dispositions, and practices of voters. The diversity of political attitudes and practices was very discernible among the participants in this study. The categories in the following typology are neither complete nor exclusive: many of the participants did not fit neatly in any one of the categories, and there were others who overlapped between them. However, they are useful in exploring similarities and differences in engagement in political discourse and practice.

PARTY PEOPLE

There were about twenty-one participants who could be described as being, or having once been, actively involved in politics. These were people who were ideologically committed to political positions, for whom political culture permeated their everyday life, and for whom politics was central to their identity and to their meaning of life. They embodied a dominant political habitus, a way of politically reading and interpreting social, political, and economic life. Some of these embodied the rhetoric and *illusio* of the political field. They embodied the same language and dispositions and the same accepted ways of struggling for the stakes to be gained through participating in the field.[10]

Consider, for example, Martin Jones. He is a former Lord Mayor of Burnby in England. After his first wife died, he married Betty, an Irishwoman. They had been coming to Ireland regularly and he had come to like it. He is eighty-six. He has lived on his own since Betty died four years ago. He is still actively involved in the local community. He is on the committee of the local Active Age Group that promotes and looks after the interests of elderly people in the county. The secretary of the county group invited him to join soon after he came to the area. Being political was part of his repertoire: he had been in politics most of his life. He was able to readily transfer his political skills to the county. As he says, "It was a scene ready-made for me I suppose when I look back, because I was so used to being in committee meetings and things like that." When it was decided that the various local groups in the county should get together for an older persons' network, the local group asked him to represent them. "And I went with another person...to this meeting and we were told...what it [the county network] was about and [that] they had to elect people...officers...and I got elected as the chairperson."

Martin worked in a big aircraft manufacturing company all his life. "The company," he explained, "had started as a family company, which had very strong connections locally and they felt that they had to contribute to the well-being of the city." In his early days in the company he became actively involved in the trade union movement and this led to him going forward as a district and then county councilor. He is proud of his record. He stood for election 11 times and was elected 10 times:

> I was well known to the people of Burnby as well as the district of Tidfield and I belonged to the Labour Party, in which I had a number of roles as well. I was active within the Labour party as well as the trade union movement and as a result of that I was elected by my colleagues to be the deputy leader of Burnby county council.

Martin developed numerous political strategies that enabled him to get elected time after time.[11] He became skilled at playing the political game. He developed the necessary volume and quality of political capital that assured his position in the field. Like many other skillful players of different games, he suggests that he had some natural talent. More importantly, again as part of maintaining his moral self-belief, he suggests that politics is more about giving and leading than about having power to command and control resources.

He went on to become Lord Mayor of Burnby. For Martin, politics is about facilitating, making connections, and being obliging. "I only ever did things that people asked me to do...I never set out to do it [become Lord Mayor]...you can't do a degree in Lord Mayorship. You know it's something that happens to you...I mean amongst any group of people, there'll be something that somebody needs. If you are in a football club, somebody has to be the captain. Now how one person becomes the captain rather than another is one of these mysterious processes isn't it?" However, he admits that he does have an ability to work with people to create change. "I make things happen."

Being politically active can, then, be seen as a kind of overcoat that children often learn to wear in families in which being politically active, debating, and discussing politics, makes the coat easy to put on in later life. Most of the participants who were involved in political party type activism were middle-class males. For them, being political was about a mixture of a feeling of ascendancy, of having the necessary political repertoire to facilitate change, or as Martin Jones put it, "make things happen."

Of course, being able to make things happen means being able to make things happen for oneself too. Betty, his second wife, had been married to a non-Catholic, but it had not worked out. When it came to organizing his and Betty's wedding, they wanted to get married in a Catholic Church. But there was a problem in that she was divorced and the church did not recognize divorce. Martin and his bride-to-be knew a priest through a local club to which Martin belonged. The club was right in the heart of Martin's constituency and, as Martin put it, "the club was important to me, as I was to them in a sense that...they recognized the value of having a member of a club who was also a member of the local council, because you could raise matters for them."

Martin likes to tell the story about how they went to see Fr. Kavanagh, the local priest, and how they explained to him that Betty wanted to get married in a Catholic Church:

> I said "look will you marry us?" "Well I'd like to," he said but he said "I'll have to talk to the Bishop," and I said "look I don't believe and you know that" because we were good friends and we did things together anyway like rugby and we'd go to rugby games and things like that, so we were good friends. And he'd often get out of a uniform and come with me you know. We were very good friends. So he said "I'll have a word with the Bishop." I said "because I don't believe...I don't wish to pretend." I said "I can't do that, but I'd like Betty to have her wish and her family's wish of course."...Well the Bishop I knew because if you're involved in public life...you meet all the people and I knew Bishop McDonald. Well I didn't know him well but because I wasn't one of his flock, nevertheless I'd meet him. And I'd done things in the city that involved him and we'd shared a few things you know and Fr. Kavanagh came back and said "Well I have to get some proof." He said and he had to get some information. Betty was married outside the church so she was married civilly. So he had to get the details of the civil marriage, which was a great help because Bishop McDonald then said, "well she was never married."

This incident with the bishop throws light on how the field of power extends beyond a struggle for money, authority, and allocation of resources and includes favors and benefits in other fields. It also reveals the network of an elite that stretches across social and cultural divisions and the repertoires and strategies—of favors requested and granted— that make things happen.

For some of the participants, party politics was almost seen as a legacy that brings with it a sense of *noblesse oblige*. Jim Nolan came back from Europe where he had a very good job and now helps his father run the family business. When I asked him if politics was important to him, he admitted that although he had no interest for a long time, things have changed:

> My family has a big history in politics and I have to say I...do think sometimes that I would like to be a representative of some sort...I'm not making

any great strives or anything like that and it is maybe something I never follow up with. In the back of my mind there is something that thinks that one day perhaps I would...like to be a representative, a public representative...And that's partially...because I see some of the people that are doing it today and I think that maybe I can do a better job myself...There's a long family allegiance if you like and I also find that in politics in general...across the world...there isn't a huge amount of difference. One's a little left, one's a little right; it's not a huge difference in mainstream politics. It's only when you go to radicals that you have your major differences. So it's whoever you nail your colours of the flag to...so I would say it's the family allegiance.

As much as family is woven into the fabric of political life in Ireland, so too is business. Brian Mason is a businessman who made his money selling and servicing gas and electrical household appliances. He is chairperson of the local branch of one of the main political parties. He is very frank about his involvement in politics. "Politics is a tool. I'm involved in politics; I have to be, because I work for government agencies and things like that. They're all politically motivated." He has a very jaundiced view of politicians. "They make an awful lot of noise, they don't seem to have any ideas...They're just a mindless bunch of fools...My own personal opinion right now is that there's nothing there. There isn't a brain among them"

He criticizes them for having no policies to deal with the recession. "We need to think ourselves out of this...and you're saying [to yourself] that...they're just merchants, political merchants out to gain political money...Everybody blames the bankers and the property developers, but you're kind of saying that part of the problem is that there wasn't any really good politicians."

The idea of people being involved in politics as a vocation, of doing it for the public good has, then, to be balanced with the notion of people becoming involved as a means toward personal ends. In many ways, the political history of Irish society can be read as the attempt over the decades, by individual politicians and the government, to balance these two impulses. The dominant clientalist approach to politics in Ireland—of politicians fulfilling the needs and interests of constituents—means that, with the exception of the Northern conflict, Irish politics has been more about responding to and managing the electorate than about ideological commitment.[12]

Miley Nolan is the father of Jim Nolan whom we spoke to earlier. They both come from a long line of party political activists. Miley talked animatedly about his grandfather's involvement in the local county council and his granduncle's involvement in national politics. "Like there would've been some of our family in the Dáil from its foundation." But, being political is not only about having power of command and power over resources. It is also about knowing what strategies of action should be employed when, where, how, and with whom. These strategies can be for personal benefit. Miley tells the story of what happened when he tried to get a mortgage for his son Brian:

> We were always into doing a bit of wheeling and dealing. You always knew somebody that knew somebody, do you know what I mean, so like when it came to my son [who had terminal cancer] and his girlfriend getting a mortgage... this wasn't going to be very possible with the medical history like he had. So I remember our doctor rang Breda [his wife] one day and says, "I have a letter here from a lending agency looking for a medical on Brian... he's not going to get a loan," and he says "I can't falsify this you know, I'd be struck off." And... through contacts and all the rest... a brown envelope with 1,500 quid in it... was sent in the application... with the medical, it was stamped in as having received the medical report, the whole lot. And what I believed happened, I don't know, the medical file disappeared out of the folder and he got his loan and everything was fine... It wasn't a big loan, small loan paying I think maybe a hundred grand or something like that maybe you know. A lot of money to be lending somebody with cancer at the same time you know but how and ever. The house has since been sold for two hundred and forty thousand so they've got their money back, everyone's got their money, everyone's doing ok, nobody's been defrauded shall we say, but... so that leaves my conscience clear but I mean the bottom line is you know, I'll do whatever I have to do to look after family. We could do this wheeling and dealing and all the rest, you might get off an old speeding ticket here, something there you know.

Political culture gives activists a repertoire for how to talk about and engage in politics, how to operate within the field and engage in various strategies of action that "get things done." In this common sense view, as Jim Nolan suggested, it does not really matter which side of the party political fence you are on. There may be, so to speak, different teams, and the divisions between the teams can be deep, but there is a recognition that everyone is playing the same game and that players take whatever advantages they can for themselves.[13]

INTELLECTUALS AND RADICALS

There are others who are immersed in political culture and for whom politics is very important, but who are not engaged in party politics. Many of the interviewees participated in politics by following events in the media. It enabled them to talk knowledgeably, take positions, debate, and discuss political issues. Ger Fennelly has a master's degree in political philosophy and lectures part-time. His interest in politics emerged when he was a student. He recognizes the gap between the theory and practice of politics, but he has not been able to bridge it:

> As a teenager I was quite apathetic and I had difficulty engaging with that world, you know, beyond periodically going to the polls, I found that I had no sort of conduit for all of my political thoughts and I think working with Bornfree [charity organization] has kind of been a way for me to feel like I have some stake in the political sphere or at least in the public sphere. Like I'm making some kind of... difference somewhere, but I have yet to align myself with a political party and it's one of my great fantasies. I find the social element of it the most difficult thing you know... I've been flirting with the idea of Labour because you need to join a somewhat mainstream political party I believe, to not be considered, you know, a loony on the fringe. Not that I don't think there's value in grassroots politics, obviously there is... and then I wonder whether I want to be involved in formal politics, you know, because there's a big gulf between what goes on there and what Jürgen Habermas writes in his books.

Radicals can be seen as adhering to an ideology. The history of Western society, and indeed Irish society, could be written in terms of what social movements arose, and what were the structural and historical circumstances that led to some ideologies rather than others achieving dominance. Whereas those involved in the settled world of party politics take a practical common sense approach to politics, as exemplified by Jim Nolan, radicals tend to be immersed in political culture that permeates the rest of their lives. Radicals tend to live within explicit, articulated, highly organized meaning systems. There is an expectation if not a demand to live according to their beliefs. Ideologies can be seen to offer "unified answers to questions of how human beings should live."[14]

As a former member of the Irish Republican Army (IRA), Nick Foley was undoubtedly the most radical of the ideologists that I interviewed. He was very wary and extremely cautious when talking about his past political life. He had not revealed his background until I asked him how important politics was to him. "Politics wouldn't be top of the agenda with me... the reunification of this country is very important to me." He then hesitated and put in the proviso "whichever way you want to look at that," pointing perhaps to the gap between political and military forms of attaining goals.

He first became motivated about reunification during the Hunger Strikes. He began to question what was happening "only up the road." His mother and father were strong Republicans. His grandfather was an old IRA man. So Nick joined up. It was a "big sacrifice... a lot of years of my life." And yet he recognizes it as one of the best decisions he ever made. He never had any qualms as to what he was asked to do. "A job had to be done and that was it.

Y'know…there was a war going on. Simple as that." He would be willing to do it again, but he does not think it will be necessary. There were times when his life was in danger. He depended on his comrades. At the time he was active, it was always a completely secret and private part of his life. Now many people know his background and his views. In the past, it led him into a number of arguments and fights in the local village. He has been asked to run in elections for Sinn Fein, but declined. "I'm just not a political person really. I mean I'm a…I mean I couldn't read books, I couldn't read policy."

Being radical and ideological and being politically active does not necessarily mean being involved in traditional political issues. Many radical ideological groups, such as New Agers and other new religious movements, hover between being political, environmental, and religious. Many people within feminism and the gay and lesbian movement are radical ideologists. Evelyn Hutchinson works as a community activist and artist. She is passionate about being feminist and gay. She lives in a remote village. Much of her life's work is dedicated to being recognized and accepted as a lesbian. She used to be the only lesbian in the village, but recently a woman, married with three children, left her husband and came out as gay. At the time of the interview, she was in the process of organizing a local parade in the village. "I've had people say to me that they don't think it should happen and that they wouldn't get involved and I'm just gobsmacked, which makes me even think that it is more important than ever that it go ahead, because it should [really] be a non-event." Getting recognition and acceptance has been a continual struggle. She told me how a few years ago the local community organization was in line to receive substantial funding from a major national body but it withdrew the application because it refused to recognize lesbians as a special needs category.

Joan Gallagher is a social worker in her late forties. She has lived in Mayfarm, the inner-city area of Dublin, for nearly twenty years. Her work is very important to her:

> It has a meaning for me in that it makes a contribution to society in terms of the education, the training, the organization and development work that we do. And then for me it allows me to fulfil myself in something that I have come to be good at as well.

She sees politics as very important "in terms of how we live and where we live":

> I believe we can affect change if we just keep plugging away at it. I haven't got the stomach for really being closely involved in party politics. I've campaigned for people along the years. I've been involved in lots of different

campaigns and protests, campaigns amendments. I suppose one of my earliest memories would have been around the Hunger Strikes in the early 80s, and then there was the ones around the anti-abortion...we were trying to make change that time on divorce, and anti-war. But I'd be aware. I'd always be aware of protests and the opportunity to say something...So I suppose the broad scope of ones to do with civil society and trying to create a society that accepts people and caters for, and allows for, difference and that we can live with those differences.

Protesting is part of her political repertoire. It can be seen as a strategy of action that can be applied to different issues. Joan feels that she has a moral imperative to protest. "I missed some of the health ones recently, just I wasn't in Dublin."

Politics for Joan provides an explanation for what life is about, the nature of power, how it operates, and how it can be changed. But it is also a model for how she should live her life. For her, politics is not compartmentalized into voting in elections and referenda, and being a listener or spectator when politics is debated and discussed on the radio or television. For Joan, the challenge is to live a political life, for politics to permeate the everyday:

Start personally and you can move out from there, y'know. I would consider it a sham to be living one way and then saying we should have a society that reflects something differently. So that if I'm talking about a society that cares for all its people equally then I need to be reflecting and I should be reflecting that in my life as well.

What makes Joan out as a radical is that she strives to live her life as much as possible according to her political ideology. What also marks her as different is the way she is immersed in the language and discourse of socialist political culture. Joan uses politics in the same way that some people use of religion to explain the meaning of their lives and to provide a model for how they should live. In the same way that some religious people have a deep knowledge and understanding of theology, of the teachings of the church, and who practice their religion regularly, Joan has an elaborate and detailed knowledge of politics and has developed a number of practices that sustain her beliefs. "The most important thing is to do good by others. Not to rip people off. Not to take advantage of other people. To look out for others and to have some collective sense...of community, and that can be as small as one's own reference group and then go on as big...as society."

Some of her key political beliefs and practices revolve around not doing harm to others and the environment: this is central to her sense of right and wrong. She argues that if we cause damage to the environment, we are causing damage to the prospects for our children. For this reason, she and her partner share a car: "Three out of the four of us cycle, we use public transport and quite consciously."

As we shall see when we come to look at the importance of religion in people's lives, Joan is also a very energetic and committed member of a group of women who meet once a month and engage in rituals that seek to evoke an earth-based spirituality. They use drums as a means of trying to connect with their ancestors and spirits of the elements. There is, then, a connection between her political and religious beliefs, but what makes Joan different is the extent to which she uses her culture to develop a knowledge and understanding of her life and how to live it. Most of the people I interviewed used a very limited part of the culture that was available to them: they were quite happy to use and adapt the repertoire that they had acquired during their socialization. In the same way that some people are happy to use a limited range of words and ideas to explain themselves, other people, like Joan use a very wide range of concepts and ideas. But what is also different is her willingness to be a cultural entrepreneur, to mix and match different elements, elements of paganism with elements of socialism. What makes Joan different was that she was willing to engage in politics to create change to make a better society.

TRADITIONAL VOTERS

Jim Doyle is a county council workman in Castlebay. Politically he has never done anything much more than vote but sees voting as a very important part of who he is and what he does. For him, it is part of being a good citizen, but it is also part of fulfilling his own self-interests. "Oh I'd vote. Oh Jesus, I'd vote. Without the votes you couldn't argue about anything. You'd have no say." He is particularly fond of elections. "I'd have the craic... I know all the politicians round about here. So like I treat them all the same. If I wanted help... that's the fella I'd vote for. That's the way I'd keep them [on their toes]."

There is a tendency to think that political talk is rational and goal oriented, that it revolves around fulfilling economic and political interests and maintaining ideological positions. However, in a settled political culture, when there is an agreed-upon opinion about how the game should be played, talking politics can become a game of party political identities, of taking positions, and then of making—almost in a staged manner—predictable challenges and ripostes. The game may be played seriously, as among politicians and among people when they participate in the media, but it also a game played none-too-seriously by nonprofessionals who joke, tease, and banter with each other. However, there is not to denying that with the recession and the changes it caused in people's standard of living the general consensus umbrella was often overturned by struggles by different interest groups, particularly during the recession, for example, between public and private sector workers.

Manus King picked up on the idea of talking politics as a game. He has a third-level education and a good job in a large transnational corporation. When he moved to Greyrock first, he felt, like many others, an outsider. As a means of integrating into the community he joined the local GAA club. He also took to going to the pub. He says, the pub "is my social life." When I asked him how important politics was to him, his immediate reaction was "it's an absolute must if you drink . . . cause what do you talk about at a bar? . . . sports and politics. It's an absolute must . . . I very rarely drink by the way, but . . . it's great banter. I get great sport out of politics."

For many of the interviewees, when I asked them if they had any interest in politics, their immediate response was "no," or "none whatsoever," but usually this was qualified by "but I do vote." Take, for example, Al O'Brien. He is a former priest who has a third-level education and works as a guidance counselor in a third-level college. He always votes and always votes for the same party. When I asked him how important politics was to him, he replied:

> I feel like I should. It [politics] should be more important to me . . . cause I feel like I should have more of an engaged interest, cause I do listen to the news and I do find it fascinating and can debate about it with people, but then again when the [public protest] marches are on, I think I was at home looking at the telly going "good on you" [laughter] . . . you should be . . . you know great for marching, so I think like. I sort of feel hypocritical so I think I should have a more active involvement, or read up more like in papers and stuff . . . I follow them [politicians], and I find it fascinating, I mean it governs our whole lives in a way. It affects everything we do, in a certain way, so I feel like I should have a more active engagement.

This was taken up by Sharon Smyth. She is a twenty-three-year-old woman who works and lives in Dublin but spends as much time as she can at home in Greyrock. She is studying to become an accountant. Like many others, she says she has very little interest in politics. "It's not important . . . my interest wouldn't lie with politics." However, she clarified: "I would vote. I think it's important to vote and I would inform myself, kind of, upon voting." She then went on to distinguish herself from those who don't vote: "Whatever the matter may be, I would utmostly always vote. And I'd say that . . . to anyone, you know, that say they wouldn't vote. But the majority of the time I wouldn't have any interest in politics. It's one of my downfalls."

For many people, party allegiance seems to have been something they inherited, much the same way that many people inherited being Catholic or Protestant. As Bridie McPhearson, an elderly woman who finished school at primary level, put it: "Well I suppose looking back on it, it was a handed down thing, you voted one side or the other." Jim O'Brien, a farmer in Castlebay, recognized that party identity and allegiance was part of the historical game of politics. "What I read about de Valera I never liked. I never liked him from day one. The result is that I'd be kind of anti-Fianna Fáil although I do think there are some very good Fianna Fáil politicians around." But he has never had any real interest or involvement in politics. "I just vote... I'm more or less a kind of a hurler in a ditch."

Margaret Mannion, the young woman who came back to live in Castlebay having lived in England and traveled the world, was adamant that she had no real interest in politics, but she votes. However, while she thinks the banter between politicians on some programs is laughable; she dislikes the game and the identities and sides that people take. She recognizes that the banter can be serious, ideological, and bitter. She remembers her childhood. "I grew up with my Mum being a Fine Gael woman, and from a real Fine Gael background, and my Dad and immediate neighbour being Fianna Fáil, and the rows that I used to listen to was unreal."

Stephen O'Brien, the young shop assistant who left school at fourteen recognizes the importance of politics. He thinks that knowing and under-standing politics and becoming involved is related to age, education, and class. While he feels an outsider and excluded from the game, he knows enough about politics to know how important it is and how some politicians are very good at getting elected. He talked about the election successes of Bertie Ahern, the former Taoiseach and leader of Fianna Fáil:

It's one thing I'm not into, but I'd know probably bits about. Like I'd know which TDs are which and who's the Minister for this and... It's one thing I'm not into but, [at] the same time like, it is a very, very important part of your life like... and there is politics type people. Like if you ask a young person about politics, they probably know nothing about it in the background I'm from. But I'm sure if you asked a posher person from a different background they'd probably know an awful lot about politics than me like. But I probably would know a good bit about it, and I probably would listen to small bits of talk like, or if I hear sections and try listening and learn as much as I can about it, cos it is a handy thing to know about, y'know what I mean. So I think it is very, very important. It is very important alright, politics, yeah.
...Like a lot of people would be shooting down the likes of Bertie Ahern. Over where I live he's like a God over there so... like the things he does over there, like it'd be hard not to vote for him, y'know like so. For example like, there's a block of flats over there and as I was telling you, there's no post going

into it. They [postmen] won't go into it 'cos they'll get attacked or something like...but the person that would go into the flats...was Bertie Ahern. So he was doing an awful lot for the community over there.

Among those who voted but were not formally active, there were some who were more critically reflective about politics, who made greater use of it in terms of their self-understanding. They may see politics as a game, but it is one which they recognize has serious consequences. Brendan Hoban, the self-employed former drug addict who is a part-time community activist, thinks politics is very important. But he is not even a committed voter: "I'd vote socialist if I was going to vote." But he dislikes politicians: "Most of the politicians that we have in our midst. I get resentful to them, y'know. When they lie and don't deliver on their promises."

He works with people whom, he recognizes, have come to be the way they are—poor, unemployed, and addicted—through social factors. He sees his work as political:

> The work we're doing...we're making political statements all the time because we're saying that people...have been affected by social determinants like y'know...All the time when I'm working I'm thinking how did this person come from this society? I'm always thinking how did these people end up like that? Do you know what I mean?...Why was he impoverished? So, if people...particularly people in power...haven't made interventions in people's lives and supported them in terms of like better housing conditions, better education, better job opportunities...particularly for people in my community...they need to answer for why they didn't do anything, or [we need to] put pressure on them, or lobby in some ways that would put pressure on them, to provide better conditions for the future, y'know.

Brendan, then, makes much greater use of political culture. He is ideologically committed. He lives in an unsettled community. Politics provides him with an explanation for why society is the way it is, and why people end up poor, undereducated and addicted. It also provides him with a model for action. But while politics provides him with meaning, and being political is part of his cultural repertoire, what makes him different is that he has never had any interest in becoming formally involved in politics.

THE SKEPTICAL AND THE ALIENATED

If going to Mass on Sunday was, and perhaps still is, the best barometer of being a good Catholic, voting in elections might be seen as the best barometer of being a good citizen. However, inasmuch as people may go to Mass out of tradition, as part of a culture that they have embodied, and yet be skeptical about the existence of God or life after death, people may vote in elections more as a habit and without any strong political conviction. Even among those who said they did vote, many conveyed a lack of interest and belief in what they were doing. Indeed they seemed to see the question "do you vote?" as almost a moral question, as if I had asked them if they paid their taxes. Bernie Young is a thirty-year-old mother of two who works part-time. She went to work after finishing school. When I asked her how important politics was to her, she said that she had "no interest really." When I asked if she voted she said "Yeah kind of." And then she added "I voted last year." I asked her if that was unusual:

> I don't know, it's not that I don't know. I just don't understand. I mean the people, there are some of them are saying one thing and then they're doing other things. They're kind of...confusing, and then you're afraid to kind of vote for them in case it's the wrong thing to do.

Her husband, Stephen, is equally disillusioned. He says he is not up to being political:

> I wouldn't really pick up the paper now and read anything or I wouldn't be too interested in watching the news, so I would be very not up (on politics)...I'm thirty-six. I'm voting since I'm eighteen; I probably have voted six or seven times.

Maise Finnerty is the forty-four--year-old woman from Mayfarm whom we met before in chapter 3. She finished school at second level and captured the moral imperative to vote with a strong sense of skepticism:

> I vote but I don't know what I do be voting for, y'know that way. I kind of say, well I'm not voting for Fianna Fáil because...even though I don't know what it's about. It just doesn't interest me.

Rosemary McManus is a self-assured, articulate woman who has her own career as a manager of a small supermarket. She was able to explain her disillusionment in more detail:

> It's a joke. It's a joke. Yes, I was Fine Gael to the backbone but...and probably if my back was to the wall, I'd still be Fine Gael. But politics, what is politics? I just don't understand politics. Cos they don't understand it themselves. I think the wrong people are ruling the country at the minute. I think it's highlighted that they are not capable of it, y'know.
>   I can't understand how a minister can come up and read everything off a piece of paper. How can he understand everything? You have to admire them like, how can they talk about everything. Y'know.

Lar Cummins is thirty-seven. He finished his education at second level. He votes, but he does not have much faith in the political system. "I think every politician is corrupt...well in every party there's a majority of politicians that are corrupt. I'm not saying they all are...most of them are. No matter who gets in it's going to be the same story."

Like some of the traditional voters, skeptical voters saw politics as a kind of game that they liked watching and following even though the recession was deepening quickly during the time the interviews were taking place. Patricia Furlong is in her fifties. She finished her second-level education and went on to work in the Civil Service before she got married. Her husband was actively involved in party politics for a number of years, canvassing for candidates in elections. She enjoys politics. "I love politics...I wouldn't get as involved—my husband would be more involved in canvassing and that...I mean at the moment now it's just fantastic to watch and listen to it." But she is dismayed by the political system, the way "the banks...have taken over the country...the politics, the corruption."

Mai Timmons is a young woman who has just begun her career as a schoolteacher. Like Patricia Furlong, she enjoys following politics, perhaps in the same way that other people follow sport. "I find it hugely entertaining and I like listening to like Good Morning Ireland and Matt Cooper [current affairs radio programs] and all those and you know it's great entertainment. Unfortunately it's not all just showbiz, it has an effect." Like many others, Mai Timmons seems well versed in political culture and is aware of its importance but, somehow, she sees it as a game that she watches but which she has little or no interest in playing.

We can say that people are alienated when they are immersed in a culture that produces not just detached and skeptical moods but also negative ones. They have no feelings of belonging. There were seven participants who could be described as complete political atheists or agnostics: they saw nothing of value in being in any way involved, let alone participating, in politics. They did not vote. They gave various reasons for not voting.

Simon Walsh is still very young. He grew up in a home in which politics was never listened to, watched, read, or discussed. Talking about politics is not part of his cultural repertoire. "Like if someone was talking to me about politics and stuff, I wouldn't have a clue." However, as we shall see, when it comes to sport, Simon makes a point of being well informed about everything that happens in the world of soccer. In the social fields in which he operates there is little honor and respect to be obtained for being politically knowledgeable or involved.

Paddy Long is the manager of a small supermarket. He has not voted recently. Again there was a sense of failing to be a good citizen. "I suppose I should vote but...I don't know...sometimes I feel it's not worth voting...who would I vote for 'cos I can't pick one from the other, there's bad and worse." Sarah Burton was more emphatic. She is a well-educated, professional woman. She feels alienated from the whole political system:

> I couldn't give a toss. I don't vote...I wouldn't have anything to do with any of them...I have no time for politics, don't trust the current environment and never did...we're beginning to see the reality of where we are now...it's not all about business. But I think there is more to come. I don't think the pain is over yet and I don't think politics can sort it. My biggest fear is that the country will become ungovernable.

CONCLUSION

When it comes to assessing the state of political life in Ireland, there are pessimists who believe that political culture is stagnant, that it is dominated by self-seeking "cute hoors" who "pull strokes" for themselves, their lackeys, and their constituents, who manipulate and manage an electorate that is passive and disinterested. They point to declining turnouts in elections and referenda and to the decline in political party membership. And then there are optimists who argue that it is not that people have become less demo-cratic but that they have moved away from traditional politics. They point to the rise of specific interest and identity politics—environmental, moral-ity, gender, sexual orientation, disability, and so forth—to the mini-publics where issues are debated both inside and outside the media and, specifically, in Ireland the appetite and willingness to engage in political and constitu-tional reform.[15]

The people who participated in this study were born into a political field dominated by the state, political parties, corporations, trade unions, the media, and the Catholic Church. All of these institutions shaped their knowledge and understanding of what it is to be political. There is a presup-posed, taken-for-granted orthodoxy about how politics operates in a mature, democratic civil society. If people want to obtain political capital, if they want to obtain a position in the political field they have to adopt the habitus and practices: they have to play the game, they have to engage in the *illusio*. Those who engage in the political culture are shaped by the webs that have been spun before and which they spin afresh themselves. In doing so, they are able to reap rewards for themselves.

Even though they are immersed in a political culture that is constantly reported on and analyzed within the media, the majority of the participants did not engage much in politics beyond discussing the issues, watching and listening to the main players, and voting in elections. Many of those who did vote had a disdainful, cynical, and skeptical attitude about politics. It was as if they felt they were involved in a game that they could only view from the sidelines, that somehow they felt that they were disenfranchised. And there was a small group of interviewees who said that there were completely alienated by the game.

An equally small group were active players, former players, or people who saw themselves as potential players. These were an eclectic mixture of party political players, trade unionists, gay rights protesters, and one former member of the IRA. Unlike the majority of the interviewees, they were willing and able to make use of the political culture, to develop political strategies that enabled them to participate in the game. In doing so they contributed to the maintenance of a democratic civil society while fulfilling their own interests.

Politics, then, can be seen as an overall part of contemporary Irish culture. Some people make use of it more than others. It is part of their cultural repertoire. They use politics, like sport and religion, to spin webs of meaning, to create and maintain bonds. It is a game they like to play and some are good at it: they can make things happen for themselves and others. But for most of the participants, politics was more of a spectator sport, which they only played occasionally when voting.

CHAPTER 6

SPORT

THE HISTORY OF SPORT AND ITS EMERGENCE AS A CENTRAL FEATURE OF Western society and culture is very complex. It can be seen as part of the pursuit of leisure and pleasure, a loosening of external and internal controls, and a quest for excitement. It became an integral part of the civilizing process, of increasing interdependence, of the control of violence, and of state formation and nation building.[1] Sport gradually became central to everyday life in capitalist societies, particularly in expanding towns and cities.

The growth of sport and other forms of popular culture is strongly linked to the growth of the media. People who previously lived in remote isolated areas with very restricted cultural repertoires became exposed to new ideas and practices, new ways of thinking and being, through newspapers, radio, and television and, more recently, the Internet. A whole new world of meaning, pleasure, and excitement opened up. Instead of having to travel to see the world, the world came to people's homes through media technology.

We now live in a global mass media age in which people follow sport that is taking place all over the world. The 2008 Olympic Games in Beijing attracted 4.7 billion viewers, equivalent to 70 percent of the world's population, over seventeen days.[2] Sports stars have become global celebrities.[3] The amount of coverage given to sport in newspapers, and on television and radio, rivals that given to politics and economics and has completely eclipsed religion.

Sport has, then, become a central part of a consumer capitalist society. People consume and are consumed by sport. In some respects, to paraphrase Marx, it may no longer be religion that is the opium of the people, but sport. Sport has become a major form of pleasure and excitement. It has become a key ingredient of personal identity and many people spend considerable amounts of time and money maintaining their sporting pleasures. But inasmuch as sport brings people together, it also divides them. Sport reproduces class and gender divisions and, more importantly, can lead to bitter rivalries, locally, nationally, and internationally.[4]

But sport is more about identity, bonding, and belonging. In Ireland, the development of Gaelic games in the late nineteenth century was a cornerstone in the growth of a cultural nationalism and the formation of the Irish state.[5] Up until then, games and sports were mainly part of an "arts of existence," a realization of the self through leisure pursuits that were developed and propagated by an aristocratic class and spread to lower classes through the zeal and entrepreneurship of cultural innovators. In Ireland, it was the English landlord class who promoted sport. Toward the end of the nineteenth century, the native Catholic bourgeoisie began to promote Gaelic games, football and hurling, as a means of creating cultural distinctions and boundaries between themselves and their colonizers. In the late twentieth century, Gaelic games played a major role in keeping the Irish diaspora connected to their homeland and their home counties.[6]

Sport has become a central feature of everyday life in Ireland. A survey in 2003 found that one in three Irish adults is actively engaged in sports, and one in three is a member of a club (including gym and health clubs). There has been a general decline over recent decades in the number of people playing team sports (particularly Gaelic) and a rise in individual sports such as swimming, golf, and cycling. The most popular sport taken up by men is soccer (11 percent) and by women is swimming (9 percent). When five-a-side teams are included, more than twice as many people play soccer (17 percent) compared to Gaelic football (8 percent).[7] But the influence of sport goes beyond the activity and participation in it. Six-in-ten men and five-in-ten women see making new friends and acquaintances as a benefit they obtain from sport.[8] Sports clubs, particularly the GAA, and also soccer, golf, swimming, and rugby clubs have come to play a pivotal role in people in communities developing and maintaining social networks.

The 2003 survey found high levels of spectatorship and volunteering. Almost half (47 percent) of the adults had attended a sports event in the previous year (almost 60 percent of these were run by the GAA). One-in-seven people attend a sporting event at least once a week. Fifteen percent of Irish adults were involved in voluntary activity for sport. The GAA accounts for 42 percent of all volunteering sport activity whereas soccer accounts for only 17 percent. In this respect, sport has become more important than religion. In 2003, the level of religious volunteering (8 percent) was almost half than that for sport.[9]

Sport has become central to identity, meaning, and lifestyle. It has become a major topic of conversation among family and friends. It has become something akin to a lingua franca across the world, particularly among men, enabling the breaking of ice among strangers.[10] It is an important form of bonding and belonging.[11] It can be seen as an important form of social capital, building bridges between people and creating social bonds.[12] But the relevance of sport reaches far beyond playing and partici- pating, it is deeply embedded in everyday life and the ways in which people create and sustain meaning. We can see this in terms of some of the other ways in which sport has replaced religion.

Previously, in Ireland time was divided into religious and secular peri- ods. The religious year was broken into different times: Lent, Easter, Advent, Feast Days, and so forth. It comprised activities such as going to Mass, Devotions, Novenas, Missions, and going on pilgrimages and retreats. The religious day was broken up into different activities: morn- ing prayers, stopping to say the Angelus at noon and 6:00 p.m. (it is still broadcast on national public radio), saying the rosary, prayers before bed, and so forth. People put up holy pictures and statues in their houses. (And, as we shall see in the next chapter, many people, particularly the elderly, still do.)

However, in recent times, for growing numbers of people, the year is increasingly broken up into sporting seasons and events. Days are taken up with exercising, playing, reading about, listening to, and watching sport. Personal and family life is interwoven with sport. The question, then, is to what extent sport has come to take on some of the roles and functions that religion once fulfilled. If religion can be defined as a unified system of beliefs and practices related to sacred things that unite people into a single moral community, we can see that there is very little similarity between religion and sport.[13] There may be shared beliefs and practices in sport but they are not unified in the same way as the teachings of world religions. There may be some aspects of sport that are sacred, such as team icons or the grounds in which they play—"hallowed turf"—but there is not the same sense of sacrilege when these are not respected. There are many aspects of sport that serve as a metaphor for life in general—playing by the rules, winning and losing, heroes, victorious underdogs, and so forth, but sport does not provide a coherent explanation for the meaning of life and, more importantly, how to live a good life.[14] Finally, while there may be sporting gods, there is noth- ing supernatural or transcendental about sport.

And yet it would not be wrong to suggest that for some people sport has become a quasi-religious activity that fills the gap left in social life due to the decline of institutional religion.[15] One of the key functions of religion is the sense of bonding and belonging that comes from participation in col- lective rituals. These rituals create a "collective effervesence."[16] Sport could, then, be seen as a postmodern form of collective consciousness, of creating a strong sense of bonding and belonging that is almost spiritual, even if it does not generate moral commitments. And while sport may not provide an explanation for life, it does create noble, heroic figures who become exemplars of character and generate honor and respect.[17] Sport generates its own rituals, rites of passages, myths and sense of sacredness, and the possibility of self-transcendence. Sport is not just spectacular, it is extraordinary and, like religion, leads to a suspension of ordinary time.[18] Sport is a source of cultural and symbolic capital. As a form of cultural capital, it operates like education and art. The accumulation of sport capital creates and reproduces class position.[19] As a form of symbolic capital, it blesses and legitimates other forms of capital in a manner similar to the way religious capital previously blessed the accumulation of economic and political capital. Fit, healthy, sporty bodies generate honor and respect. They have become a form of secular salvation, a sign of being one of the elect in the same way that pious, humble, puritan bodies were previously a sign of being one of the saved. For many of the participants, there seemed to be no conflict or contradiction between their sporting and religious lives. However, it became clear that for some participants their sense of identity, passion, and commitment to sport was far stronger and stood in stark contrast to their lack of interest in or commitment to religion.

What needs to be understood is how sport operates as a source of bonding and belonging within families and communities, and among friends. What we need to do is to see how sport operates as a key ingredient in forming identities and creating and maintaining webs of meaning. As we shall see, similar to politics, sport is a key cultural ingredient in some participants' lives; it is central to their identity, to how they communicate and relate to others. For others, mainly women, it has little or no importance. We will also see, however, that there are other women who have a developed an interest in watching, following, and talking about male sports. The question is, to what extent is this a part and parcel of their symbolic domination or is it more of a cultural strategy that they use to create and sustain webs of meaning.

FAMILY SPORT

Peter Flynn is passionate about soccer. He played for Ireland as a youth. He got a trial with a top English club. He was fifteen. But it didn't work out. He thinks back as to what might have been. "I could have made it, probably, maybe, who knows but I could have made a living out of it." The problem was, as he says, that he was "too far into the social things." Nevertheless, he did get to travel around the world. "I was in most European countries. I was in Russia, in the States…but they're all in my imagination now." He remembers in particular being in a beautiful village in the South of France, "but as I say it was all just a blur to us. I don't remember anything." The team was flown in and out to play the matches. They rarely got any time to do any sightseeing.

When he came back home he played for a well-known Irish club. Most of his close friends are those he played football with growing up. He is forty now and is very involved in the local club in Mayfarm. He still plays in the over-thirty-five league. He says it is demanding, especially if he has been out on Saturday night. "Sunday morning...is a killer...As we say, if we played Tuesday night we'd win the league every year."

He was managing a team up to the end of last season. He had been managing teams on and off for the last ten years. He is still up and down to the club regularly. The previous evening there had been a big celebration as they had opened a new pitch for which they had been lobbying the Council for nearly thirteen years. He got a great thrill from seeing the young people training on it. "So, I was saying like, people done it for me all my life so...put something back in y'know that kind of way. It's great to see the young guys, under 7s, under 8s, under 9s, down there, so they were all training last night. It's great for them, y'know."

He says that there is always something to be done at the club:

We've pitches up in Morristown that we use on the weekend. We have to get them marked. Y'know putting up nets, things like that. I mean just 'cos you're not a manager doesn't mean you can't do anything. You can go up and put the nets up or cheer them on from the side-line even, y'know, that kind of way.

He thinks he has learnt a lot from football. For him, doing a good job on the pitch translates into work:

I actually always...personally always...tried to be good at what I did and I'd say that from a young age, from playing football and all of that. I was always very confident with my own ability.

He can be emotional, particularly when playing football. "I was always very argumentative on a football pitch." He would feel lost without football. It's embedded in his social life. He was quite definite about what gives him pleasure and satisfaction in life:

Soccer would be the main thing, social aspect. I mean we go out and have a few pints at the weekend. Friday night it would be probably more so...or probably Wednesday night it would be the Champions league football or something like that, I'd be meeting my mates for a pint.

Soccer is also deeply embedded in his family life:

> My son plays for the team. It's actually...when I say the family thing, it's actually a very area-orientated football club. Like you'll see the wives of the players or the girlfriends of the players, the kids of the players and all wearing the Blackhall tracksuits and it is a very area-orientated thing like even going out when we played the cup final, we beat Rockfield last year in the cup final, like there was probably 600 people at it...for a small area...y'know what I mean. Like my wife would have a Blackhall tracksuit, my son would, my daughter wants one. So family, and it's a really area-orientated thing [as well], y'know.

When I asked him if there was anything he would feel lost without, he was quick and unequivocal: "Football definitely. My wife and kids, family like, but as I say, I was managing a team up to the end of last season."

Family life is big for Peter. His father died eight years ago. He had not been well for years. He had heart trouble. Initially he got over it by going to the pub, then by getting back into the football. It took a year or two to recover. They were very close; his father regularly came to watch Peter play.

For Peter, sport, family, and community are interlinked. He believes that a family that does sport together stays together. His mother is hale and hearty. The family recently celebrated her eightieth birthday. He also keeps in contact with his uncles and aunts. "I have one aunt in particular now I'm very fond of. She only lives round the corner actually, but we kind of make a...if we were going out for a drink she'd be invited as well, y'know that kind of way." He and his brothers and sisters are mindful of her. "If we were somewhere local someone would collect her or ring her and bring her out, she's only down the road. She lost her husband there recently as well."

He met his wife when he was fifteen. He jokes that if he had murdered someone, he would have been out by now. But they make sure to go out together at the weekends. He has a son nineteen and daughter twelve. He plays football with his son. He takes his daughter swimming but that is coming to a halt: "She is starting to look at herself in the mirror. She is not the little girl she once was." But they make it their business as a family to go away on holidays together. They were off to Florida for Christmas. He is delighted that his son still wants to go away with them.

Peter works in a small construction company. There are seven of them. He says he "would be more or less the senior worker in it bar the boss." But there is no big turnover of staff and "we're all mates more so than colleagues." He has been working with the same "mates" for the past eleven years. Peter likes his work. He gets annoyed sometimes at work when the younger lads take the attitude "ah just leave it, it's alright" over little things—things that Peter would have to change "to make sure the job was done right."

It was through sport and his involvement in his local soccer club that Peter became interested and involved in politics:

I'd be very interested in politics and it's sharpened my brain in the last few years 'cos we're after been dealing with Dublin City Council and we've been turned over so many times, as I say...to get a [soccer] pitch done. We've been told so many lies by different people and I've seen the way they operate y'know so. I actually buy *The Irish Times* now and I do take a keener interest in it, like even this credit crunch and all now, like I do, I do tend to read that now.

He votes for individuals rather than parties. He would vote for the local Fianna Fáil man not, he says, because he is Fianna Fáil but because "he gave us a great dig out with the pitch."

We can see Peter then as having used soccer as a means of developing an identity and sense of self in his family, his local community, and among his workmates. It is something that he is good at. He has status and position in the local club and in the community. He has symbolic capital and uses this and his social capital to maintain his position. He sees sport as the means of living a good life, of being attached and attuned to his family, friends, and colleagues. But he is also good at family life, looking after his wife, his kids, his mother, and aunts. And he is good at his work.

He feels most calm and relaxed at home. He likes to go in for a pint after work and sit down and read *The Irish Times*. In particular, he looks forward to Friday evening and calling into the pub, and sitting quietly and doing the crossword: "just sitting down there for an hour and just completely chilling out. Two or three pints and you go home then, y'know that kind of way." The pub, family, community, work, and sport are all webs of meaning that are closely interwoven with each other.

Peter is caught up in a long-term process of change wherein more people are spending more time playing, watching, and talking about sport. For much of the twentieth century in Ireland, there were conflicts, often bitter, between the guardians and promoters of Gaelic games and those who sought to play "foreign" games such as soccer and rugby. This was the cultural context in which Peter Flynn grew up. Every morning when he went to school, the yard in which he played was an ongoing site of struggle in which the Christian Brothers, who had been the traditional promoters of Gaelic games among boys, sought to get the boys to play their games. Peter Flynn knew, understood, and operated within this culture. He knew that come half past eight every morning, the soccer ball would be taken up and replaced with a Gaelic one.

However, inasmuch as the Christian Brothers were agents of change, so were Peter's parents. Even though he was attending a Gaelic football school and probably would have excelled at playing Gaelic as much as soccer, they encouraged and supported him in his desire to play soccer. He grew up in a well-to-do working-class area in which, as he says, "we never got everything we wanted, but we never kind of wanted for anything, y'know that kind of way." However, when it came to Peter playing soccer, his parents were very supportive: "Football was always a big thing in my life. My ma and da always encouraged it, always. I always had the proper equipment." Even though he was one of six children, his parents were insistent that Peter be encouraged to fulfill his dreams and ambitions.

In other words, the cultural context in which Peter grew up was one in which children were permitted and encouraged to challenge the dominant norm of the Brothers who ran the local school. It was a culture in which there were strong bonds between parents and their children, something that Peter has made part of his own family practices. Peter's parents thus used culture to become small but significant agents of secularization, informalization, and individualization with sport as the vehicle for transformation.

SPORT AS A MODEL FOR LIFE

There were some participants who, like Peter Flynn, saw sport not just as form of pleasure and excitement but as a model for life. For them, much of social life, particularly when it came to work or politics, was about playing a competitive game in which players learn to create and maintain their advantage. Jim Nolan picked up on this notion of sport being a model for how to live a good life, particularly in relation to being successful. He is in his early thirties. After university, he went to work in Europe and met and married a woman from New York. He came back to Ireland to help his father run the small company he owns and to build a house in the field behind his parents' home:

> I've played sports from when I was very, very young...just to be part of something that is winning. That doesn't always mean that...the result is wining but that you're moving forward and you're going in the right direction. That you're positive, that you basically give it your all; you know what I mean and that success isn't always winning. You know success is that you've tried your hardest, you've done your best and that's the way you've done it. So you know I don't always mean success as in...five-nil or thirty-nil or something. I just mean success in that you've pushed hard and you've done it and invariably if you do, you know...you will be successful in what you do, if you push hard.

Danny O'Brien is in his early twenties. He recently completed his degree but has been working in construction. He lives at home with his parents.

His brother emigrated to Australia a few months previously, and with the recession developing, he is thinking of going out to join him. He is not very religious. He says he believes in God, but it is not a strong belief: "I suppose I was taught to believe in God, in national school." But he does not go to Mass much and he has outgrown the habit of praying.

But sport is a different matter. He grew up with the GAA in Castlebay. "My father was in charge of a football team when we were young... from under 8 I suppose or whenever we started playing... he was in charge of us the whole way up through under 16 and under 18 and the under 21 as well [until] about 5 years ago." Danny's team won the County Intermediate Championship two years ago. This elevated them into the Senior County Championship. Last year they managed to stay up, but Danny thinks this year is going to be difficult as they have no manager and two of their leading players, including his brother, have emigrated. He made most of his friends through football. He has hopes of making the County team but he is tempted to join his brother in Australia:

> I'd like that [to get into the County team]...I suppose you'd be in the spotlight then...I'd like to be a county player alright...I've trained with them a couple of times...under 16 and minor, but like I never made the panel. You never know, in a couple of years now. But it takes a lot of dedication too...takes up an awful lot of time...maybe in a few years time...come back from Australia and put my mind down to it for 3 or 4 years. It'd take that. It'd take one year to get right in shape and the next year to try and train for them and try and get picked, get on a panel.

Sport is central to his life: "I think I'd go mental without it." Nothing really stresses him except losing matches. "I like to be winning playing football. I feel competitive like that." His life revolves around Gaelic football: "it's all based on football." When I asked him if has any major disappointments in his life, it all came back to football:

> No nothing too major...just the football again...the odd final now...the under 21 the championship...that was the main one...we lost the quarter final to a team from Brona...it was our last year together. That was fierce disappointing so it was. We were expected to win, we had a good chance of winning that year, but things went sorta downhill on the day for us.

We can see, then, how much Danny was shaped by the sporting culture into which he was socialized, and how he makes use of sport to create meaning and a sense of self, and how it is woven into his everyday life. God may not be in his heart, or on his mind, or on his lips, but football is.

One of the key ways that sport mirrors life is in terms of identity. As Durkheim argued, from the very beginning of social life, human beings have divided themselves into different groups, clans, and tribes. This system of classification became central to developing alliances and trading. There were, for example, tribes that identified themselves with the air, and within these tribes there were those that identified themselves with certain birds, for example, the eagle or hawk. Then there were others who identified themselves with the earth, or water, and so forth. This system of classification and identification is reflected in sport in which some participants and spectators identify with specific sports such as soccer, rugby, Gaelic football, and hurling, and, then, within these, with particular teams. Now while social relations are not tied to particular teams or sports, identities along with ways of being and communicating are often linked to teams. People, for example, might play and watch soccer, but may belong to or support different teams. Even though their identity is with different teams they can still talk about soccer with each other. But it is more difficult for people who, for example, participate in and follow sailing to talk to those who participate in and follow swimming, even though they are both water sports.[20]

Adenike Ajayi is thirty-six, married, with three children, and lives in Mayfarm. She and her husband are both from Nigeria. She studied accountancy and came to Ireland in 2002. She had no connections or contacts before arriving. She is used to adapting to different cultures. She was brought up as Muslim but when she was twenty-two she decided to become a Christian—the original religion of her mother who converted to Islam in order to marry. Adenike and her family are now strong Pentacostalists. They are also strong supporters of English soccer but each of them supports a different team:

> My husband is into football. So there's always a discussion around football over the table...supporting different teams...my colleagues as well at work are into football, and we talk about it at home, and we talk about in at the office y'know. So I get drawn into that...Now I support Chelsea, and my son is Arsenal, my husband is Liverpool, my daughter is Man U. My husband come back home from work. We're sitting down at the table, talking about how his day has been, how my day was...So then we are much relaxed, and we are watching football. We talk about football as well.

What makes the Ajayi household different is the almost deliberate way in which they use soccer as a means of creating and sustaining family bonds and relationships among themselves and for Ajayi with her work colleagues. It is as if they recognized that talking about and following English soccer was a way of being attached and attuned to each other and integrating into

Irish society. It may well be that while cultural insiders like Peter Flynn have a natural feel for engaging in sport—it is second nature to him—for the Ajayis it was an acquired taste, language, and lifestyle.

Hannif Mustar has a similar story. He is a thirty-two-year-old Muslim from Egypt. He came to Ireland to study music but ended up working as an assistant in a shop. Growing up in Egypt, where English soccer is shown on television, he always followed Manchester United. Six years ago, he started working with a man from Poland. They became close friends and they began watching soccer together. However, his friend supported Liverpool and so Hannif switched his allegiance: "I liked Liverpool just for him." Now when Liverpool is playing Manchester United, Hannif wants Liverpool to win. There is no doubt that the pleasure Hannif gets from watching soccer sits comfortably with his religion: it is an elective affinity or symbiotic relationship. He is a deeply committed Muslim who prays every day. He says: "I still love my religion. I still do what I can do. Like, I don't drink. I don't eat pork. I never had sex outside marriage, only two times ok [laughs]."

Sport then acts as a language and practice that people use to become and remain attached and attuned to each other. Patricia Furlong is fifty-nine. She lives in a rural area outside of Hillbrook. She has three children, two girls in their early twenties and an eighteen-year-old boy. The girls are studying at university, the son lives at home. He plays Gaelic football. When I asked her how important sport was to her, she was quick to respond: "Love sport, I love [the] Premiership in England." She follows Manchester United, but she says she would watch any of them. She watches the highlights of the matches on RTE television on Saturday nights and then, again, later on BBC and, she says, "I might get up on a Sunday morning and he [Mick her husband] might have it on again and I'd watch the same thing again and we'd discuss it, do you know. Mick loves it as well. I love the rugby—the 6 nations, now I love that."

Stephen O'Brien is twenty-seven. He is in a steady relationship with his partner. They have two children. He works long hours, six days a week. He is passionate about Gaelic football and the Dublin team. He used to play with the local club. He gave it up because he could not balance training two nights a week and playing on Sunday, with his family responsibilities. Now he contents himself by supporting Dublin. It has become a major source of meaning, pleasure, and identity for him. He goes to away matches during the year, but it is the home matches that he likes best. "The main thing in the summer I would look forward to would be...the Dublin matches and like things like that. I'd even go as far as booking my holidays around the Dublin matches like so they don't clash with Dublin matches." He has hundreds of used tickets at home. They are all from Croke Park and, specifically Hill 16 (an area of Croke Park stadium where "die-hard" Dublin supporters gather). He has tickets from "all this year, all last year, the year before, the year before, the year before, all them like." He has all of the Dublin shirts for each season. He told me that there was a new one coming out the following Thursday. "I'll be going into town and getting that."

Because he works so hard, has two children, and is saving to buy a new house, he does not get out to the pub as much as he used to with his girl-friend or to meet his friends. But it is different when it comes to Dublin matches. "Yeah but when the Dublin matches come around, I manage to go out for a few pints with them and that's alright like."

Simon Walsh is the twenty-one-year-old youth worker from Mayfarm that we met when we were looking at the importance of family and place. He lives at home with his parents. He plays soccer with Blackhall, the local club in Mayfarm. He also plays basketball. He sees sport as central to his sense of self. It is about being informed and knowledgeable, about being up-to-date with what is happening so that you can talk about it with friends:

> Sport is really my main thing. If there was a conversation about sport, I could get into that conversation like that [clicks his fingers]. In the newspapers, I'd probably read the headline on the front of the newspaper and then go to the back page... I really like to know what's going on with all the clubs and stuff like. Who's being sold and to which team. So it's really a strong thing in me to know about the sports and stuff.

We can see how playing sport and being knowledgeable about what is happening in the sports field, particularly soccer, is an important form of cultural capital for Simon. For many people like him, sports capital has replaced religious capital as a means of gaining honor and respect among his network of friends. In the same way as people are respected for their knowledge of saints, popes, bishops, and priests and all that was happening in the Catholic Church, Simon obtains respect from being informed about what is happening in sport and being able to talk about it knowledgeably.

Although, as in any field, there is always a competitive element to being involved in the sports field, there is also an element of bonding and belonging, of creating and maintaining meaning. Indeed, as I argued in chapter 2, the two are inextricably linked. As in a gift relationship, playing the game of watching and talking about sport can be strategic and competitive, but if some strategies are deemed too instrumental and calculated, there is the danger of the shared meaning being undermined.

Matt Flynn is a brother of Peter Flynn who we met earlier. He is forty-five. He too played soccer as young lad, but not as well as his brother. He used to do gymnastics and karate, but, as he says, "the old joints" have got the better of him and he has become lazy. But sport is very important to him. He likes to go to boxing competitions but his main pleasure is watching soccer on the television in the pub with the lads, especially when Ireland or Manchester United are playing:

> I love watching United, I love watching Ireland…We go down to the pub yeah. If we got tickets now, we'd go over to the match. But other than that now we'd go down to the pub, and have a bit of banter, y'know the usual…great bit of craic…The banter does be flying, depending on who's playing y'know…everybody hates United except the chosen few, shall we say. So the stick would be kinda lashed out of it left, right and centre.

Lar Commins, a Dubliner who migrated to live in Greyrock, reflected about the camaraderie that comes from watching football with his friends. "I think sports is very important between me and my friends as in watching football on the telly, 'cos that's when you bond. That's when you bond with your friends and you go in and have your arguments and nearly kill each other."

While it was mostly men who played and watched sport, it would be wrong to think that sport is some male macho preserve. We saw how important it was to Adenike Ajayi and Patricia Furlong. Women too can become as passionate and involved as men watching it. Evelyn Hutchinson, who we met in the chapter on family, lives on her own in a small remote rural village in which she tried to organize a gay parade. She likes to go the pub, particularly to watch rugby. This may be a part of a cultural strategy to develop her gay identity, but it is also a major pleasure:

> I love sport. I haven't played much of it. I'm a passionate rugby nut…I follow…like Munster, Leinster, Connaught, Ulster and Ireland. Yeah, definitely follow Ireland. Screaming down the pub like, I have to be restrained. I think it's the nearest thing to war without intentionally going out to damage someone, y'know what I mean like. It's that brute force.

No Interest

As with religion, there were many participants, mostly women, who did not watch or participate in sport. They varied between those who were simply disinterested—who found it boring and uninspiring—to those who saw it as having become too big a phenomenon in society. When I asked these participants if they had an interest in sport, most responded immediately and said they had no interest at all. Danielle Burton is the separated mother we met in the chapter on money and success, who lives with her two young boys. She does not follow or participate in any sport except for kicking a football around with her sons. Then there were participants like Fiona Stephens who has no interest except when it comes to watching the Olympics. Other people referred to keeping fit and healthy, and how they liked to walk or cycle, but were reluctant to consider themselves as involved in a sport.

In the same way that atheists might have considered themselves to be outsiders in the heydays of the Catholic Church's dominance of Irish civil society, Jim Lennon felt that he was peculiar for finding sport boring:

> First and foremost I wasn't a lover of sport [when he was young]. Maybe I was lazy, that's what I put myself down to. But then...I was playing music with the lads. The sports field was there, music was there, right. And I was also afraid of getting hurt and I wouldn't be able to play... Sport wasn't important to me. I found it quite boring and for a long time I didn't like myself for that. Not cos I didn't choose it, that's ok, but to find it boring.

In many respects, Jim Lennon's comments reveal how much sport has become a dominant, normative part of Irish culture. He feels guilty not because sport is not part of his cultural repertoire but because he cannot see how other people could become so passionate and excited by it.

And then there were those who were more critically reflective about the role of sport in society. Donal Murphy lectures in the college in Falderry. He has no interest in sport but he thinks that it plays a crucial role in society:

> It's very important in terms of the world. I think it's a terrific thing; it keeps everyone just sorted, you know, in their place...Otherwise there'd be madness. There'd be just anarchy...we need a soother in our mouths...in the same way as Marx called religion as the opium of the people...absolutely I think sport is that.

We met Anne Fogerty in the last chapter. She is deeply committed to politics. She is positively disposed to sport, but she thinks that it has become too dominant in everyday life, particularly in the media. "In fact I turn off the radio. But actually it's probably wrong to say that. I think sport is a brilliant thing. I just think it's all out of proportion."

CONCLUSION

Sport may not be the new religion in Ireland—it does not unite followers into a unified system of beliefs and practices that provide any overall meaning of life or how it should be led—but for many people in this study, sport has become a major ingredient that they use to create and maintain identities, to form bonds of belonging, and to spin webs of meaning in their lives. For many people, sport is a language that facilitates communication and enables collaboration. It is seen as a good form of self-discipline and training for the competitive world of work and education. But most of all perhaps, it is a form of pleasure and excitement.

As we shall see in the next chapter, most of the participants did not seem to be directed or guided by religious teachings in their everyday lives. There was little concern about death and salvation. They were not actively seeking to discover any meaning or explanation of life. Their lives revolved more around habits, ways of being, of working and fulfilling duties and responsibilities, mixed with forms of comfort, consolation, relief, distraction, and pleasure. The rhythm of life did not have a strong religious dimension. For many people, the rhythm of their life was based around family, work, and sport. It may well be that, for them, the meaning of life is not about questioning it, about developing a coherent set of ideas, beliefs, and principles, but rather about living it within different webs of meaning. This brings us back to the notion that everyday life revolves around habituated practices. We develop rituals and routines that provide us with a sense of security, well-being, and happiness, and we develop ideas, beliefs, and values that accommodate and facilitate these rituals and routines.[21] People take pleasure in many different activities, watching television, shopping, gardening, dancing, eating, drinking, and so forth. However, of all the shared pleasures in contemporary Ireland, sport is probably the most popular one. It is in this sense that sport has become the opium of the people.

Sport, then, helps reveal how people's lives are shaped by structural and institutional forces, particularly by the market and the media, and how the events and activities that they produce become important ingredients in the creation and development of webs of meaning and identities. And, as we saw with Jim Lennon, sport has become such a dominant, almost taken-for-granted part of Irish culture that those who are not part of it feel guilty for being different.

CHAPTER 7

RELIGION

THROUGHOUT HISTORY AND THROUGHOUT THE WORLD TODAY, RELIGION
IS the rock on which the meanings of people's lives are built. It provides
an explanation of life, of its meaning and purpose, and serves as a moral
guide on how to live a good life. Religion provides a definite worldview.
It does this through a comprehensive and systematic ordering of ideas. It
sets the tone and character of a good life, its qualities, ethics, and aesthetic
styles. It establishes long-lasting moods and motivations.[1] In Ireland, particularly during the nineteenth and twentieth centuries, the Catholic Church
established a monopoly over religion and the meaning of life. Its teachings
and theologies provided a detailed, comprehensive worldview. Its symbols,
beliefs, and practices became key ingredients in the webs of meanings into
which most Irish people were born and suspended and the webs they spun
afresh in their everyday lives.

As we shall see, many of the people I interviewed have used and adapted
the symbols, teachings, beliefs, and practices of the Catholic Church to suit
their own ends. Some of them are quite traditional and orthodox in the
way they use these Catholic ingredients, and there are others, whom I term
cultural Catholics, who while they use some of these ingredients to create
a sense of bonding and belonging, are less committed to core beliefs and
practices. Yet others are creative in the way they mix and match Catholic
beliefs and practices with ingredients from other religions. But I also found
a good number who have become distanced, disenchanted, and alienated
from Catholicism and the institutional church. And while there were obvious traces of Christian thinking in the way they saw and understood themselves and the meanings of their lives, they were willing and often anxious
to dispose of the legacies of the Catholic Church in the way they understood
themselves and approached life. There is, then, a huge complex variety to
being Catholic in contemporary Ireland. Every time people embrace or let
go Catholic beliefs and practices, they add to and recreate the rich mosaic
of webs of meaning.

Contemporary Ireland is a very different culture to what it was 50 years ago. The Catholic Church is no longer the colossal institution that once presided over Irish society. Despite the best efforts of its leaders, together with many of its dedicated laity—particularly those working for the state—the church has not been able to stem the decline in its power. The number of new entrants to all forms of the religious life dropped from 1,409 in 1966 to 33 in 2005. In the thirty-five years between 1970 and 2005, the number of priests, nuns, and brothers halved, from 33,001 to 16,333.[2] This decline in the number of religious personnel was reflected in the decline in the control and influence of the church in education, health, and social welfare. It was no longer able to control the legislation that the state—albeit mostly run by Catholic politicians—introduced particularly in relation to health, sexuality, and the family. By the first decade of the new century, there had been a shift in the balance of power between church and state. Instead of the state and politicians being accountable to bishops and priests, the state began to investigate the church and the ways in which it operated, particularly in relation to clerical child sex abuse.[3] During the second half of the twentieth century, the church also lost its ability to limit and control the media. Until the 1990s, the symbolic dominance of the church in Irish society meant that it was able to avoid being investigated by the media. This changed dramatically with the clerical sex scandals. What was once a taboo subject—the sexual practices of celibates—was forced into public debate in the media. At the same time, bishops and priests were compelled in and through the media to confess to the sins of the church and to provide explanations for their actions and policies. The media effectively began to replace the church as the social conscience of Irish society.[4]

The media was also central to the erosion of the picture that the church painted of Irish society, to the meanings it created and maintained, and to the moods and motivations to which it gave rise. The messages of the media, particularly those imported from abroad, helped erode the habitus of self-denial, humility, piety, and chastity and replace it with ones of desire, pleasure, and self-fulfillment. The media were a central part of the new flow of cultural globalization that began to sweep through Ireland, particularly in relation to communications technology, travel, and the penetration of the market through advertising. During the last half of the twentieth century, Ireland slowly moved from a Catholic form of capitalism to a fully developed Western form of consumer capitalism.[5] These structural transformations and long-term processes of social change were reflected in changes in the Irish Catholic habitus, in what Catholics believed—particularly about God, salvation, and life after death—and how they practiced their religion.

At the level of religious affiliation, it might appear that little has changed in the last fifty years. The proportion of the population who identify themselves as Roman Catholics has declined by only 10 percent—from 94 percent in 1971 to 84 percent in 2011. While the number of atheists, agnostics, and those who identify themselves as having "no religion" has grown steadily in recent years, they still account for only 6 percent of the population.[6]

Moreover, despite the sex scandals and changes in the institutional church, the level of religious belief, particularly in relation to belief in God, would seem to have changed very little. In 1973/74, 96 percent of Irish Catholics said they fully accepted belief in God. Thirty-five years later, in 2008, 92 percent believed in God—85 percent said they had always believed in God, and 7 percent said that they used not to believe, but that they do now. This does not appear to be significantly different from the 96 percent in 1973/74 who said they fully accepted belief in God.[7] However, what may have changed is that the nature and strength of the belief. In 1973/74, only 4 percent of the respondents chose categories that expressed some doubt about God's existence. In 2008, more than half (51 percent) of the respondents expressed some doubt.

In addition to Irish Catholics increasingly choosing for themselves which institutional beliefs and practices to accept and engage in—an *à la carte* approach—there is also an indication that they are willing to mix and match Catholic beliefs with those from other world religions—a *smorgasbord* approach.[8] There is also definite evidence to suggest that while Catholics may still believe in heaven, they are not inclined to see the church and, in particular, its teachings and receiving the sacraments as a necessary means of attaining salvation. The numbers attending Mass each week has declined steadily from 91 percent in 1973/74 to less than four in ten in 2008. The decline in the number of people attending Confession has been more dramatic. In 1973/74 almost half (47 percent) of Irish Catholics went to Confession at least once a month. Within 15 years (1988/89) this had declined to 18 percent.[9] It may be that this represents what could be termed the "protestantization" of Irish Catholicism, that is, of Catholics devising their own path to salvation: while believing in core Christian beliefs, they do not belong to the church or participate in its rituals and practices in the same way as in previous generations. There are indications that the decline in the level of participation in Baptism, First Holy Communion, Confirmation, and church weddings and funerals has been much slower. For most Irish Catholics, these still seem to be central to their Catholic identity.

Of the one hundred people that I interviewed, ninety could be said to have been brought up as Catholics, although the strength of their religious socialization varied significantly. There were seven who were raised as Protestants, two as Muslims, and one as Hindu. Although I will make references to them, I will concentrate on those who were raised as Catholics. I have divided the Catholics I interviewed into Orthodox, Cultural, Creative, and Disenchanted. This is an analytic device: these are ideal types to help categorize a broad range of beliefs and practices. In reality, there is sometimes a movement from one to another or blend of two or more types.[10]

ORTHODOX CATHOLICS

Orthodox believers are those whose understanding and conception of God, and ways of relating to him, are closest to church teaching and practice. They use standard prayers, and engage in traditional practices, particularly going to Mass. In this sense, they both believe and belong. This was the most common group—forty-three of the total ninety participants who were brought up as Catholics could be classified as traditional or orthodox. They used the same Catholic culture into which they had been socialized to weave their webs of religious meaning. They may have had their doubts about some of the church's teachings, but there was little or no evidence of any major critical reflection, let alone challenge or resistance to these teachings. It was as if, when it came to being religious, they had a bagful of Catholic beliefs, values, and practices, which they were adept at using to create and maintain the meaning and purpose of their lives.

We met Sarah Gilsenan when we were looking at the importance of family. She is a devout Catholic. She was very attached to her mother who was also a devout Catholic. In her apartment, she has pictures and statues of her favorite saints and others, including "The Holy Face," "The Child of Prague," and "Our Lady of Fatima." She talks to God every day. She feels his presence. For her, talking to God is mainly saying traditional Catholic prayers every morning and night. But there are also others to whom she prays—guardian angels and saints. "I say my prayers every morning. I say them every night. If I have any problem or if I'm in the car I'll ask my guardian angel to get me parking, things like that." When she prays, it is usually to one of her three favorite saints, the Mother of Good Counsel, Padre Pio, or Francis Xavier.

Sarah became devoted to Padre Pio through a woman at work. "He was alive at the time and she used to write to the convent and it was her who told us [about him]." The origin of her devotion to the Mother of Good Counsel is, she says, simple: it is the name of the local parish church. The devotion to Saint Francis came about because "we always did the novena of grace, always, all my friends and myself in St. Joseph's. That was a big thing, every March." Again, when she refers to "the" novena, she assumes that I will know that she is referring to the "nine day solemn novena." She talks animatedly about a Catholic world that for her was dominant, vibrant, and embraced by almost everyone. "It's not the same. Like years ago you couldn't even get into the church... They'd be out in the car park and in the school." Sarah grew up in a world of churches, masses, saints, and novenas. In those days, priests were celebrities. Sarah lives out her life in a web of meaning that was developed through her mother, but sustained by a myriad of Catholic friends and fellow workers who populated her everyday life. The world of saints and their differences creates a shared understanding and way of adapting to the mysteries, miseries, and misfortunes of life. There were differences in the saints they followed. Sarah's mother was devoted to St. Rita, the patron saint of the impossible. However, Sarah did not seem to have the same fondness as her mother for St. Rita.

It was mostly her mother who collected all the medals, statues, and holy pictures in the apartment. Sarah inherited them. They seem to have become part of Sarah's habitus, an unquestioned orthodoxy. And yet there are nuances in her belief about them, almost some doubt about their role or importance. When I asked her if the statues, pictures, and medals gave her a sense of peace and calm, she said that she did not think so. "I inherited a lot of them I suppose, and then you feel guilty if you throw them out... You would just find it hard... when they're religious pictures, to just discard them." The prayers she says, the statues, and pictures are all part of her everyday religious life. She is so deeply immersed in her Catholics beliefs and practices that she cannot imagine how she, or anyone else who was brought up Catholic, could live without them. "I don't know how people survive without their faith, cos I couldn't."

She goes to Mass, mainly just on Sundays but she does "stop in" at the local church now and then to light a candle. She likes to give thanks for what she has: "particularly my good health." She explains that going to Mass on Sunday is "only one hour a week. It's the least anyone can do." She does not see it either as a penance or a duty. "I see it as a way of life." She enjoys it most times. She likes the peace.

She hopes that when she dies "it is just like that," and she snaps her fingers. "And I hope I go to heaven." When she thinks of heaven she thinks of being reunited with her mother and father. She thinks she will recognize people she knew. "To be honest I don't think too much of it, about it (heaven). I just hope that when my time comes that it will be quick." But she lives for today. The idea of hell "never even enters my head." But she thinks that for all the wickedness in the world that there has to be somewhere else for evil people to go to when they die.

Orthodox Catholics are more likely to to turn to God, Our Lady, and the saints for help and consolation in times of trouble. Imelda O'Kane is forty-four. After she left school, she worked in a large department store in Dublin for nineteen years. During the years of the Celtic Tiger, she, like many others, moved to Greyrock. She lives there with her husband and three children. Times were good in the early days and she gave up her job. But recently her husband's business failed: she has been through some very troubled times. They ran into serious difficulties and could not cover day-to-day expenses. When her husband turned to his sister for help, she refused him. At times like this, Imelda turns to Our Lady.

> If I'm feeling very vulnerable and very upset—you know 'cause I do cry a lot. I'm afraid —I go to the church. And I sit beside Our Lady's altar and I can see the crucifix as well, and I ask Our Lady for help. But I say a Hail Mary or I bless myself. I say please God help me get through this and...he does, I calm down then and I just get on...do what I have to do.

The shared webs of Catholic meaning in which Imelda is suspended means that she is skilled in knowing what to do and say when it comes to illness, tragedy, and death. The previous evening, she had gone to visit an elderly man who was dying:

> I put the rosary beads around his fingers and the daughter-in-law had gone off and I just blessed myself and I said a decade of the rosary. Now I don't know whether he could hear me or not, but I held his hand and I held the rosary beads and I said the decade of the rosary with him. Then she [the daughter-in-law] had come back over and out of the blue—she'd tell you herself—he blessed himself—and this man is losing consciousness the whole time—and he blessed himself and he said "we're finished." So if God is not around, I don't know who is.

When I asked Imelda what happens when she dies, she invoked a very traditional Catholic image:

> I hope that at some stage, whether it'd be hundreds and thousands of years that I will eventually get to see God, and I will get to see his face, and just be able to see the man that has made me who I am. And I will meet up then with my mum and dad and all my family and just be happy.

Although Imelda Kane and Angela Doyle, whom we met at the start of this study, were both middle-aged, middle-class suburban women, most traditional Catholics were older and lived in rural areas.

Jim Doyle is in his late fifties. We met him when we were looking at the importance of politics in people's lives. He lives with his wife and two dogs in a small cottage in a remote rural area. He works as a laborer for the county council. But he has been out of work for almost a year, recovering from treatment for cancer. He lives with his wife, Mary. They do not have any children. He is devoted to his two dogs. He says "they're nearly like kids." He walks down to the sea with them every day. He says it is his only pastime since he gave up playing cards. He got the younger dog because the other one was getting old: "I thought if anything happens him, we'd be all down in the dumps, with me not well, and the dog gone. So I thought I'd get us a young dog, to keep shuffling with, y'know like." He likes to go to the local pub: "I enjoy the few pints. I like the craic that goes along with it."

The culture in which Jim lives and the webs of meaning that he maintains are interwoven with the webs of meaning that he inherited from his mother, brother, and sister. He is devoted to them. He sees them all at least every second week. He has a good number of friends, some of them workmates, but, he says, he is not particularly close to any of them. It seems that those webs are based more on banter and craic.

When I asked him if he believed in God, he said:

> I have to say I do. Cos I go to Mass and that, y'know. And I think that's what keeps you doing... [from doing] wrong y'know. Well, I prayed a good bit once I got sick. Y'know. But beforehand I always... I was brought up a Catholic, y'know. Like my father and mother, they sort of rubbed off on me and I didn't go away from it like... I'd have friends, priests and nuns that I knew. And I respected what they did and that like. I suppose I would like. If they were believing in God, I sort of wouldn't go off and say well you're codding yourselves.

When he was diagnosed with cancer, he employed a common Irish cultural strategy, he took to the drink. "I suppose I downed a good few bottles of whiskey and downed a good few pints of Guinness... when I was told it, y'know." He was very worried that he was going to die. He says he knows some people who gave up drinking once they were diagnosed, but he kept on. "I'd often sit down here (in his living room) at night and I'd take a bottle out. I wouldn't be talking now about one or two drinks. I'd have a good few, y'know." Before he went into hospital for his operation, a friend gave him rosary beads and told Jim they once belonged to Padre Pio. Jim still has them.

Like many other orthodox Catholics, he is able to blend his Catholic beliefs with non-Catholic ones. He believes in faith healing—it was a faith healer who helped him give up smoking—and he believes in piseogs (fairies): "I wouldn't go against them." There are certain things he would not do that were contrary to fairy folklore. He would not move house on a Friday, and he would not cut wood or use nails on Good Friday.

Although, like Imelda Kane and Sarah Gilsenan, Jim could be described as a traditional orthodox Catholic, he did not have the same belief in life after death. He wove a web that was humorous, skeptical, and philosophical, all at the same time:

> *Tom*: What happens when you die?
>
> *Jim*: Well I worked with more fellas like, and one of them reckoned you come back as something.
>
> *T*: Do you think that?
>
> *Jim*: Arra, I wouldn't say like. Once you're gone, you're gone. We used to be working like, and I enjoyed working. Bejaysus, we'd be out early one morning and you'd see a crow on top of a pole nearby you, or a tree like, and he'd be squawking away there and one of the boys would say, well "that would be an old foreman anyways," and they'd say, "why?" And he'd say "Well, you'd hear him fucking shouting now [laughs]. Y'know." No, no. I think when you're gone, you're gone and that's it.
>
> *Tom*: Do you believe in heaven and hell?
>
> *Jim*: Well I suppose that's what sort of keeps people sane, y'know.
>
> *Tom*: Does it keep you sane?
>
> *Jim*: Well I don't know [laughs]. I'd be as sane as them all and that, y'know.
>
> *Tom*: Yeah. So you're just not sure. Do you think there is a heaven?
>
> *Jim*: The only way I look at it is, as I says, there must be a mighty place 'cos I never seen anybody coming back to tell us [laughs]. Y'know, they're not giving away the secret, y'know so.
>
> *Tom*: And what about hell?
>
> *Jim*: Well I wouldn't know about hell. I'd say hell was sort of thrown in there to frighten people y'know.

Jim is adept at using Catholic culture. He has learnt when to show respect—to his relatives who are religious—and how to keep the Catholic web of meaning going with his workmates with whom there is greater distance on these issues. He is highly skilled at spinning these webs of Catholic meaning.

Jim finished school when he was fifteen. His meaning of life was shaped by the same traditional Irish Catholic culture that shaped many of the other people I interviewed. He uses that culture, which includes the pub and drinking as much as going to Mass, praying, and walking up and down to the sea every day, to create and sustain the meanings of his life. The culture he uses may be, like his language, quite limited, but the meaning he creates and sustains with it is rich and rewarding. He is skilled at using different cultural frames and strategies to sustain himself. Outsiders, particularly academics and intellectuals, may not fully understand it, but there is a logic to his practice.

LIFE AFTER DEATH

There is an ambiguity at the heart of being Catholic. Following the church's rules and regulations is central to getting into heaven and not going to hell. However, there is little evidence that the church places much emphasis on telling the laity that their lives revolve around this struggle to attain eternal salvation and avoid eternal damnation. There is equally little evidence that the church constantly reminds the laity about the pleasures of heaven and the pains of hell.[11] It is not perhaps surprising then that, like Jim Doyle whom we met above, many of the participants were ambivalent, confused, and skeptical when it came to the notion of heaven and hell and what happens when you die.

It is difficult to know if there has always been a level of ambiguity about about life after death, even among die-hard orthodox Catholics. Like the notion of God, of Jesus rising from the dead, and of Our Lady being assumed into heaven, it was in the realm of faith and mystery rather than scientific fact. But it may well be that the decline in "hell-fire" sermons and the promotion of the concept of God as a figure of love—as opposed to an authoritarian, fearful figure who judges and condemns—has changed many Catholics' notions of heaven and hell.

Survey findings indicate that Irish Catholics have a very strong belief in life after death and in heaven. However, among my Catholic participants, only twenty-eight could be classified as definite believers in heaven. They could be seen as fundamental believers who have an unshakable belief that heaven exists. However, for most of the Catholic participants, it seems that heaven is more in the realm of mystery, of being a nice thought rather than a definite reality.

Consider, for example, Sylvia Cummins. She is forty-three, married, with a baby daughter and a nine-year-old boy. She believes in God, and that Christ rose from the dead, and that the Holy Spirit intervened on her behalf after a major operation. She goes to Mass when she can, but she does not see herself as particularly religious. "It's just the feeling I get from going to Mass more than anything. The Catholic thing doesn't bother me at all." She is not sure what happens when you die:

> No one has ever come back to tell us what it is, but I honestly do think that your spirit does live on somewhere. Do you know what I mean? I don't know... if there is a heaven, but like I mean none of us knows until we get there. But to be honest with you I definitely think there's something there. Do you know what I mean?

Carol Flynn is the young, happy, confident graphic designer who we met before, who lives with her parents on a remote farm. When I asked her if she believed in God, she immediately said yes. But, then, laughing, she said "and I also believe in the fairies. I'm kinda open to anything." When I asked how she would describe her relationship with God she said: "I think I have a brilliant relationship with God actually, and I was only speaking to mom about it the other night. She's very religious—my parents are both very religious and we've had a very good catholic upbringing." However, while she believes in God she is more skeptical when it comes to Jesus being the son of God. "I would like to believe that Jesus is the son of God but I'm not willing at the moment to say that I do—if you understand what I'm trying to say." She goes to Mass most Sundays with her parents. It is part of a family tradition. "My grandmothers went to Mass, their mothers went to Mass, and I kinda like to keep it on, keeping something in my life that they had in their life." But she is not legalistic about it. She didn't go to Mass the previous Sunday: she was a "bit hung over." When I asked her if she believed in heaven, she replied:

> God, wouldn't you love to think there's a big cloudy heaven that you could float around in, big harps and everything. I don't know and I'm quite happy to wait a long time before I find out I suppose is the answer to that. I don't fret about it. I'd love to (believe). I really would. I think…my grandfather died nearly two years ago now and he was an absolutely brilliant man and we all loved him very much and I'd love to think that he's keeping an eye on me now 'cos I was too young to know my two grandmothers when they died. And I'd love to think our neighbour John who died last year is there like. You would genuinely love to think they're keeping an eye on you.

Other committed Catholics seemed to accept that the concept of heaven was important to give meaning to life and to provide comfort and consolation at death. Collette Phillips is the fifty-five-year-old mother of six children who we met when we talking about money and success. When I asked her if she believed in God, she responded: "I do but I wouldn't be hugely religious, but I do believe in God yeah." When I then asked her if she talked to God, she said: "No if I have a problem I talk to the Blessed Virgin, I would pray to her." She goes to Mass but not "every single Sunday." If there was a clash between going to Mass and a rugby match, "the rugby match would probably come first at the odd time, you know." She is skeptical but, despite what she says, quite practical when she reflects about heaven:

> When you think of heaven it doesn't sound that practical like that everybody's going off to this place, you know, up there somewhere, but I think…you need

to think that there is a heaven, because I think death would be very frightening if you didn't think you were going...somewhere...I think people need to think that they'll live forever somewhere, you know and if you thought there was no heaven or no afterlife, I think...I think you miss something in your life, you know.

Mai Timmons is the young primary schoolteacher who, like Carol Flynn, lives at home. She believes in God and talks to him as a friend. She often feels the presence of God, particularly at Mass. She believes in all the main teachings of the church, that Jesus rose from the dead, and in the immaculate conception of Our Lady. And yet, when I asked her how important it was to be Catholic, she said "it's probably not that important to be honest." She went on to say, "Like I don't define myself as a Catholic...not that I could say. 'oh tomorrow I'll be a Sikh,' but like my beliefs are my beliefs...I like the community of the church and the solidarity." She does not believe in hell. When I asked her what happens when one dies, she said:

> I believe you go to heaven. My ideas beyond that I think grow very vague...but I don't find that problematic, because I think you know we're not meant to understand that...I used to think heaven was the cloud that you looked at where the sun hit and I still probably to a certain extent think that heaven is, you know, up there somewhere...that, you know, you're reunited with the people you've lost.

Delia Slowey is a very practical, hardworking woman, but she is also a skeptic. She lost her daughter and her husband within a year of each other. She is a lukewarm believer. She believes in God, but she did not turn to him when she suffered her tragedies. She says prayers with her teenage children, but nothing more than that. She has a Sacred Heart picture in her house and a statue of the Child of Prague. She carries two medals with her. They do not give her any comfort or consolation, but she would not throw them out. When I asked if she believed in heaven, she said: "I don't know why but I do...Well we are led to believe that great things happen or good things will happen, I don't know." When she thinks of heaven, she thinks "about something cloudy and white and mystical." But then, when I probed her about what happens when one dies, she said: "Oh you just go away in a box [laughs]. What happens...I don't know. You die. That's it."

Many of the orthodox Catholics did not believe in hell. Siobhan McManus was one of the oldest people I interviewed. She pointed to the decline in hell-fire sermons. "Well there was one time we were afraid of hell. We were always brought up to it, that we'd be burnt in the fires of hell. But now, sure, everything has changed. Everything has changed. I don't know if there is any hell in it at all. I don't know."

Some participants picked up on a notion that hell is not a separate space to which one goes after death, but that it is more a place of mental unhappiness here on earth. Orla Feeney, a deeply committed Catholic, conceived of hell in terms of loss. "Then to me hell is just the total absence of God. I don't know whether it's physically a place of burning or anything as is portrayed, but I do think it's being without, being forever without the presence of God in your life."

A number of participants captured the contradictions involved in everyone going to heaven. Frank Flynn, the grandfather of Carol Flynn whom we mentioned earlier, believes that there must be some sort of punishment in the next life for criminals as it wouldn't be fair for "the good person" if there was not. Veronica Walsh, a forty-four-year-old single parent whom we will meet in the next chapter, echoed this:

> The way I look at it is, we'll say, people that have done serious wrong in their life and people that have lived a fairly good life anyway, you know a normal life, not getting into trouble that kind of thing and they both die. Well I...I can't see that the two can be together.

It would be wrong to think that it was only the laity that was uncertain about heaven and hell. Brian Doheny is the sixty-six-year-old priest whom we met when we were looking at family life. When I asked him if he believed in God, he laughed, as he said he knew from having received the topic guide in advance that this question was coming. He said he did "absolutely," but then qualified it saying, "not in God is God. I think Jesus is God, I think He's my friend and...I try to be his colleague and friend too." He says that friendship with Jesus varies: sometimes he is close and sometimes not. He feels closest when he is ministering to the very ill. When I asked him what happens when one dies, he said:

> All being well, all the little knots and pains and aches will be gone and I'll be back to pastures fresh and lovely where we need nothing, where everything is just relaxation and calm and delight.

When I then asked him if he would recognize people from his life, he responded by saying "hopefully...otherwise my preaching would be in vain." When I then asked if getting into heaven depended on what people did in this life, he responded:

> I think I'm much more positive about the notion of a heaven rather than a hell. I think it'd be pretty hard to get into hell I'd say. You'd want to really be a committed baddy to make it to hell. I think the notion of the Lord's love

and forgiveness puts us all to shame, in our own view of people, you know
and that you'd want to be really, really a bad apple to get left out.

MAGICAL THINKING

Magical thinking, basically the notion that supernatural or transcendental
forces can be marshalled to bring about change in this world, is endemic
to being Catholic. It ranges from core beliefs such as the bread and wine
being transformed into the body and blood of Christ, to miracles and the
direct intervention of God and the saints in the lives of people.[12] Magical
thinking revolves around the belief that God, Jesus, Our Lady, and the
saints can and do intervene in this life. Among the participants in this
study, twenty-five believed in miracles. This varied from a quite firm belief
for some, to a vague and fragile belief for others. There were a few people,
like Bernie Young, who said they had personally experienced a miracle.
Bernie had scoliosis as a child. Her mother had to take her to the hospital
every week for a checkup. Then her mother took her to Knock (a pilgrimage site). "I got the blessing of the sick and then when I went back to the
hospital...for another check-up [but] they couldn't find anything. They
said that it was like I never had it."

Fergal Heuston is a dedicated Catholic. He goes regularly on retreats and
pilgrimages. One time he was in Lough Derg (a penitential pilgrimage site).
A relative of his wife had just given birth to twins who were thought to be
blind. "I really, really prayed strong to heaven for them, and it turned out it
was [just] very, very severe glaucoma...I believe that that was a miracle."

There were some participants who believed in charms, fortune tellers,
or horoscopes. Linda Grey, a young woman living in Castlebay, is not religious in any traditional sense: she believes that God is a force of energy. But
she has had a couple of experiences with fortune tellers who have told her
things about people and events that were "frightening" "ridiculously dead
on," "things that I have done in my life that nobody knows and would have
no way of knowing."

Some participants were superstitious. They said, for example, that they
would not walk under a ladder, or thought that breaking a mirror or seeing
an injured bird was a sign of bad luck. Jim O'Brien said he does not really
believe in fairies. But he said, "I certainly wouldn't do anything to annoy
them [laughs]." And when it comes to a lone hawthorn tree in the middle
of a field: "I certainly wouldn't pull one of those or break it or do anything
like that with it."

Some superstitious beliefs seem to take hold more than others. Seven
participants mentioned their concerns when they saw a single magpie. The
folk belief on sighting magpies is in the form of a rhyme that goes, one for

sorrow, two for joy, three for a girl, four for a boy, etc. It goes on up to ten, but most people only know the first four signs. Like two other participants, Angela Doyle knew that if she saw a single magpie, the trick was to salute or greet it, as this would cancel any bad luck.

The most common form of magical belief and practice was in faith healing and cures. There were sixteen participants who believed that a variety of illnesses—including whooping cough, eczema, colic, ring worm, thrush, warts, and burns—could be successfully treated by faith healers or by people who "had the cure." There were a number of different treatments including spitting, burying coins or beads, or licking the stomach of a mankeeper (a small Irish lizard).

Danny O'Brien lives in the west of Ireland in Castlebay. He told me that he had the cure of the burn from a mankeeper. He told me: "they're very small...you find them on the mountain...and eh, if you catch one and you lick its stomach you get the cure of the burn. My father caught one, one time and when I was young and I licked its belly. If I got a burn now on the hand and I licked it...I don't know if it's my own mind or if it's actually true, but it wouldn't be sore after."

It would seem that for many of the people I interviewed, there was no bold line between the realm of institutional religion and the world of cures and faith healing. It is not so much that the two overlap, but rather that they have their own time and place. When I asked Brian Doheny, the priest, if he believed in magic, charms, or horoscopes, he said "I don't feel very strongly about them one way or another." However, he said he did believe in cures and faith healing. "I have experienced that...some of them really work, so then you've got to have faith in some of them." When I asked him how they worked, he said "I just don't know. I believe that it's some qualities or gifts, or herbal remedies that are passed on down through generations, and some of them work incredibly." When I asked him if it was related to God, he said, "Whether it's God or Jesus I don't know."

There are, then, Catholic and non-Catholic forms of magical beliefs and practices. The question is how they interact. Is there a time and place for them both? More importantly, perhaps, is how do they interact with rational scientific knowledge and practice? We get some insight from George Flynn. He is a farmer/motor repair man who lives in Castlebay; he almost died a few years previously when a machine fell on him.

George has been on pilgrimages to Lourdes and Medjugorje with his wife, who is also a devout Catholic. He talked about seeing a vision of Our Lady. "I had a vision one night up in the local grotto. A good few of us had the same vision so we all couldn't have seen the one thing wrong." Some years previously, he underwent a surgery on his appendix that went wrong. He was certain he was going to die. His lungs had collapsed. His whole body had swollen up. The doctors could not control his bleeding. His body was not able to heat the blood that he was being given. His family was told that he did not have much time to live. He tells the story:

> and then my cousin came in to say goodbye to me and he asked me why they couldn't cure me in the hospital and I said I was bleeding and they couldn't stop it...and he said there was no problem there...I was in intensive care at the time...he said "sure John Adams in the North, he's able to stop any blood," he says. He went on with some rigmarole...some cow cut her juggler and John Adams cured it...So he rang John Adams and he was going to do the cure at 6 [o'clock]...the Angelus bell rang and that was six o'clock and so I blessed myself and I happened to release wind and it was the first wind I had released...I think I was nine weeks in intensive care at that stage...it was the first wind I released.

Soon after, the bleeding stopped. George is convinced that it was the intervention of John Adams that saved him. When I asked him if Adams was the seventh son of a seventh son, he said he did not know as he had never met him. "But I do owe my life to him." He was not sure of the provenance of the cure but, when I asked him if he thought it was Christian, he said "I'm sure it was. I wouldn't have it done if I thought it wasn't Christian."

It would seem that instead of being rationally differentiated, magic, religion, and medical science are easily enmeshed in George Flynn's mind. He insists that it was not his prayers, nor Our Lady, but the faith healer John Adams that cured him. However, to what extent would it have been acceptable for him to have been in a hospital in which doctors, nurses, and surgeons, engaged in faith healing and magical beliefs and practices? It may be that George Flynn tells this story as part of his role in creating and maintaining myths that he sees as central to understanding life, to any attempt to bring some meaning to the arbitrariness of life chances, and to building and cementing the bonds connecting his family and friends together.

THE CHURCH

The Catholic Church in Ireland has been overwhelmed by an ongoing series of clerical child sex abuse scandals. It is difficult to make direct links to the scandals and the ongoing distancing of Catholics from the institutional church.[13] The type of legal-orthodoxy, of a strict adherence to the rules and regulations of the church, had been on the wane for a long time.[14] The question, however, is to what extent did the scandals weaken or threaten the faith and support for the institutional church among traditional orthodox Catholics. Many of the orthodox Catholic participants made reference to the scandals within the church. Some were deeply affected. Bride McPhearson, the elderly devout Catholic who lives with her friend Orla Feeney, said the scandals were "dreadful...it was horrendous, but the good priests that are out there have to suffer for the wrongs of the others." She insisted, however, that the scandals had not affected her faith.

Phillip Dunne, the dentist, felt the same. He still strongly identifies with the church. "I was just very disappointed with the way they dealt with it...I would just accept that it's a big unwieldy organization." Nan McCormick, the fifty-eight-year-old shopkeeper, is a dedicated loyal Catholic. "I was born, baptized, confirmed, made my first Holy Communion, so I'm proud of it and I'm no more different anyway you know. It's the way my mother and father brought us up and I think they brought us up [as] good Catholics." She brought up her children in the same way. She thinks that the church has been a positive influence in her life. However, she thinks that the scandals mean that the church no longer has much influence in Irish society. She says "a lot of people have questioned it [the church] and are sad over it more than anything else." When I asked her if the scandals had affected her own relationship with the church, she said, "No, not with the church, I'm still going; it's the house of God as far as I'm concerned."

Not so long ago, the church and its clergy were considered to be sacred. People may have sinned, they may not have followed church teachings, but they did not openly challenge the church or its bishops and priests. However, the profanity of the scandals broke the sacred ring that protected the church. What was once unspoken is now being said. Orla Feeney is the seventy-six-year-old woman who lives with Bridie McPhearson. Orla was born in Ireland; her family emigrated to America when she was two. She returned to live in Ireland four years ago. She and all members of her extended family are very committed Catholics: many of them are priests and nuns. She is very critical of the church: "There are so many changes that need to be made and the institutional church is not facing up to it." She says the church needs to publicly acknowledge all the wrongs that have been done and to stop "trying to hide it all." She thinks this has to be linked to fundamental changes such as priests being able to marry and women being able to become priests.

Orla Feeney represents a more robust, rugged type of individual Catholic that is more common in America.[15] She is willing to confront the church on fundamental issues. We can see this process of Catholics distancing themselves from the institutional church, of being critical and challenging, and of deciding more for themselves what is right and wrong, not just generally, but within the church itself, as part of the individualization of Irish Catholicism. People like Orla may be orthodox, but this does not mean that they toe the institutional line on all of the church's teachings.

Perhaps the best indication of the decline in the power, influence, and respect for the church and its priests is reflected in the experience of Brian Doheny. He is the mild, well-mannered priest we met above. He spends much of his days praying and looking after the sick and elderly. He talked about how he had been deeply hurt by the "child abuse saga" and how it had undermined his faith and ministry. He has had some traumatic personal experiences regarding the collapse of the honor and respect of priests. The worst were the couple of times that he had been in Dublin just after the stories about pedophile priests first emerged, and he had been "spat upon and insulted." He no longer wears his clerical collar when he goes to Dublin. We can see this decline in the physical distance between priests and laity as part of increasing informalization. The formal authority of the priest, often linked to fear and deference, is rapidly disappearing.

When I was designing the schedule of questions, I thought that when I asked participants how they decided what was right and wrong, that many of the more orthodox Catholics would make reference either to their Christian faith, church teachings, the Bible, the Ten Commandments, the gospels, and so forth. In fact, many had difficulty trying to think of an answer. It was as if it was something that they had not questioned or thought of before. Take, for example, Siobhan Byrne. She is sixty-eight. She is an orthodox Catholic. She believes in God, says the rosary and other traditional prayers, and has her favorite saints. When I asked her how she decided what was right and wrong, she said: "Jesus, you'd know, what's right and wrong, do y'know what I mean. Right and wrong like...which way will I put it...I always tried to be right. I know we're not all perfect but I mean well, if you'd do something wrong you'd correct it. That's all I can say about right and wrong."

Other orthodox Catholics referred to notions such as "gut feeling," "instinct," "part of your inner being," "part of your make up," "by the way I feel," "upbringing with my parents," "learning from experience over the years." George Flynn, the farmer we met above, said: "Well I think what's right and wrong is a very easy thing to judge because I think everybody knows within their head what's right and what's wrong...people are trying to justify wrong to right but they still know inside in their head what's wrong." This reveals the complex relationship between how people are shaped by culture, by institutional discourses such as the Catholic Church, and how they use that culture. Much or most of the ingredients that these participants used to decide what was right and wrong would have been shaped by their Catholic upbringing, but it is not something which they have thought about. It has become second nature to them.

In some respects, looking at the comments of orthodox Catholics, we can see that all that was once solid and institutional about the Catholic Church in Ireland is fragmenting. In the days of legal-orthodoxy, when priests acted as moral policemen and Catholics were more likely to follow the rules and regulations of the church, there was a strong connection between church teachings and what Catholics saw as right and wrong. The question now is to what extent does the church still act as the social or moral conscience of Irish Catholics, even orthodox Catholics.

CULTURAL CATHOLICS

Being Catholic is often not so much about embracing all the institutional teachings of the church and adhering to its rules and regulations, but more about embracing a Catholic habitus—the open, flexible, adaptable, dynamic way of being Catholic—that adapts to changing cultural conditions. Members learn to adapt their Catholic beliefs and practices to meet their other needs and interests and the exigencies of their everyday lives. As much as citizens of the state do not follow to the letter all its laws, there is always a gap between the institutional teachings of the church and the way these are interpreted and put into practice by members. For many Irish Catholics, being Catholic revolves around embracing a cultural heritage, a general orientation to life that they inherited, and that they, in their own form of adaptation, willingly pass on to their children. They may willingly send their children to Catholic schools, often because they have no option, but there is no great passion or enthusiasm for the church and its teachings. This is particularly the case with teachings on contraception, divorce, and abortion. But it also relates to practice, to the importance of the sacraments, praying, and going to church. I identified nineteen of the participants as belonging to this category of cultural Catholics. They neither strongly believe in the church nor feel that they belong to it.[16]

Stephen Young and his wife got married six years ago. Three years ago they moved to one of the new calm, comfortable, modern estates of Greyrock. Stephen sees himself as Catholic but is ambivalent about his belief in God:

> Yeah, I do and I don't, yeah I do. I'm Catholic, but believing in God is...yeah I suppose I do but...you know when you look at things and you kind of say it's like a wish, you know, "come out and help me" and it doesn't happen, so you know, you kind of do it yourself.

He feels he should go to Mass more often, not just for the kids, but also because he feels great afterward. He also feels they should make a better effort as his son's first Holy Communion is coming up and then his daughter will be doing it the following year. If he does go to Mass, it is usually on Saturday night as the traditional Sunday fry is a big thing in their house. He works as a fitter and drives a good deal in his job. In the four vans that he has had during his time on the road, he has always had his picture of "little Mary" there to protect him, and he thinks she does. He has no real idea what happens when you die: "Now again they say, if you're good you'll go to heaven." When he thinks of heaven, he thinks of gates, white suits, and a good time.

Matt Flynn lives in Mayfarm. He is forty-five. He is separated from his wife and lives with another woman. He has three children in their late teens and early twenties. He works as a courier. His life revolves around his family, his work, sport, and meeting friends in the pub. "I'm actually content at the moment now to be quite honest with you. As I said to you, kids are doing alright. Partner and myself is alright. So everything is hunky dory at the minute y'know." He brought up his children as Catholics and sent them to a Catholic school.

When I asked Matt if he believed in God, he hesitated:

> That's a hard one. Yes I do actually believe in God. But em... Well, I was brought up to think God is a divine spirit transformed into a man that walked the earth, and it's pretty hard to understand because you have all this Darwin's evolution theory... On one hand you're being told God created the world, and then all of a sudden you're told it's the big bang theory and all this sort of carry on, y'know. I believe God did actually walk the earth.

But when I asked him if he talked to God, he replied: "No, I have to say, I don't practice religion now to be honest with you." And yet, he admits, the moment there is "any sort of bother at all... the first thing always out of your mouth is, 'oh God, God help me', do you know what I'm saying?" Like many other participants, he referred to how he had been brought up as a Catholic, how he had embodied the beliefs, and how they had become part of who he is. "I bless myself every time I pass a church, but eh as regards to practice my religion, no."

Although he was brought up as a practicing Catholic, he never fully embraced it. He went to church regularly up until he was about fifteen or sixteen. "I thought it was extremely boring." It did not do much for him:

> Actually it went in one ear and out the other to be quite honest with you. You just... it was like going through the motions. You went to 11 o'clock Mass, or half 10 Mass every Sunday morning, and went up, got your communion... and went home, and that was the end of it as far as I was concerned.

Many respondents made a direct connection between no longer believing in God and no longer going to Mass or other religious ceremonies. Maisie Finnerty is the forty-four-year-old single mother with two children who we met when we were talking about the importance of family. When I asked her if she believed in God, she responded:

> I used to be very...I wouldn't say "holy, holy"...but I always went to Mass and I'd go on holy days and y'know Lent and things like that but I haven't been to Mass in God knows when...like it probably was, the last time I was there was for a funeral. I don't know [what]...has stopped my going. Now I don't not believe in Him. Like I've my own prayers, I say my own prayers, I'd always bless myself and like I have a cross in my house, I got my house blessed and all. I got the monk to come out and bless it, a friend of ours, y'know things like that. But I don't know what...it wouldn't be out of laziness cos I don't stay in bed, so I don't know why.

But while she has her doubts about God and has stopped going to Mass, she still prays and talks to God:

> Well I know most people probably kind of pray to God when they're kind of looking for something. You know that way or if they are kind of "why oh why" and all that, which I have done myself...I do, I pray at night yeah.

She also prays to Jesus and Mary. She says traditional prayers like the Our Father and Hail Mary. And she believes in guardian angels. "I believe in guardian angels. Cos when I find a white feather I always say that's a sign, y'know the way you find a feather as a sign and I always say that's them, that's my lucky feather." She doesn't have holy pictures in her house, "just the statues of the angels, y'know the guardian angels." But she has loads of medals: "I have them everywhere [laughs]. You'd find them in a bag, you'd find them in a purse or there's one in the end of my garden."

Jim Nolan, a thirty-two-year-old company director, from Hillbrook, described his faith as follows:

> I can't say that I directly believe that there is a man up there called God, do you know what I mean. I believe that there's a being if you like and I believe in...I believe that the morals that are instilled through the Catholic religion, which is the reflection of what Christ and God is, are good morals. So...I've used that as kind of as my guideline through life.

But despite his doubts, Jim Nolan had his son christened and intends sending him to a Catholic school:

> I would send my son to a Catholic school because I believe in the morals and just what it instils you know, the values that it instils. I believe in that. I think

they're good and they're correct you know what I mean..... Well, it's part of Irish culture you know what I mean. Lesser to an extent now, but it's still a big part of Irish culture.

He links this to the importance of family and bonding and belonging:

Religion in its essence is the result and cause of huge conflict in the world yeah and we've seen...[that] in Ireland, but if it wasn't religion it would be something else. So I think it is a thing of good, I think it's a thing of where people can get together, congregate, where they can, even if they're not praying, if they're just concentrating on something or thinking about something or reflecting, then I think that's maybe, that's not a bad thing, you know what I mean? It's also possibly a time when people get their family together sometimes. The only time when a family might be together is when they go to Mass on Sunday and sit down at Sunday lunch afterwards.

Again it is important to recognize the variety and depth of belief among cultural Catholics. What characterizes them is a distancing from the orthodox, from what used to be called "the simple faith," that revolved around ritual practices. Being Catholic is less about salvation and getting into heaven and more about identity and a sense of shared meaning, bonding, and belonging.

Fiona Stephens is married, with four children; the eldest is thirty-one. She is a schoolteacher, reaching the end of her career. She enjoys her work. When I asked her if she believed in God, like many others, she said she did, but conflated it with practicing. "Yeah I do. And I'm not a practicing Catholic anymore, I used to be." But when I asked her if she talked to God, she responded: "I do. I talk to my Dad." She explained: "God isn't real...I turn to God in times of trouble and times of 'please God don't let this happen or please let this happen.'" She wishes that God was more present in her everyday life, but she always finds herself "running against time." She continues: "It's a busy life; I've had a busy, busy, busy life...I've reared four children. I've taught since I was nineteen, as I said without a career break. I kept my hobbies going, trying to keep myself going and my family going."

Then she reflects and says that it is "not that there's no time for God: there's maybe no time for formal religion." Her growing lack of attachment to the church led to contradictions in her work as a schoolteacher:

I mean, here I am. I've taught for thirty-seven years of my life. I've taught religion, I've taught all classes for First Communion. Seventeen years I taught First Communion, first Confession, till one day I suddenly thought "what am I doing," [to] these six year olds. I'm telling them about all the things they've done wrong...and I said "I can't do this anymore"...and I brought all my children to Mass…and dragged them to this, that and the other. Easter ceremonies and the lot, until…one by one by one, they said "no, it's not for me" and I was the only one going to Mass myself. And then things just got…soured or something, disillusioned.

When I asked Fiona if she believed in heaven, she dithered. "I do believe in an afterlife, definitely. I'm actually toying with Buddhism. I love the whole Buddhist [belief]…Maybe reincarnation, get another chance at it. I don't want to die…I believe I'm going to be somewhere."

But Fiona has major problems with the church, particularly in its teachings about women. She says "there have been horrendous things happening in the church and the power of the church" but she lost her faith over a simple thing. She was turned away from St. Peter's in Rome because her skirt was too short. "Cause my knees, my arms were being shown and I thought oh my God, I have been a Catholic all my life, taught religion and "no, no, no, no out"…I was furious. I can't bear the male dominance of the Catholic Church. I can't bear the power and the pomp and the wealth. That's exactly where I lost it." And yet she sees the church as has having been a positive influence in her own life and in Irish society. She was heartbroken when her daughter-in-law decided not to have her grandson baptized. "Every time I go to see him I just want to baptize him myself in the bath, [and] I'm only washing his hair."

It used to be that mothers and teachers worked in unison with the priests, nuns, and brothers in socializing each new generation into the world of God and the Catholic Church. The more the church loses its influence in families and schools, the more the Catholic habitus—the Catholic model of what life is about and the model of how life should be lived—will continue to give way to more personal, privatized ways of being spiritual and moral. It would seem from the results of this study that this privatization is linked to an increasing disillusionment with the church. In some cases, as we shall see below, this disillusionment is turning to resistance.

CREATIVE CATHOLICS

Creative Catholics are more diversified and imaginative in their conceptions of God. They are religiously musical and adventurous. They are more open to alternative ways of being spiritual, and to reaching out to the supernatural and transcendental. They tend to explore and engage with beliefs and practices from other religions. These are the *smorgasbord* Catholics who mix and match their Catholics beliefs with other religious beliefs. They may identify with being Catholic, but they seek religious and spiritual fulfillment— and guidance on how to live a good life—in other places besides the

666

church. These Catholics do not have any coherent consistent belief system that comes close to resembling Catholic dogma.[17] There were a number of participants who, like Fiona Stephens above, toyed with the idea of reincarnation, but none who could be categorized as firm believers. I identified seven creative Catholics among the participants.

Rosemary McManus is a fifty-two-year-old woman who lives in Castlebay. She was brought up as a Catholic, married a local man, and had five children. She experienced tragedy some years ago. One of her three sons was killed in a car accident not far from the family home. She is a deeply spiritual woman who passionately believes in God, still prays to Catholic saints, but has little or no time for the church. She has more time for ark angels, crystals, and Reiki. She prays to God every night. She is confident that her prayers will be answered. "Now he mightn't give you everything you want but if you're patient, he'll give you everything you need." She feels that God has intervened in her life. Indeed she had a vision of the car accident three days before it happened. She does not feel any anger or bitterness. Six months before her son died, she was talking to God and she said to him that she was sick and tired of rearing her five children. "Y'know, I'm handing them over to you. And I said to him afterwards, 'I didn't expect you take one of them back.'" She feels that God has taught her a lesson.

She has crystals in the house. There is one that has special importance. "There's a little crystal out there [in another room] that shows me the rainbow all the time. That reminds me of Liam all the time. It's an unbelievable crystal in that room. That room for me is very meditative."

She feels that some people are more attuned to God and are able to channel his powers for healing. She herself used to be a Reiki master and was able to heal people. Like many other people that I interviewed, she believes that some people have the power of curing ailments such as burns, ring worm, thrush, and colic. She herself has the cure for thrush.

While she still calls on St. Martin to help her, she is far more likely to call on her ark angels. When I asked her how many she had, she responded:

Well it depends on how many you want in a situation. If it's looking after your house you put one on every corner. Y'know. Depends on how many you want on the night or in the situation. Y'know. They might be busy.

Joan Gallagher is the forty-nine-year-old woman we met when we were talking about politics. She was educated by nuns when she was young. She is a social worker, married, with two children. She does not believe in god. She inherited Christian values but is not sure if they are still really Christian. She has adapted them over the years. She believes in the spiritual: that we are spiritual beings. She is certain that there is more here than just us. She is part of a group of seven women—what she calls an earth-based spirituality group—that meets once a month. They connect with ancestors, spirits, and the elements. They sing, chant, and drum. The group started eighteen years ago and she has been in it for thirteen years. It is based on ritual; they have no core beliefs:

> We start by invoking the spirits, the north, south, east and west, and then we might go either from there into drumming and movement, or movement on its own, or chanting, so it's quite a natural flow into what just comes out of that, or what somebody proposes. Then we'd usually have some chanting and or singing and sometimes we'd have a cleansing ritual with some sage or water in which we'd put some rosemary, either ordinary water or blessed water if we had it. And then around the Celtic festivals we would have extra like sounds coming up. We'd celebrate Brigid in February. We'd go out for some of the festivals, like the solstices, winter solstice, summer solstice.

Joan is not certain about what happens when you die. She is sure that there is something more. "I have a sense of spirits. I have a sense of my father being around, not in any physical manifestation, but I do have a sense of spirit and staying on."

Like many others, Evelyn Hutchinson hesitated when she was asked if she believed in God. "I don't know if I believe in God and Jesus and all this stuff and that there's God up there to punish you and send you to hell or purgatory or heaven or y'know, but I've been brainwashed into it." She was brought up as a Catholic, sent to a convent school and, at one stage thought she might become a nun. "I have been indoctrinated by Catholics, but no, I wouldn't see myself as a Catholic." She dallies with belief in reincarnation. She regularly says "Oh my God" but recognizes that it was part of the vocabulary she grew up with. For the most part she sees herself as being part of an energy. "I think we're all energy. I would be kind of like, there is a universe but I don't know what it is, whether it's God or whether it's our collective energy or whatever." She feels connected to this energy when she is in a local fort (copse) that "has these incredible trees and that to me is like a cathedral or church." She does not know if she can communicate with this energy. She sees it as an embodied but transformed legacy of her Catholic upbringing "every night I get into bed and I go thank you so much for my warm, dry, secure bed and I really appreciate it." She does not believe in lucky charms, but she often carries a stone in her pocket as a reminder of the fragility of life. "I feel it and I want to just be aware, be thankful." She does not believe in life after death, heaven or hell. When she dies, she will be cremated, and, she says, that will be it.

DISENCHANTED CATHOLICS

The last type of Catholic I identified are disenchanted Catholics. There were twenty-one in this group. Most of these may be seen as religiously "unmusical." They have little or no identity with God, the church, or being Catholic. Many neither believe in core church teachings nor have any sense of belonging to the church. If they do believe in a god, they have an image and conception far from church teaching. Disenchanted Catholics tend to be more critically reflective and, unlike cultural Catholics, are less willing to "go with the religious flow." They find it difficult to embrace Catholic tradition. Some are even angry with the church. Among others there is an ideological opposition to the church: they are concerned about its power and want to challenge and resist it.

Anne Fogarty is a primary schoolteacher. She was brought up a Catholic and she used to go to Mass, confession, "and everything like that." When I asked her if she believed in God, she was quick to respond; "No." When I asked her if she had any wobbles in her disbelief, she was equally adamant. "No, not one. Not even that much. Not a bit, no. It was very liberating I must say. It was great." However, she said being religious was more out of habit "because you do believe what your parents tell you." She read and she explored, and once she accepted the arguments of Marx and Darwin, she realized that there is no God, no salvation, and no life after death. She came to realize "that actually this is it, y'know, enjoy it and get the best out of it that you can." She admires the new generation of Irish Catholics. She thinks they do not have any of the hang-ups that she and her peers had when they were growing up:

I mean, that you weren't allowed use contraception, no abortion, y'know, you couldn't have sex before you were married, you had to have a heterosexual relationship, you had to be monogamous, all of those things and y'know it was so drummed into you that it took you ages just to shed all that, the guilt that you would feel around it, y'know.

She thinks that the Catholic Church has had a completely negative impact on her and on Irish society. However, these are her private thoughts and she has to constrain them. She works in a Catholic primary school: over 90 percent of primary schools are still under the patronage of the Catholic Church. "Even in this day and age," she says "I would not be spouting out that I'm an atheist."

Hannah Thompson is a thirty-year-old lecturer. She is a committed atheist. She began to lose her faith in God when she was about fifteen. It mainly came from reading, particularly science. She began to realize that God was not the truth. But it was difficult. It was "hard to let go of...you know, that belief that there is something out there." Her parents "still blindly accept what the Catholic Church teaches as right and wrong." She realizes how upset her mother would be if she knew that Hannah was an atheist. She detests people who force their beliefs on others and for that reason is not a proselytizing atheist. She has become a detached outsider:

> Even though I haven't practised in a long time I'm still familiar with what happens every Mass, every Good Friday and all the rest. And you start to see it from the outsider's perspective as well and realising, "God" yes how crazy is it...I say God. I still say God a lot [laughing] how crazy is it that...people kiss a piece of wood on Good Friday as part of a religious ceremony.

Hannah sees the Catholic Church—in her own life and in Irish society—as old baggage that has to be gotten rid of. The power of the church is much more evident to her when she goes down to her fiancé's home in Clare. But she says it is not very noticeable in Dublin. She thinks that the influence of the church has been in relation to morality, in teaching people what is right and wrong. But she says: "if the only thing that is stopping you from committing murder or from stealing something or whatever else is the belief that you will be struck down and go to hell, that's not the right reason. You need to have a better reason; you need to have a more developed morality to be a decent human being."

This notion of fear was echoed by Brian Mason, the successful businessman who left school when he was very young. He thinks the church subjected people to "ignorance for far, far too long and only because they knew no better...It's like, you know when you're young, your parents [tell you], don't go out there, there's a big, big dark man out there, he's going to take you away. Well the Catholic Church done the exact same thing, and we were afraid of the dark, and we were afraid of the light, and we were afraid of everything."

The power of the church in education, particularly its ownership and control of primary schools, leads to increased cultural contradictions. Donal Murphy is a forty-year-old media executive. He was brought up a Catholic, and has reared his children as Catholics and sent them to a Catholic school:

> So I think religion for kids is really important, whatever religion it is, it doesn't matter, you know. But I despise the Catholic Church with every bone in my body, you know...everything since 300AD, 400AD, they've just been a rotten, corrupt institution.

What makes Donal different, and in many ways creative, is his dedicated search for meaning and spirituality and a willingness to search outside the

Catholic box. Like many others who spoke about God, certainty is mixed with doubt, ambiguity, and confusion. He says he is very spiritual. He became a Muslim for a while, "did the whole worship thing." Now he thinks he is closer to Carl Sagan and the notion that "we are the God," but this he thinks is quite close to the Sufi Islamic or Buddhist perspective.

However, what Donal Murphy's quest reveals is the absence among disenchanted Catholics of any desire to search for new ways of being religious.[18] Indeed it would seem that there is little attempt by most Irish Catholics to stimulate and invigorate their religious beliefs and practices. It may be that the church's domination of the religious field for so long has led to a form of religious disability. The laity were, for so long, spoonfed their religious beliefs and values by the church, that there is little desire or appetite to seek out new ways of being religious.

OTHER RELIGIOUS PEOPLE

The way some of the orthodox Catholics talked about God, can be contrasted with two non-Catholic participants. Adenike Ajaya was probably the most passionate, enthusiastic, and committed religious believer that I interviewed. She was born and reared in Lagos, Nigeria. After finishing school, she studied accountancy. She had a prosperous middle-class upbringing: her father was a civil servant, her mother worked in business. She has five brothers, one younger than her. Her parents were orthodox Muslims. But her mother had converted from Christianity. When Adenike was twenty-two, she decided to become a Christian. It was a big move. "I just knew that it [Christianity] was the way of life for me." One of her brothers and many of her friends also changed religion.

Her life revolves around God. He permeates her life. She feels she is in his presence every day. "When I close my eyes to pray I feel the presence of God. My everyday life really...is centered around God and I suppose even being able to go to sleep and waking up this morning, it has to do with God, it's all around God." She recently suffered a tragedy which she found difficult to talk about, even with her husband. But she found consolation in God and her religion.

> Initially I was angry, then afterwards I was...yeah, I was in tears. Then I decided to pray, and I was praying and I was reading my Bible more. I was going to Fellowship. I was meeting Christian brothers and Christian sisters and that kind of helped me really.

She loves to sing when she is praying, and she feels the presence of God more intensely. She does it with the Fellowship and at home, sometimes with the children. In the Fellowship they begin by singing, then they pray, then they read the Bible. She sings different songs and hymns. She sees herself as a spiritual person. Being spiritual for her is all about connecting with and praying to God. To be spiritual "you have to believe in God, you have to believe that Jesus Christ died for our sins, and was resurrected and as a result all our sins have been taken away...and the Bible is there to guide you on how to pray."

Although her belief in God is very strong, she is not certain what will happen when she dies,. "I don't want to think about that. I don't know. I don't know really. But I believe that when I die, I would go to heaven. I suppose it's not crossed my mind yet. The time is not right yet."

Hannif Mustar tries to live the life of a good Muslim but he finds it difficult. He grew up in a town in Egypt. Both his parents are still alive. He has one brother and two sisters all of whom are married with children and still live in the same town. He is thirty-two. He came to Ireland to study music, but he had to give it up after a year as he could not afford the fees. He now works as a shop assistant. He is a devout Muslim:

> My wife is Irish. I will never tell her to be Muslim. I will never tell her what to wear. Jean, "you do what you like. I do what I like. As long as you don't harm me and as long as I don't harm you. You have your own religion, I have mine. I do what I want, you do what you want, and we're all happy."

He prays at least twice each day, in the morning and at night time before he goes to bed. Muslims have five prayers a day but he is only able to do the first and the last. "As soon as I get in the car, I have to pray for a least ten to fifteen minutes, no radio, no music on...If I didn't do it I feel the day is messy. I didn't do my prayer today and that's what happened. I probably cut my finger, I probably hurt my hand." He thinks that it is his own fault because God told him that he had to pray at least five times a day. He feels God punishes him if he does not pray.

He feels in touch with God when he has a problem. He sits on his own and talks to God. He talks to him as a friend. He does not feel God talks back to him. He has never felt he is in the presence of God. When I asked him how important Mohammad was, he said: "Everything, more than my Dad...more than anything in my life." He reads the Koran. He follows the teachings and rituals. This year he only did ten days of the fasting of Ramadan but previously he did the thirty days. He feels guilty in handling pork and alcohol, both of which are sold in the shop.

When he dies, he says he will be buried in the ground, then God will punish him for the bad things he has done and reward him for the good things. "I will be in heaven sometimes, I will be in hell sometimes. Some people will go to hell forever, some people will go to heaven and never leave it." He believes that in heaven you can always have everything you wish for. "If ever you wanted to see your Dad or anyone, he'd be just there in front of you. If you wanted to eat something, it's just, it's heaven... Hell is just full of fire which is more stronger than our fire, seventy times... it is just an ocean full of fire." This makes him frightened "big time." "If I ever do a mistake I always feel guilty." But he knows that God may forgive him.

CONCLUSION

The majority of the participants grew up in a relatively settled, homogeneous culture and society. For most of the twentieth century, the vast majority of Irish people were white, English-speaking, and Catholic. Being Catholic was part of the air that people breathed. Without their Catholic beliefs and practices, they would have been like fish out of water. Catholic dispositions, attitudes, and values were woven into everyday family and community life and from there they penetrated into civil society, the media, social and cultural organizations, political parties, the civil service, and the state. By the middle of the last century, the Catholic Church had gained a monopoly not just over the meaning of life, but over morality and spirituality as well.

Belief in God was created and maintained by a whole array of symbols, words, and practices. In addition to God, the Irish Catholic world was full of references to Jesus, Christ, the Holy Ghost, Our Lady, and the panoply of saints, angels, and martyrs. This world of Catholic language was maintained in houses, schools, hospitals, welfare homes, and many public spaces. Ireland was also festooned with Catholic imagery, pictures, statues, medals, and crucifixes. Catholic churches dominated most towns and villages with the laity journeying back and forth regularly to attend Mass, Holy Communion, Confession, Devotions, Novenas, Missions, Benedictions, the Stations of the Cross, to light candles, or just to pray. All of these symbols, words, spaces, and practices gave way to a peculiarly Irish Catholic conception of God that was different from but similar to the Irish Protestant conception, the general Christian conception, and the conception of many other religions. In Catholic Ireland fifty years ago, there was regular reference to "god-fearing" men and women. There is little or no evidence from this study of such fear among contemporary Irish Catholics.

The homogeneous orthodox world of Catholic Ireland is fragmenting. In general, people are used to thinking in opposites, of being either believers in God or not, of believing in life after death or not, of being either Catholic or not. The findings of this study suggest that issues of both believing and belonging are much more nuanced and complicated. There is evidence of increasing doubt and uncertainty about God. It appears that, increasingly, God is seen less in personal terms and more as a spiritual force or energy. This may be related to a greater debate and discussion about God and the meaning of life in the public sphere and the media. It is in this sense, perhaps most of all, that Catholic Ireland has become secular.[19] Belief in God, which was once taken for granted, has become problematic. Many of the participants referred to how different they are from their parents. Many of them inserted phrases such as "that was what we were taught" or "that was what we were led to believe." The decline in the influence of the church in everyday life, combined with people living in a secular rather than a religious time, means that the conception of God is no longer part of the modern social imaginary. Religion is no longer the basis for common action, except in some families and small groups.[20]

Survey data suggest that the level of salvationary belief among Irish Catholics is high, with over 80 percent saying that heaven "probably" or "definitely" exists and just over 50 percent believing in hell. And yet, this study suggests that when you probe, there is a considerable level of doubt and confusion. Even among orthodox Catholics, there is doubt about what happens when a person dies. However, it may well be that this doubt has always been a characteristic of religious belief, and that it is revealed more in personal, in-depth qualitative interviews. Whatever may be the level of belief in life after death, there is plenty of evidence regarding magic among Irish Catholics, of faith healing, cures, and of God and the saints directly intervening in this life. However, even among orthodox Catholics, particularly among the elderly, there was a sense of God being compartmentalized into religious time and place and of being related to through traditional prayers.

There was very little evidence from what most of the participants said, even among those who were orthodox, that religion was a major ingredient in the webs of meaning that they spun each day. There was no impression from any of the respondents that getting to heaven and avoiding going to hell was a major preoccupation in their lives; nor did they seem to live god-filled lives. It was more that religion was one of the meanings in which they were suspended and which they spun themselves, sometimes daily, sometimes just occasionally. But, as with many other webs of meaning, there was a sense in which, again, even among the orthodox Catholics, that there was a time and place for religion—there was going to Mass, saying prayers (mostly traditional), christenings, weddings, and funerals—and everything religious should be in its proper time and place.

What has changed, then, is that most Catholics, including orthodox Catholics, do not regularly use Catholic symbols, words, images, and gestures to create webs of meaning. They do not invoke religious language. They do not exclaim "Jesus, Mary and Joseph" when they are frightened. They do not bless themselves. They do not assume that everyone else thinks like they do. Religious time and space has become compartmentalized, personalized, and privatized. This compartmentalization is linked to a greater detachment from the institutional church. However, it was not just that many Catholics are no longer going in and out of churches to Mass, devotions, novenas, and many other services, or are distancing themselves from church teachings, or are being critical of the church, particularly in relation to the child-abuse scandals; it was more that they have developed nonreligious explanations for the meanings of their lives and chosen their own paths on how to lead a good life. We can see all of this as linked to a rise in religious individualism. Even if people still believe in God and life after death, the nature of their beliefs and the practices that relate to these beliefs—how they realize themselves as spiritual and moral human beings—are become increasingly personal and private.[21]

CHAPTER 8

LOVE

WE BEGAN THIS STUDY WITH ANGELA DOYLE. I CHOSE HER BECAUSE IN many ways she revealed how quite an ordinary middle-aged, middle-class woman was shaped by the culture into which she had been socialized, and how she used this culture to develop her social position and live a fulfilling and meaningful life. She, like most of the participants, is suspended by strong webs of meaning spun around, in and between family members, friends, and neighbors. There is nothing particularly odd or special about her life. Her days revolve around caring for her husband, children, and parents and, beyond them, reaching out and attending to the needs of the parents, teachers, and pupils in the local school—she is president of the PTA and a member of the local GAA club for which she used to act as secretary. Like many others, she has her own trials and tribulations—particularly her alcoholic father. But the impression I got was that she is generally happy and content in the cocoon of love and care in which she is enveloped. There were others who were less happy and content, who had suffered great tragedies, losses, and illnesses: Miley Nolan, whose son died of cancer at a very young age; George Flynn, whose daughter almost died in a road accident and then he himself nearly died of an accident on his farm; Rosemary McManus, whose son died in a car accident; and Simon Walsh, whose brother committed suicide by a drug overdose. There were others who were abused as children, who suffered from illness and disease, who spent time in prison, who were involved in bitter rows with loved ones, and so forth. And then, finally, there were all those who had their share of disappointments, anxieties, and concerns about their family, their careers, and love lives.

We can see all of these as part and parcel of the meanings of life. But what is remarkable is how almost all of the participants, despite the slings and arrows of outrageous misfortune, have not fallen out of the webs of meaning in which they are suspended. They are sustained by the love, care, and concern of others. It is these strong bonds of belonging that provide comfort and consolation, that give them a sense of purpose and identity, and that enable them to flourish and be happy. This love and concern seem to provide a form of ontological security, a sense of meaning and purpose. It is this ability to continue to spin webs of meaning even when faced with the arbitrariness, injustice, and meaninglessness of life that makes these participants similar to every other human being. However, as we saw in the previous chapter, what has changed in Ireland, as elsewhere in the West, is that the ingredients that are used to spin these webs of meaning and the ways in which they are structured—the institutions, contexts, and codes that shape them—have become less religious. When the participants told me their stories, there was little or no mention of religion, of God, Jesus, Our Lady, saints, priests, nuns, or brothers. It is in this sense, in the absence of a religious rhetoric, of religious symbols, gestures, and practices, in telling stories about death, illness, tragedy, and loss, that love has become secular and replaced religion as the core meaning of life.[1]

If we are to understand how the participants in this study are able to develop a sense of self, to live in families and neighborhoods, to go to work and participate in public life, we need to understand how they create and maintain their webs of meaning. There is a difference between the strong webs of meaning that are spun between loved ones with whom people are emotionally close and intimate, and those that are spun between colleagues, members of organizations, and strangers as a means of getting things done. But there is a connection. If the webs of meaning spun at home between loved ones are not strong, if they become weak and fragile, they may not be able to sustain the individual. Insecurity, anxiety, and depression can affect a person's ability to spin webs of meaning at work and elsewhere. People sustained by strong bonds of belonging are more likely to be able to deal with the outside world and the tragedies and misfortunes of life.[2]

Webs of meaning are strongest when members of a family or group are deeply attached and attuned to each other. They are physically and emotionally balanced. They generate feelings of happiness, contentment, and well-being through operating in the same place, sharing tasks, doing the same things together. Attachment emerges from deep, enduring feelings of contentment that come from intense, intimate communication, and cooperation. It is embodied love. It is manifested in the ordinariness of everyday behaviors, in touching, hugging, caressing, smiling, laughing, teasing, and joking. Attachment often emerges when people are busy doing things together. It is as natural as the air they breathe. People become used to each other. They would be lost without each other.

In addition to becoming attached, loved ones become attuned to each other. Couples, parents, children, siblings, and intimate friends are able to read and interpret each other's mental and physical messages, their words, gestures, and emotional displays. They are on the same wavelength. They see and predict each other's needs and interests. They are able to put themselves in each other's shoes. In this sense, they are able to "make love" with each other. And if and when they become out of tune, they are able to reach out, to talk things through, and describe and reflect on their differences and difficulties.

The other main ingredient of love is attraction. Although people can be attracted to each other based on character, personality, wit, intelligence, and wealth, attraction is generally associated with sex and passion. Attraction is central to couples finding each other and falling in love. It can also play a crucial role in keeping a couple together. However, generally in long-lasting loving relations, intimacy and companionship based on attachment and attunement become more significant than sexual attraction.

It is important to remember that love between couples is only one form of love, and not necessarily the most significant. Love between parents and children, sisters and brothers, and between good friends can often be more important. Moreover, the love that, for example, a young couple has for each other will often be sustained by the love they each have for their children, parents, siblings, friends, and other loved ones.[3]

What makes love central to the meanings of life and to being able to spin strong webs is that it is founded on emotion. Love is not rational and scientific. In rational bureaucratic organizations there is a demand to control emotions. But love revolves around being able to express feelings and being able to critically reflect and talk about them. Not only would it be difficult, it could also undermine the strength of the bonds between loved ones, if emotions could not be expressed.[4]

It would be wrong, however, to think that all strong webs of meaning are necessarily emotional. The bonds between group members, colleagues, and friends can often be intense and intimate without being emotional. Consider, for example, the bonds of meaning spun between monks in monasteries or soldiers in armies. They spend a good deal of their everyday lives spinning webs of meaning through shared rituals, doing and saying the same things, but with a strict control on their emotions.

We have become accustomed to thinking of love stories as having a certain structure and content. There are stereotypical images of a couple, generally young and beautiful, being completely subsumed in each other, doing and saying romantic things. Indeed, if couples are to find each other, if they are to fall in love and get married, there is often a need, particularly in modern, urban, cosmopolitan society, for them to engage in the language and practice of romance.[5] We can see, then, that while being romantic has become an almost globalized discourse and practice deeply embedded in consumer capitalism, it has enabled couples from different religious, racial, ethnic, and class backgrounds to find each other and stay together.

Is love central to the meaning of the participants' lives? In this chapter, I try to unravel and explore the nature of the bonds between loved ones and how important these bonds are in understanding the meaning of their lives. I try to find out how attached and attuned they are to their loved ones, how they love and care for them, and how love fits in with the messiness, arbitrariness, and upheavals of their lives.

LOVE STORIES

The vast majority of the participants had lovng relationships. While there was a great variety in whom they loved and how they loved, almost all of them loved and cared for their loved ones and were themselves loved and cared for. The more romantic love stories were not of complete strangers falling for each other, but rather of couples from the same neighborhood and social background coming together. Many, like Angela Doyle, married someone they had known since they were a child or adolescent. Although I suspect that many of these couples may have been romantic in their relationships, none of them talked about this, mainly perhaps because, as with their sex lives, I did not inquire into personal, intimate areas unless they raised them. But there was plenty of evidence of what could be called real, practical love that revolves around caring and being attuned and attached to loved ones.[6]

Take, for example, Stephen O'Brien. He is the twenty-seven-year-old Mayfarm man we met when we were looking at the importance of sport. He has a partner, Sheila, who is also twenty-seven: they have two children, a son aged eight and a daughter who is four months old. Stephen and Sheila are saving to buy a house. Sheila and the children live with her mother. It is messy and inconvenient: balancing loving and caring for each other with the need to earn a living, and save to buy a house, is hard work. "It's hard at the moment as I say. I come home after work, get changed, go over there. I kind of stay [with Sheila's mother] 3 or 4 nights of the week at the moment, 'cos she's got the baby, the kids like, and things like that."

We are inclined to think of young people "falling" in love as if somehow they were out of control. However, becoming romatically involved with someone necessitates balancing love with other interests. Consider, for example, Carol Flynn. She is a twenty-three-year-old graphic artist who lives with her parents in a remote rural area. She has a steady boyfriend. He moved up from Dublin recently and bought an old farm house that he is doing up. She goes down and stays with him three or four nights a week. She says that she loves it that her boyfriend is close by. But she also likes living at home. "But I'm just loving it and they seem to love having me at home. I pay my rent…my mom comes home from work every day—six o'clock. I have the dinner ready. I have the fire pumping. I have the house clean and that's kinda how I pay my rent. I look after the laundry and, you know, the running of the house." We can see how Carol moves easily between webs of love spun between her parents and her boyfriend.

There were many other examples of bonds of love being sustained within other complex webs of meaning. Remember Hannif Mustar? He is the thirty-two-year-old Muslim we met at the end of the last chapter. He lives with his Christian wife. He is devoted to his family back in Egypt, particularly his father. He spends an hour on the phone to him every day. Hannif has a son whom he has not been with for over five years but whom he contacts occasionally through Skype.[7] Then there was Linda Grey, a twenty-five-year-old woman who has a sixteen-month-old boy and who lives with her partner, Paul, who is not the father of her child. She had known Paul for more than four years but has only started going out with him just over a year ago. Like her, Paul used to be in another relationship, but been separated for five years.

For many people, one of the major chances they take in life is when, after falling in love, they take a leap of faith and make a life-changing commitment to someone that often involves sex, marriage, children, financial commitments, and becoming involved in new webs of meaning. Falling in love has become one of the big stories of modern Western culture. There is a demand if not an expectation to fall in love. Because it is such a big chance to take, and because for many it is a lifetime commitment, people make a big story out of getting married. The engagement, the hen and stag parties, the ceremony, the reception, the photographs are all part of making the commitment public and helping to make the leap of chance into a success. We are bombarded with love stories in books, films, television soaps, and serials. They have become the parables through which we know and understand love, and they enable us to be loving, romantic, and caring. However, as we know, not all of those who fall in love end up happy.

Take, for example, Rafa Tendelka. He is a forty-two-year-old single professional who grew up in London. His parents were both very successful professionals. Rafa was sent to boarding school from the time he was six. Both his parents were Hindu: he comes from a long line of Brahmins. In the absence of an appropriate Hindu school, he was sent to a Christian school. When he was there, he fell in love. He is critically reflective about it now, but it was overwhelming at the time. "Like when you're young you get to develop a crush on someone and you fall in love…it was a very young age. It was a girl I knew in school and one could describe it as an obsession but it's not."

His parents were very strict and told him he could have no girlfriends until he had graduated from university. Despite his insistence that he was not obsessed, it seems that he was clearly infatuated with this girl, but he was not able to communicate his feelings. "I was never able to tell her how I felt about her, but... I would know when I was going to bump into her because a few days before I would get premonitions and dreams." He was certain that they would marry, but then she went to live in South Africa.

He met someone else. It did not work out, but it took him eight years to end the relationship. In the meantime, he took up Reiki. Then one morning, almost twenty years after the girl had gone away, he had a spiritual experience. "I had this Reiki visualization... looking for the one thing that was missing from my life and it was this woman. I... suddenly flickered alive in her womb and I knew it was a womb because it was all grey pulsating walls." Soon after, he learnt that the woman had come home to England. He tried to make contact with her but found out that she was married. He became very depressed. Some months later, he found her address and tried again to make contact. This time he discovered that she was pregnant and was about to give birth. He linked his visualization to her pregnancy. "Everything," he said "kind of slotted into place because I was experiencing the whole birth thing." Rather than trying to forget the experience, he concentrated on it. He resolved to "build and continue that experience and just work at it... and then the experiences become bigger and bigger and then began to separate themselves from this woman."

Rafa Tandelka's long story reveals, how, at one level, he was born into webs of meaning in which there was an expectation that he would follow in his parents' footsteps: he would, as they had done, sacrifice his career for love until he graduated and developed a professional career. It reveals how rejection of his parents' webs of meaning led him to have strong emotional experiences that became part and parcel of developing new webs of meaning.[8] We can interpret his story in terms of him being caught up in a confusion of religious meanings, being isolated in a Christian school, and becoming infatuated with one of the girls. The spiritual experiences did not emerge from nowhere. They were deeply embedded in his practice of Reiki. They were part of his cultural repertoire and his style. They were key ingredients in the spinning of his webs. However, rather than dismiss his visualization of being in the woman's womb as disturbing, he used it as a means of coming to terms with his loss, of creating new webs of meaning. We can see here how culture not just shapes the strategies that he used to pursue the relationship, but also creates sensations and emotions, and is then used to interpret and make sense of these experiences. In this sense, culture provides the ingredients that generate the experiences and emotions of love, the values and beliefs that direct the way these experiences are turned into strategies of action, and the mechanisms through which these actions can be interpreted, reflected upon, and made meaningful.[9]

We tell each other stories every day. Some stories are more significant than others. As we have seen, many of the most important stories in the participants' lives revolved around illness, loss, death, and tragedy. For many others, like Rafa Tandelka, it revolved around love. Falling in love can create webs of meaning that last a lifetime.

In many respects, this was what happened to Phil Durkan. I met her in an old folks club to which she belongs. Like many of the older people I interviewed, she was hesitant in the beginning, tending to be "matter-of-fact," to give short, staccato answers to my questions. She was not used to being interviewed. She was happy to help out but, at the same time, she was uneasy and uncertain. She wanted to get back to her friends. But as the interview progressed she relaxed.

She lives on her own in the inner city of Dublin where she was born seventy-three years ago. Her mother was from the same inner-city area; her father was from Cork. Phil's father had a mixture of occupations: first, he was a taxi driver, then, he had his own shop, and then he joined the army. Her mother had twelve children, only five of whom survived childhood. There are four still alive. Her two brothers and sister live in the area. She sees them regularly.

Phil finished school at fourteen and went to work in a factory. She saw her life chances as being fairly limited and straightforward: "Just go to school and learn as much [as you can] and go to work. That's it, y'know, just be happy in life, that's all." When she was sixteen, she went to England. She lived there for thirteen years. It was there that she met Michael, the love of her life. They had a baby boy together. When she became pregnant again, she came back to Dublin. Michael came over to Dublin a little while later.

But the relationship did not work out, and Michael returned to England. She decided not go with him: she stayed at home to look after her mother who was ill. Her mother recovered. Eventually, when the children were able to go to school, Phil went back to work, and her mother looked after her two children. She never saw Michael again.

She and Michael never married. When I asked her why, she said that it was not because of religion—they were both Catholics—but more to do with her mother and Michael's father. "My mother didn't like him nor his father like me...I was 7 years older than him, and his father told him he was much too young...He was only about twenty-one. I was twenty-eight."

Soon after returning to England, Michael emigrated to Australia. She found out that he had various relations with other women and eventually married one of them. In her struggle to come to terms with this, Phil questioned the legitimacy and "true meaning" of his marriage. "Oh, he went with women over in Australia, but [he is] not married now. He didn't get married in a Catholic Church or anything. He just got married in a registry office. That was it." She insists that she was not saddened by him marrying, even though she talks about the separation as if it had happened recently. There seems to have been little contact between Michael and the two children. Phil tells the story of the time her daughter first met her father:

When his mother died, my daughter was 34 years of age and she met her father for the first time...And when she met him she told him out straight, she said, "I don't know you," she says. "I know you're my father but I don't know you," she says. "My mam is both mother and father to us," she says, "always has been and always will be. She worked very hard to rear us..." she says. "Therefore why should I fall over you," she says, "I don't know you."

She says that in a subsequent communication Michael said he admired the way his daughter was so straight and honest with him. He began to phone his daughter regularly. It seems, however, that he never phoned Phil:

And the first thing he asks [his daughter] is how am I? How is your mam keeping? Always asks about me, y'know, even when I was in hospital and my son was over in Australia. He went over to see about his house and he happened to say to my son; "how's your Mam?" And he says "my mam is in hospital", and he says "what? 'Did you not think of ringing me to tell me," he says. And he rang my daughter. "Well" she says, "to tell you the truth dad" she says, "I lost your number but," she says "I thought John [her brother] would have rang you and told you." He says "I'd have been on the feckin' plane, first plane home," he says. "If anything ever happens your mom ring me immediately," y'know.

So I asked Phil if she was still very attached to him. "Very attached...Never went with another man after that." When I suggested that she was still a young woman at that time, she said that it "didn't bother me." She then elaborated:

The reason I never went out with a man was because I told him out straight that I would never put another man over my children and I kept my word on that. I never have and I never will put another man over my two children.

The fact that she and her partner never married is one of the major disappointments in her life. "I would have liked to have been married. I would. Although we're still friends, but still, y'know." After she returned to Dublin, her life revolved around her children. She had no time for hobbies and self-indulgence:

> I had to bring up my two children, y'know, and I had to work and rear them up and that, and then my mother died, and I still had my two children there, and I had, y'know, a bit of a hard life, y'know that way. But I never went outside the door. I never went out without my children. They were with me seven days seven nights a week. I didn't know what it was to go out to the pictures, anywhere.

Phil's life now revolves around her family and friends. Her son has four children, one of whom recently had a baby: "that's my first great grand-child [laughs]." He lives in Australia, but not in the same part of the country where Michael lives. Her son has become the communication conduit between them. Her daughter is also married and has a sixteen-year-old boy. Phil talks about her daughter as being the rock of her life. "My daughter looks after me…My daughter's never away. She was never in Australia."

Phil had a major heart operation sixteen years ago, and more recently she got an ulcer on her leg; she says, it was "touch and go that I'd live. They didn't know whether my leg would come off or not." After her heart operation, her daughter took over looking after her. Her daughter said to her: "Mam you've done enough, she says and you're not doing anymore, she says. She looks after me. She makes sure I go out and enjoy myself."

A number of years ago, Michael's Australian wife came to Dublin on a visit. Phil explained what happened. "My partner [Michael], he has two daughters from the other woman that he's with, and she was home on holidays and my daughter brought her up to see me. She was delighted, y'know she never met me." When she was leaving, Phil gave her two of her Lourdes medals for their (her and Michael's) two daughters. "And their father was delighted and they still wear them y'know, they say 'that's from my nanny' and if someone asks them they say, oh my nanny gave them that, and they couldn't make out who's their nanny, y'know."

Although Phil is a devoted Catholic, she is less committed to the church. She told me the story of what happened when her daughter was born in 1964. She went to the local church:

> Made the arrangements and all. Went over that Sunday to have her chris-tened and there was 4 other babies being christened. Went in, y'know the way the priest says your name, and my sister was standing for my little one and he says, "Oh I'm sorry, you must stand back" he said, "that's an unmarried mother," he says. We do those people first. And I walked out of the church. I walked out of the church with my child and I went home and my mother was alive, and my mother says "Well God that was quick" she says.

Soon after the priest called to the house and said that her daughter could be christened but not in Michael's name. But her son had already been christened in Michael's name and Phil told the priest, "I said I'm not going to have my children with two different names." The priest said that the solution was for Phil to change her son's name to Durkan. "'But,' I said, 'why should I do that?' I said. But the thing is I had to do it because they wouldn't christen my daughter, y'know."

I asked her if she had any dislike of priests after that. And she responded immediately: "Oh no, I don't, oh no... Don't get me wrong." She then told me a story about a local priest. She says, "he was a bit of an alcoholic," but she insisted he "wasn't bad to anyone, only doing damage to himself." He used to be seen regularly with a well-known nun from the area. One night the priest "took bad" and had to be taken into hospital. Phil went into the hospital later with the priest's sister. They were sitting outside the room when the priest's sister turned to Phil:

> Do y'know, I'm dying for a smoke," says she, "but I've no matches," y'know. I says "hold on Fr. Jim smokes," I says, "I'll ask him for matches." Oh, I nearly passed out. I just [knocks on table] done that and I opened the door, oh for God sake, there was him and her (the nun) locked in one another's arms. I nearly passed out [laughs] I closed the door real quick. Now, she was shifted to another place, and he left the priesthood. He's married now; has four children or something.

Phil seemed to use this story of the ordinary, human priest caught up with desire and pleasure—who perhaps mirrored her own story—to counteract the rigid, hierarchical attitude of the priest who refused to baptize her daughter. In telling these stories, she is also capturing the Catholic culture of the time, into which she was socialized, which shaped her life, and to which she is still committed.

What we can see here with Phil is how, despite the events of her life and losing the man she loved, she clung to the cultural ingredients into which she had been socialized, and to her repertoire of cultural strategies. She was deeply attracted and attached to Michael. But she was also attached to her mother and she felt compelled to return to the webs of meaning of family. She uses these ingredients to tell her story, to explain to herself and others what happened

MARRIED LOVE

Because emotions are such a key ingredient in building strong webs of meaning, love can be messy, chaotic, and riddled with conflict as much as it can be peaceful and happy. Lovers, couples, parents, and children go through emotional upheavals. Sometimes their relations are settled, and sometimes they become so unsettled that they separate. Many of the participants had moved in and out of relationships. Some had encountered major difficult times in their relationships, others seemed luckier. What is of interest, however, is how participants dealt with the various trials and tribulations they encountered, and how they struggled, succeeded, or failed to remain attached and attuned to their loved ones.

Consider, for example, Patricia Furlong. She is a fifty-five-year-old mother who lives in Hillbrook with her husband and three children. She has two daughters at university and a son who is in his final year at school. She had a happy childhood and learnt about love and caring from her parents. She grew up on a farm in a comfortable home, with good food and "anything that you really needed." Her mother was "a very loving person." She says that her father "would have been loving but he wouldn't have known how to show it." She explained: "He'd never tell you he loved you but a Saturday morning he would always bring everyone tea to bed...and Sunday morning he would always cook a fry...he nearly always did the weekly shopping."

Like many other women in this study, Patricia gave up her job to stay at home and look after her children. She thinks she may be a bit scattered but, she says, she is devoted to her children. "I'd always have the priorities right...food and the clothes clean for the children." She reflects: "A lot of women mightn't dedicate a lot of time to their children as I would, but I suppose that's what I would have taken from childhood."

Patricia developed breast cancer when she was in her early forties; her son was four years old at the time. She said she coped with the treatment until it was all over and then she became very depressed. She was, she says, "in a black hole and there was nothing at the bottom but only death."

Now she is very concerned about one of her daughters who has been suffering from depression and anorexia since her early teens. At one stage her daughter was hospitalized. "Well she wasn't eating anything," and she was having "suicidal thoughts." Her husband was less willing and able to look after their daughter's needs. She said she had to "make all the moves." She made "all the appointments with the psychiatrists and the doctors."

Patricia's husband, Mick, was also one of the participants in the study. He too grew up on a farm, but it was much smaller than the one on which Patricia had grown up. Life, he says, "wasn't that easy...it was very poor times...a bottle of milk going to school was a luxury." His family was unusual because he was only one of two children: his father was against large families. Mick talked fondly of his father and how he used to take himself and his brother to county football matches. They did not have a car and so the three of them would be brought "maybe off in a cattle truck...there was lots of men there, but there was no other children there bar my brother and myself." I interviewed both Mick and Patricia in their home. I interviewed Patricia first. During my interview with Mick, he made no reference to his daughter's anorexia and he made only a fleeting reference to Patricia's depression. This was in response to my question about what worries and anxieties he might have had. He talked, instead, about his money worries. He had a small business, and he was seeing how recently many other businesses had gone under because they were "over-borrowed." He then mentioned Patricia's illness.

> You know my Patricia was ill years ago, she probably mentioned that and you know I came through that flying, it didn't seem to worry me at all at the time, well it worried me all right but you know I had no doubt that she was going to be ok.

It may be, of course, that Mick was not used to talking about "women's" problems. It was not something he had learnt. He also had difficulty talking about private family matters. When I asked Mick had there been any disappointments in his life, he became hesitant and then told me the story about his married brother who had an affair a few years previously. He found it difficult to talk about it and express his feelings of annoyance, disappointment, shame, and embarrassment:

> My brother did have a bit of trouble a few years back there. He had an affair, you know...She was on a bit [in age]...it would've disappointed me...like not so much in him...anyone is human you know. I remember when I heard about it first and when I went to talk to him on it. I said the first thing "look it, I'm not going to be judge and jury over you or anybody else, because that's something I don't believe in doing." No one knows what causes people to do it. It would've been a big surprise, you know...His wife stuck with him anyway.

He was very worried that his brother's daughter would have got to hear about it; "there could've been a word dropped...you're in a very close knit community you know what I mean and it would've drifted back to him...I would've been regretful for him and his wife's sake that it happened right. I would be very, very, very concerned for them not for me or anything, but for them."

Mick is bound up in strong webs of love that are interwoven with family and community. Although he referred to himself when talking about his wife's depression and did not mention his daughter's illness, or express any emotion about it, it would be wrong to think that he is not deeply attached and attuned to them. He learnt to love and care from his father. When I asked him what he would be lost without, he mentioned his eyesight and how he would not like it if he could not read the paper, watch television, or read a book. But then he said: "I suppose the loss of my wife now would be the biggest thing."

Mick may not be able to talk about his love and affection for Patricia, possibly not even with Patricia herself let alone with me but, like Patricia's father, he demonstrates his love more through what he does than through what he says. People develop strategies of being caring, loving, and affectionate. They develop their own cultural repertoire and style of loving. Just as how no two people are religious in the same way, no two people love in the same way.

We saw this when we were looking at the way participants spun webs of meaning through sport. Patricia and Mick spend a good deal of time watching, reading about, and discussing English soccer in a way that was quite unique among the participants. The webs of meaning that Mick spins at home with Patricia and the children are interwoven with his involvement in the small business and farm he runs, his participation in local politics, his attendance at Mass every week, and going down to the local pub for a couple of pints.

I have concentrated on Patricia and Mick as a means of trying to capture the bonds of love and the difficulties in maintaining strong webs of meaning in everyday life, of dealing with the events that could undermine, if not severely damage, the webs. Although they seemed deeply attached and attuned to each other, they both had different interests, issues, and concerns and different ways of talking, or not talking, about them. They were suspended in the same strong web of meaning, but they used different ingredients. They acted out their different roles in the same play, on the same stage, everyday, but they had different capacities, strategies, styles, and repertoires.[10] And, as we saw, the web of meaning that Patricia and Mick have spun is suspended in the web of extended family and community. We can see how, for Mick, his brother's affair could not only have easily destroyed his own marriage, but also his undermined relations in the extended family, the wider community, and Irish culture generally, which has traditionally seen marriage as sacrosanct.

MOTHER AND DAUGHTER

For some participants, an event—an accident, incidence of abuse or violence, the loss of a job, or a business—changed the direction of their lives. It meant that their experience, meaning, and understanding of life were pushed down a different track. Often it led to a change in their disposition and attitude to life. Sometimes the results were catastrophic. Consider, for example, the case of Veronica Walsh. She grew up in a large family in rural Ireland with six sisters and one brother. Her father was a small farmer. When Veronica was twelve, she started working part-time in a pub. She used to ride a bike in and out to the pub, often at night, often coming back late in the dark. "I'd come home from school, get something to eat and I'd get up on my bike and ride four miles into work and I worked for four hours and got on to my bike again and rode home and did my homework after that." She did three years of secondary school but she left to go and work in pubs and restaurants. She eventually got to work in a well-known, local hotel and was trained to be a "silver service waitress." One day she slipped and fell on the stairs and broke her ankle. She was rushing to go out to a local folk concert. She was in a relationship. She was young, happy, and excited. An ambulance was called to take her to the hospital but it crashed on the way. She developed dystonia, a chronic neurological disorder, as a result of the accident:

> So I damaged my arm and hand in that and the dystonia travelled right through the whole side and my neck went down onto my right shoulder. It was like that for six years and I had...injections into the muscles in my neck and that released my neck. But as you can see my leg, my foot is turned like that. They tried those injections for my leg but they didn't work,

She laughs at how quickly her life changed. She is forty-four now. She lives with her teenage daughter. The relationship with her boyfriend continued after her accident. They married and her daughter was born five years later. For the first year, they lived with her parents. Eventually, they got their own house but things went from bad to worse: "The day we moved into our own house was the first day he [her husband] beat me...and it got worse and worse." They eventually separated when their daughter was four. It was only then that she discovered that there was another side to her husband. "After we broke up I found out that he had been going out of the house at night, he was taking underwear off clothes lines and looking in windows at people and the Garda got seven bags of women's underwear in our attic."

Veronica uses a wheelchair. She lives in a small house with Felicity who is now sixteen and is attending the local secondary school. Five years ago, she herself did the Leaving Certificate and she got three honors. She has worked part-time, on and off, for the county council. She used to have ten hours, but after a series of operations, she had to reduce her hours to three a week. She loves it and wishes she could do more. Her boss is wonderful:

> The boss is very good to me. I hurt my back there a while ago and the boss will come down for me and collect me for work and bring me home and

there's not too many bosses who will do that and she'll ring me to make sure it's a day I'm able to work and if, you know if I was in bad form or...I have leg ulcers all the time and then if the nurses haven't come on time, she'll say to me, "sure we'll leave it till tomorrow.".

Her everyday life revolves around her daughter to whom she is completely devoted: she comes "one hundred per cent before anybody...I'd be completely lost without my daughter." She is happiest when she is able to care for her daughter. "Once I can get up in the morning, once I can be there to call my daughter in the morning, to get her out for school...to just sit at the table and be there with her and talk to her before she's heading off, I'm happy." She hopes that when her daughter finishes school she will go on to college. That will mean looking for more social services on top of the personal assistant, home help, and other services that she has already. But she wants to feel that her daughter "can go and do what she wants." She has two very close friends and, if anything should happen to her, they would be the people with whom her daughter would go and live. Her former husband is now in a relationship with another woman. Veronica has full custody of their daughter. He was granted access for four hours a week, but he rarely takes it up. She thinks that his new partner's three children are more important to him.

Her parents come and do things for her, but she is not close to them: "they'll come in and ask me 'do I need anything,' but they'll have their shopping done and they'd be on their way [home], [laughter] so I usually say I don't need anything." She never felt loved as a child. It was a cold, harsh regime for herself and her siblings, particularly the older ones:

> Different things happened when we were young, that shouldn't have happened, I suppose, happens in a lot of families...It was harsh and it would've been physical and it was very tough. It was a life that I wouldn't like to see. There's no way I would like to see my children do it or anybody else's I suppose. But then lots of families I suppose did the same you know at the time...You would never be told you had done well, no matter how well you did at school or anything else. You would never get a hug; we'd never be told you were good or anything like that. That just did not happen.

She has a couple of sisters who live in the area and one of them comes to visit her and she is close to her. She has another sister in America, the eldest, to whom she is very close, but she has not seen her for twenty-one years. She says phlegmatically: "that's her life but like I keep in good contact with her." But above all, it is her two friends in the town to whom she is closest and on whom she is most dependent. If anything happened to her, she knows it would be they that would look after her daughter.

Her biggest disappointment in life is the breakup of her marriage. But the second biggest disappointment is the way her parents treat Felicity. Her sister has three children and her parents dote on them. However, they are never happy with anything that Felicity does and, Veronica says, they are always looking for her to do everything. She thinks it goes back to when she was a child but then, she says, " I suppose really, [it] is to do with my disability. They don't know how to cope with it." She thinks that it is related to some sort of denial, because two of her first cousins have the same disability. So they say "you know 'it's not in my family, so it has to be in your family' and that kind of thing."

Her life is full of pain. "I have a lot of pain and I live with it twenty-four hours a day. So…that can make you stressed at times you know…when you go to do something and you realize you can't do it…I always try and keep busy and I've always said…I've always…lived with the ideal that there's always somebody worse than myself." Most of all it is her commitment to her daughter that has kept her going. She says that there have been many times, particularly when another one of her many operations has failed, that it is the thought of her daughter that keeps her going: "I always know I have to be there for her."

We can see from Veronica's story, how webs of love, caring, and bonding become frayed and fragile and complicated and entangled. Events happen and the webs of meaning are easily pulled asunder by anger, frustrations, and disappointments. Veronica has managed to overcome the tragedies of her life and build a loving, caring relationship with her daughter. Her story is also a reminder of how webs of meaning depend on life chances.[11] Most life chances relate to when and where we were born, our gender, class, religion, race, ethnicity, and so forth. They relate to our parents, siblings, and teachers. Within this broad category of life chances, much can depend on chance meetings, encounters or events that send us down a different track and lead to the creation of new webs of meaning.[12] However, as we can see from what happened to Veronica there is another realm of life chances that turns people's worlds upside down. These could be deaths, illnesses or losses, or tragic accidents. In these cases it was not about the meaning of life being shunted down a different track, it was more about it coming off the rails completely. There were many participants who had experienced tragedy in their lives but almost all of them became enveloped in new webs of love and care they spun afresh with loved ones.

Veronica's story also revealed the ways in which webs of love are interwoven with webs of religion. She believes in God and prays to him. But, she says, that she is only religious "to a certain extent." Even if she could get up to the local church, she would still not be going "seven days a week or anything of that sort." But she prays, and her daughter does as well. Her prayers vary between talking to God as a friend and saying traditional Catholic ones. She thinks that God may have intervened in her life, but is not certain. She has often said a few prayers and then "things sorted themselves out, you know, that kind of way." When she is in hospital, she always goes down to the oratory and spends time there. "It's not that I would be mad religious but you know I still like to pray and talk to God and you know." When I asked her if she thought God could have made her life any different, she said: "Well I suppose he could but...who's to say that if he made me different that it would be any better. It could be worse."

We saw in chapter 5, how most strong webs of meaning are spun in families. We discovered that many of those who lived on their own were also enmeshed in family relations. Moreover, family webs of meaning extended beyond parents and children. There were numerous participants who mentioned the strong bonds that existed between them and their uncles, aunts, grandparents, brothers, and sisters. What was noticeable, however, was the number of women who were very close to their sisters. Many of these women referred to their sister as "their best friends."[13]

Anne Fogarty is the schoolteacher in Mayfarm we met earlier. She grew up with three brothers and two sisters. They all live in and around Mayfarm. She is particularly close to her two sisters and to one of her brothers. "One of my sisters is my best friend. She lives around the corner from me, and my other sister lives relatively close. I'd see one of them every single day and sometimes twice and three times a day. We're very close." When I asked her who were the most important people in her life, she immediately said her sisters—she has a partner but she does not live with him. She explained the nature of her relationship with her sisters: "[if there was] anything that I needed to talk about or if I needed help, I know that I could just literally contact them and they'd be there for me...and we're like-minded, we have the same value systems. They are all strong socialists and we'd be very active politically...We'd debate lots of things but [on] the core issue we'd agree."

Inasmuch as there is enormous variety in the ways couples love and care for each, in the ways they build webs of meaning, there are myriads of ways of belonging and identity built around parents, children, siblings, and friends. Rather than thinking of family and friends as separate, it is better to think of people moving between webs of intimacy that include family members and friends. Many of of the participants, like Veronica above, talked about friends with whom they shared problems, concerns, and confidences. They were their soulmates. Collette Phillips lives on a farm with her husband.

They have six children. Her husband and children are the most important people in her life, but she has a number of good friends, some she has kept since childhood. "Only two nights ago I was out with two friends for dinner and my sister. Like we would keep in contact. I have some good friends and then I have new friends that I have made here, friends that were very good to me when I was ill last year." She has one special friend, with whom she works, and Collette says she could talk to her about anything.

And then there is Joan Gallagher. We met her when we were looking at the importance of politics in participants' lives. She is a social worker, married with two children. They are the most important people in her life along with her mother, her four sisters, and a group of friends whom she met when she was at university. She described the network of webs of meaning that she has created with them and their children:

> [We] have remained very close to each other, very supportive to each other, we're always there for each other. If anything happens we have sort of an innate sense of what we need from each other and how we can support each other. We've been there for each other's children as they've grown up and all of their children.

As we saw when we were looking at the importance of sport, there are many friendships that have less to do with being intimate and more to do with enjoying good company and sharing mutual enjoyments. Peter Flynn developed and maintained strong friendships through his involvement in the local soccer club. He works in a small firm with seven employees who had worked together for over ten years. He said that they were "all mates now more so than colleagues." Again, as with Collette Phillips, this shows that the webs of friendship extend beyond family and friends to neighbors and work colleagues.

Many of the participants still had friends from their childhood and adolescence. But there were others, like Manus King, who has no friends from this period in his life. His father was a guard and they moved around a lot when he was young. He never built a circle of friends. He has only realized the importance of friends since he moved to Greyrock. Like Angela Doyle, he became involved in the local primary school. "In the last four years, I would either know or...be well known, by I'd say 80 percent of the village down there, because I'm on the school board now."

SELF AND OTHERS

Human beings can realize themselves as "selves"—that is as individuals with their own personal identity—only in and through others. This is what culture does when people become embedded in relationships and webs of meaning.[14] An important element in building loving, caring relations and strong webs of meaning is an ability to see and understand oneself, one's cares and concerns, in relation to other people's care and concerns.[15] The majority of the participants were deeply embedded in webs of meaning that revolved around caring, looking after, and thinking about children, parents, and friends.

Some of the participants seemed less dependent on being attached or attuned to others. Remember, for example, Brian Mason from Castlebay whom we met in the chapter on family. He was never close to his parents, he is separated from his wife, and he has five children and a brother and sister whom he rarely meets. He seemed to deliberately keep people at a distance, not wanting to become attached, as if, somehow, the bonds of belonging might strangle him. When I asked him who was the most important person in his life, he responded: "I've no idea where we're going to go with that. If you can figure out that piece, you're talented. I don't honestly know." He told me that when he goes on holiday, he likes to bring someone. When I asked him why he said "bring." He said that he liked the company but that he wanted it to be "his" holiday. He went on to explain:

> To get involved with somebody that you would like, I presume the word you are looking for is love that you would like to love... is too complicated yeah. I would prefer a safe distance, always.

While the strategies of Brian Mason shed interesting light on the ways in which the self is realized through others, he was very much an exception. None of the other participants seemed to adopt such a rational, calculated, instrumental approach to their relationship with other people.[16] The vast majority were deeply embedded in loving, caring relationships. In this sense, the rather pathological, rational, strategic approach to relationships adopted by Brian provides a contrast to the more dominant interest in love: to love, and be loved.

Indeed, for some, the care and concern for others extended beyond those in their immediate webs of family and friends to who can be called "generalized others." We can see this love for "fellow human beings" as quite distinct from the love toward one particular person.[17] Brian Doheny spends most of his days looking after and caring for his sick and elderly parishioners. "I feel that I have a role in my parish with people. I've tried to visit all of them who are in hospitals, no matter where they are, as regularly as I can within reason. To just be with them at their... at their weakest times you know."[18]

Anne Fogarty, whom we met above, wants a revolution. She is politically active. She campaigns, protests, and used to be a member of a radical socialist party. She is an active trade unionist. She defines living a good life in terms of changing the way human beings relate to each other and to the environment. When I asked her if she had three wishes what would they be, she said: " I'd wish for a revolution in Ireland, a revolution in the world. That would be my first one... you know there's enough wealth in the world for everyone to live a very nice life... I don't think there's any necessity for children dying, or wars to happen, or anything like that. So I suppose that would be my first wish definitely." For her, the possibility of living a good life is put in the context of others being able to do the same.

PETS

Webs of meaning are woven around attachments not just to other human beings, but to a variety of other phenomena. People become attached to places to their homes, pubs, cafes, and neighborhoods. They become attached to groups, sports teams, and nations. When I asked participants what they would feel lost without, many mentioned their phone or car.

However, what emerged during the interviews—which I had not antici-pated—was how many of the participants were attached to their pets. They were an intrinsic part of many participants' daily lives. Not only were their pets an outlet for caring, particularly for those who lived on their own but, it seemed, in many families the pet was a mechanism for maintaining bonds of belonging. In the same way that parents communicate and bond through their mutual love, care, and concern for their children, pets were often an object of mutual attachment through which family members would talk and relate to each other.

There is a long history of the relation between human beings and pets and, in particular, how some animals moved from fulfilling particular chores and tasks to becoming objects of affection.[19] It is this emotional con-nection between human beings and pet animals that makes them significant in understanding webs of meaning. Pets are a source of company and solace. They provide occasions of joy and long-term happiness and can instill a sense of well-being.[20]

Evelyn Hutchinson lives on her own in a small village. She is one of the people whose mother was addicted to cigarettes and alcohol for most of Evelyn's life. Her mother died eleven years ago. She rarely saw her. The last time she saw her was at her brother's first anniversary Mass: "I remembered [then] I had loved her at some point in the far distant past."

When I asked Evelyn who she would feel lost without, she mentioned close friends, particularly one in Dublin. And then she mentioned Frodo, her dog. "I know that he's not a person [laughs] but he is a little personality isn't he?" She explained that up until recently her father had been the focus of her attention. He had died last year. He had lived with her for three years and then the last two years of his life he had been in a nursing home. She had visited him regularly. It was around this time that Frodo, a stray, had come to live with her. She was dubious about keeping him. However, one night some local lads came up the drive to the house and Frodo ran out barking while they were making off with her bicycle. Evelyn saw Frodo as the hero who had saved the day and prevented a possible break-in and attack. She says that Frodo and her two other dogs, Barker and Blimey, along with her two cats, Coy and Dainty, bring her most pleasure and satisfaction in her everyday life.

Attachment to pets did not seem to be related to gender, age, class, or where people lived. Maisie Byrne lives in the inner city of Dublin with her partner, her daughter, and her pets:

> I'm an animal person and I love my animals. That's my haven, y'know what I mean, nature and anything like that. I love my dogs, now they would come before any man in my life, y'know what I mean [laughs]. I have…two dogs and a cat. And the dog he's thirteen now. I've always been around a dog and I love them.

Mark O'Neill has always had dogs. He is the shopkeeper who is devoted to his family, to his business, and to making and spending money. He says that while he has many acquaintances, he has no friends. But he has always had pets. Recently he got a very large, very exotic, pedigree dog of which he is extremely proud. It seemed to me that in the same way that people talk about trophy cars, Mark liked to talk about his trophy dog:

> It's a huge thing. It's a big monster of a thing. It's nice. It's a big baby…I always had dogs but this dog is good. Like this dog is…without sounding like one of those nutty dog people…we've had her a few months, she's only wet in the house once, she bangs the door when she wants to go out, if we were sitting here now she wouldn't beg food, she just sits there.

His children tease him that he puts the dog before them. He likes being out and about with the dog. It is part of the family. They took the dog to a big pet exhibition. "I wanted to socialize her with all the other people, everyone petting her and all and she was fantastic." In some respects, it is not just that the dog is a subject of conversation and care, it becomes a symbol of the family, something about which he can feel proud.

Patricia and Mick Furlong, whom we mentioned about earlier, also have a family dog to which they are devoted. Again, it was something we had not talked about during the interview, but at the end of all the interviews, I asked participants if there was anything that we had not touched on that was important or meaningful in their lives. And it was then that Patricia told me a long story about their dog Rosc, how they got him and how he got into trouble. Rosc took to going off on his own and coming back filthy and exhausted. A local farmer said he was chasing and worrying his sheep. This is a serious issue in farming communities and so Patricia felt she had no option but to have Rosc put down. So she brought him to the local pound. Having to put Rosc down caused huge heartache in the family, particularly with their youngest daughter. But then another farmer phoned to say that he had seen Rosc out wandering in his fields and he had never seen him chase or worry his sheep. So Patricia phoned the pound and, luckily, they had not put Rosc down, and they were able to go and rescue him. "It was the St. Patrick's weekend last year on the Friday evening and we got him. Now we have to walk him every day. We have to bring him for the walk so he won't stray. But he's lovely. Yeah, he is nice alright."

This is a story that seemed to have become central to the history of the Furlong family. Like many of the other stories that I was told, it seemed to me to have been told many times before. It was told with appropriate emphases and gestures. As with many stories, the story of Rosc and the sheep seemed to have become a mechanism to understand the arbitrariness of life and the strength of the bonds of belonging between people and pets.

LOVE AND MEANING

The image that has emerged within this chapter, and from most of the participants that I interviewed, was that almost all were suspended in strong webs of love that they spun each day with those for whom they cared, and to whom they were deeply attached and attuned. It is in this sense that love has become the secular religion of contemporary Ireland. The other picture that emerged was that while most participants were suspended in these strong webs of meaning, there seemed to be little need to or interest in developing a strong, coherent explanation of life.[21] Very few participants had a definite explanation of what their life was all about. Instead the majority had vague, unresolved, incomplete understandings of the meaning of their lives. Life was something they lived rather than thought about. It was full of trials and tribulations, illness, tragedy, and death, and while many reverted to a religious explanation in those times, most lived their lives wrapped up in the meanings that they spun with those that they loved and cared for.

Consider, for example, Al O'Brien. He was one of the few who did seem to have thought about the meaning of his life. He is the fifty-year-old former priest who now works as a counselor. He believes in God. He says that God is "someone I can relate to." While he is a practicing Catholic, he does not use the teachings of the church or the language of Catholicism to understand life. He married soon after leaving priesthood. He is devoted to his wife. She is the most important person in his life: he would feel lost without her. When I interviewed him, she was away on business for three weeks and he said he felt "half abandoned at this stage." When, at the end, I said that the interview had been an attempt to capture the meaning of his life, I asked him if there was anything that we had missed. He said no, that we had touched on "most of the kind of key areas" in his life. But then he said that the questions I had asked were "not questions... I ... perhaps engage with all that much nowadays... You sort of spend so much time trying to cope with the mundane things and you don't find yourself going on long retreats and things to kind of struggle with all ... these issues."

And, then, there was John Philbin. He is a sixty-two-year-old man who lives in Castlebay. He was abandoned by his mother and grew up in an orphanage and industrial school. He still bears the scars of those days. He grew up without love and finds it very difficult to make love: to love, and be loved. "It's very, very hard to get close to anybody because you're all the time thinking 'well are they going to drop me as well?'" He does not have any good friends. He is afraid that if he ever made friends with someone they would turn on him. He has a dog, "a little hairy thing... She is only a Pomeranian type of dog. Her mother was Pomeranian. But like, like they say, you always love animals 'cos you know that they're never going to fail you." When I asked him if had any worries or anxieties, he said:

> Well that the family would disown me or something, y'know what I mean. That my wife would... You see at the end of the day, I probably don't trust women because of the earlier things y'know and I'd be afraid that my wife would leave me or something. I'm always trying to satisfy her, which some-times... [it's] a failure... because I try too hard.

Yet he is quite emphatic about some things. He believes in God. He prays and feels close to him. He says that his belief has got him out of a lot of situations. "My religion is still important to me. As I say, I was born a Catholic and I'll die a Catholic. I was born Irish, I'll die Irish. Y'know what I mean." Finally, when I asked him what was the meaning of his life, he was equally emphatic. "The meaning of my life is to make my kids happy, my wife happy more or less...if I knew they were happy, I wouldn't mind dying. Y'know."

Finally, let us consider Brian Doheny. He is the priest we have met before. His life seems to revolve around his devotion to his religion, his family, his parishioners, and his pets. When I asked him at the end what he considered to be the meaning of life, he responded by saying, "I thought we were finished and now you ask me the real question." He then continued:

> Impossible to answer... I suppose for all of this life, from the moment birth unfolds... and from my perspective at this stage coming towards the end of that life, I would say that it just means... relating really, really well with people, or making an effort to relate to people. Being kind to people, express-ing our appreciation or love for people in their goodness to ourselves. And the talk now about the carbon footprint. The meaning of life is doing something positive with gifts and the talents that we have. And I know that's all very woolly and fuzzy and horribly miserable in everything but....

What is perhaps most noticeable in Brian's explanation is the absence of any religious language. While he perhaps encapsulates the Christian mes-sage that God is love and that his model of a good life is to love and care for others, he does not invoke any reference to the scriptures, the lives of saints, and so forth. It also reveals the fuzziness about his thinking. He is not able to articulate a clear, consistent, coherent explanation. He can only give an approximate understanding of the meaning of life. But clearly, for him as for most of the participants, it revolves around love.

CONCLUSION

There are many webs of meaning in our lives. These are spun with fam-ily, friends, neighbors, colleagues, and members of the public we meet in everyday life. Some webs are deep and long-lasting, some are shallow and temporary. They are all spun in different contexts, at different times, and in different places. They are all part of the fabric of social life. When these webs of meaning wear thin, become frail, or collapse, it can lead to misun-derstanding, conflict, and violence.

Creating and maintaining these webs of meaning require great skill, which is acquired during socialization and developed during adult life. It is a skill that everyone needs to survive, but some have developed it more than others. Some are better at communicating, making and creating bonds, and loving and caring for others. Most of us need these strong bonds of love and care. We need to be wrapped in strong webs of meaning, based on love, in order to be able to operate in the other webs of meaning that are more ori-ented toward attaining money, success, and status.

What emerges from these interviews is that for most participants, the strong webs of meaning in which they operate are not spun around religion. There was little evidence that religious language or thoughts were in the minds of people as they lived their daily lives. There was little evidence that religion was a key cultural ingredient used to create and sustain meaning. There was, however, plenty of evidence to suggest that the strong webs of meaning in their lives were built around love and care for others.

CHAPTER 9

CONCLUSION

When we think of Ireland, we often think of a piece of land represented on a map, an island at the edge of Europe. If we can imagine a large CCTV camera suspended over the island, we would see thousands of people moving in and out of different places in rural areas, towns, and cities. From a distance, they would look like highly sophisticated ants, busy, coming and going, as they fulfilled their daily tasks. If we examined the images over a number of weeks, we would see that most people move in and around the same place, engage in the same habits, rituals, and routines of daily life, meeting and interacting with members of their family, friends, neighbors, colleagues, acquaintances, and various strangers. They develop ways of being, ways of saying and doing things, in their homes, workplaces, schools, offices, shops, cafés, and pubs and other places in which they operate. Much of their everyday life is habitual. It involves encountering the same people, doing the same things, retracing the same paths, and recreating the same meanings and understandings, all the time having different conversations, talking about different experiences, telling different stories.

What would emerge from the images of this fantasy camera is an enormous sense of order, of people weaving in and out of confined spaces, of making complicated maneuvers like they do on a motorway, yet rarely colliding; all the time moving in, out, and around each other with ease. We can see these movements as part of a complex choreography. Despite the large number and enormous variety of the movements and interactions, there is relatively little dispute, let alone conflict or violence. The choreography reveals the sophistication of human beings as cultural actors. Everywhere people go they are able to communicate, to respond to each other's movements, gestures, and words, to keep the meaning going and make social interaction mutually beneficial.

One of the simple questions at the core of sociology is: How can there be such order? How is it that human beings are able to communicate and collaborate with such ease? How are they able to create and maintain shared meaning? The simple answer might be that they have been socialized to think and act in the same way. They have been inducted into the same culture, into speaking the same language, into being able to read, interpret, and respond in a similar way to the thousands of complicated signs and symbols that they encounter in the various interactions in their daily lives. They become experts in reading and interpreting each other's actions, in reading between the lines of what is said and done, in being able to decipher the meanings of gestures, of knowing the difference between a twitch and a wink, and in making judgments about people's intentions and motivations. They present images of themselves through what they say and do and, at the same time, they read and interpret the images that others present to them. In all of this, there is great intuition, imagination, and creativity.

People may have been socialized into the same culture, but they were never socialized in the same way. People may have similar beliefs, values, and attitudes, but they are never used in the same way. It is through the agency of individuals, through their ingenuity in adapting and blending the cultural ingredients through which they create meaning, that culture is constantly being reshaped. Even though there is a great similarity in what people do and say in everyday life, social interaction is a world of small, subtle and important differences.

I have suggested that the best way of capturing this complexity of interactions is to see people as operating within webs of meaning. People are socialized into webs of meaning that they re-spin and keep going, all the time making small adjustments that, over time, change the structure and content of the web. They spin these webs using many of the same cultural ingredients as their parents did—the same ideas, beliefs, codes of behavior, ritual practices, and so forth—blended with other cultural ingredients that they have picked up elsewhere and made their own. Many of the cultural ingredients are Irish. They come from knowledge and information they receive, from conversations, reports, and stories in the media and, increasingly in new social media, about what has happened to whom, when, where, and how. These are filtered through and blended with existing attitudes, beliefs, and values. These national cultural ingredients are disseminated and filtered in local places, among family members, colleagues, neighbors, and friends. They become mixed with more local ingredients. These local and national ideas, beliefs, and values then become blended with ingredients from other cultures around the world, that flow into Ireland through the media, the Internet, and people traveling in and out of the country.

The webs of meaning that people spin give a sense of purpose and security to what is essentially arbitrary and meaningless. They provide an ongoing, mainly unquestioned explanation for their lives and a guide as to how they should live their lives. They provide a map of what they can say and do to whom, when, and where. These webs enable them to fulfill interests and achieve goals, to get an education, earn a living, fall in love, get married, rear children, shop in the local supermarket, and chat and gossip with neighbors.

The problem in trying to understand and interpret these webs is that there are so many of them, and that they are interwoven with each other. If the CCTV camera pointed at Ireland was infrared, we would see an incredibly dense, intricate tapestry that has been spun for generations. Some of the webs are thin and frail. Some, like disused railway tracks, are hardly ever used. Much of everyday life in Ireland, as elsewhere, is taken up with short interactions between loved ones, friends, neighbors, colleagues, acquaintances, and strangers. These webs of meaning are often spun over a short period of time to enable communication, collaboration, and cooperation. They often involve adhering to codes of behavior, and accepted ways of saying and doing things that do not cause offense. They involve being polite, knowing when to be serious and when to be lighthearted, when to be humorous, and when to laugh, tease, and joke. Webs of meaning that are fragile and temporary are interwoven with stronger, more permanent ones spun within families, neighborhoods, workplaces, and so forth.

Trying to capture and interpret these webs of meaning is very difficult. The webs may appear to be the same, to change little from day to day, but they are being constantly spun afresh. There are variations in the ingredients that are used, in what is said and done, in the language and gestures that are used. They are different because each web is constructed with different feelings and emotions. It is never the same person who speaks and acts. What is said and done and the type of webs that are spun depend on whether the participants are happy, sad, angry, excited, or anxious, and so forth. As much as it is impossible to enter the same stream twice, it is impossible to enter the same web of meaning twice. The meanings of the webs depends on the social field in which people are operating, the institutional setting, the general context, and the specific interaction. The webs of meaning between a husband and wife will change depending on whether they are alone or with their children, whether they are in the privacy of their home or in a public space. Context, therefore, is extremely important.

And yet, despite the number and variety of the webs, despite all the changes in the symbols, words, and gestures used in the webs, and the differences in people's interests, moods, and motivations, people are generally able to move easily between the various webs within which they operate.

This is because they are able to read and interpret what is said and done, to judge and evaluate other people's motivations, emotions, and interests and, most of all, because they want to keep the meaning going.

MAKING USE OF CULTURE

When we talk of Irish culture, or indeed of any culture, there is a danger of making it into something that is shared and common, that enables people to be a member of Irish society and, consequently, marks them out as being different from members of other cultures. However, as we have seen from the people I interviewed, there is often as much that divides people culturally, as binds them together. There were, for example, considerable differences in the extent to which people were political, sporting, religious, and so forth.

It is perhaps useful to think that there are many shared, core ingredients that people I interviewed use to spin their webs of meaning. Everyone, for example, spoke English. Everyone was polite and civilized, and followed the taken-for-granted rules that govern communication and conversation. Everyone had enough education to understand and respond to my questions. At another level, there were many shared beliefs and values, deep-rooted dispositions into which they had been socialized and which they took for granted. These related to basic human rights, such as the right to freedom, privacy, private property, and so forth, and to values and beliefs about marriage, family, children, education, and democracy.

The participants may have used the same language and symbolic forms, but they used them differently to develop their cultural strategies, different ways of being, saying, and doing that helped them develop personal cultural styles and, through them, different identities. It was as if they were all part of the same play, but they had each developed their own personal roles and characters, with their own particular ways of speaking, being, and presenting themselves. The roles they play, the persona they adopt, are acted out in different social interactions. It is these forms of being, these cultural repertoires and frames, the various scenes in which they engage from hour to hour, from day to day, that become the webs of meaning in which they are suspended.

Not only do the cultural ingredients vary, but they are not necessarily used in a consistent manner. Inasmuch as culture is not a unified system of beliefs and practices, neither do individuals use culture in a logically consistent and predictable manner. They can switch beliefs and attitudes. They can move from one way of thinking about something deep and personal, for example, about what happens when you die and, almost within the same moment or realm of thought, they can move from a belief that there is a heaven, to a belief that when you die there is nothing. Many of the participants had quite ambiguous, inconsistent, and sometimes contradictory beliefs, particularly when it came to religious beliefs. It may be reasonable to expect that a Catholic theologian will be logical and consistent in his arguments, but the beliefs and practices of ordinary Catholics do not have the same logic. But just because they are contradictory and inconsistent does not mean they are illogical. It just means that we have to try to discover what that logic is for them. Most of the participants were quite willing and able to live with ambiguities, contradictions, and uncertainties. They were flexible, adaptable, and dynamic rather than rigid and consistent in their beliefs and attitudes about the meanings of life. There was also plenty of evidence to suggest that many of the people I interviewed were skeptical about the beliefs and values they held and the practices in which they engaged. Many of them, for example, operated within webs of political meaning but were doubtful about the intentions of politicians and the nature of the political game.

PLACE AND FAMILY

The importance of place to people, particularly the neighborhood in which they have grown up and where they live now, has perhaps been underestimated. This may be because the stories and reports in the media, experiences of travel and migration, and generally, the compression of time and space, give the impression of people living in a highly mobile, interconnected, globalized world—that we all live in the one place. However, while there was evidence of people having lived abroad or in other parts of Ireland, the more general picture was of people being rooted to the neighborhoods in which they grew up. Indeed, most of the participants still live in the same neighborhood. Some of the people I interviewed had grown up in other countries and although they were suspended in webs of meaning in the neighborhoods in which they now lived, they were also deeply engaged in and attached to the people and neighborhood in which they had grown up and developed their identities and sense of self.

This attachment to place was evident throughout all the interviews but it was stronger in Mayfarm, the inner-city working-class area of Dublin, and Castlebay, the rural area in the west of Ireland. Many participants in these areas had gone away to work and live abroad, but had returned home, often to rear a family. Many, particularly in Mayfarm, had experienced violence, conflict, and personal trauma and tragedy, but were still deeply attached to the locality. It was as if they were so bound up in the webs of meaning into which they had been born, that they did not have the desire, interest, or perhaps the resources, to move elsewhere.

The webs of meaning spun around place are closely interwoven with those of family. Family is important not just for those who live together, but for members who live apart. Families preside in their absence. Family members are often deeply attached and attuned to each other even if they only speak on the phone and do not see each other very often. While most of these family webs of meaning were positive and sustaining, many were spun with tensions, conflicts, and negative feelings and emotions. The webs of family life included troublesome children, alcoholic or abusive parents, and problematic siblings and relatives.

It would be wrong, however, to think that people live in either settled or unsettled families. It would be better to see individuals moving in and out of webs of family meaning most of which are spun in emotionally settled times and others that are spun in unsettled times. Moreover, tensions and difficulties can affect some family members and not others. There was plenty of evidence of families bonding together to help not just deal with, but also love and care for, a problematic member.

And this brings us to love. Again due to the media, marketing, and advertising, we often tend to think of love as being romantic love, of passion and sex, and people falling in and out love. These are the mythical love stories that are the central theme of much of popular culture. And yet the overwhelming evidence from this study is of the existence of a strong, prosaic, practical love that revolves around people being deeply attached and attuned to loved ones, of caring, looking out for, and thinking about them. These were the strong webs of meaning at the center of most participants' lives. These were the core webs that enabled them to move in and out of the many other webs of meaning.

CHANGES IN STRUCTURES AND PROCESSES

The cultural ingredients and the ways in which people in contemporary Ireland spin webs of meaning are very different from those spun fifty or a hundred years ago. There have been major structural transformations in the Irish economy and in society that have led to changes in the content and structure of the webs of meaning. The ways in which Irish people create meaning have changed along with the ways in which they earn a living, who they live with, their housing conditions, the means of communication, and so forth. They are also linked to shifts in the balances of power between institutions for example, the European Union, the market, and the state. However, these structural transformations are not outside of culture. They take place in and through people creating and maintaining meaning. The changes in the material conditions of people's lives are filtered and mediated through the cultural ingredients that they have inherited, adopted, and adapted and that they use creatively every day to spin their webs of meaning.

The most important transformation in Irish culture has been the demise in the power and influence of the Catholic Church. This can be linked to the rise in the power of the media in civil society—its domination of the public sphere—and its messages of liberal individualism and hedonism. The dominance of the media can, in turn, be linked to the increasing penetration of the market into everyday life. The goods and services that people consume can change their meanings, identities, and sense of self. These changes are linked to the infiltration of global cultural flows into everyday life. As a result of these changes, the participants in this study, along with most other Irish people, had access to a far greater range of cultural ingredients with which to spin their webs. They developed new habituses, new ways of seeing, understanding, and being in the world.

In addition to structural transformations, the participants were also caught up in long-term processes of change, particularly the globalization of Irish culture and also increased informalization and individualization. Informalization revolves around the lessening of the psychic and emotional gap between people. This is linked to a diminishing of power imbalances, which in turn facilitates greater interdependency. In Ireland, in previous decades, there was an emotional, psychic gap between parents and children, men and women, teachers and pupils, lecturers and students, bosses and workers, doctors and patients, priests and laity, and so forth. These relationships were more formal, with greater limitations and constraints in the way they addressed each other and about what could be said and done between them. The diminishing psychic gap between people was reflected in the places where they met, in the nature of their talk, in their gestures and their touches. These cultural transformations were linked to an increased demand and expectation to be open and frank and to express feelings and emotions. This involved learning new skills in relation to what can be said to whom, when, and where. It involved new forms of communication and trust.

In this study, this process of informalization was probably most evident in the wide range of people who were willing and able to talk openly and frankly to me, an unknown academic. But it was also evident, for example, in the way Angela Doyle related to her mother and talked about her father. "Well, I tell everybody my father's an alcoholic." She recognizes the decline in power of priests and that it is hard for some, particularly the older ones: "they think they're God nearly, you know what I mean that they have this almighty power over you and they don't anymore." It was also evident in the ways many people were able to talk about and confront the abuse they had experienced as children. Often during the interviews, when participants began to talk about sexual abuse they had encountered, they became reticent, concerned about confidentiality and anonymity. But they were still able to talk about it.

The Catholic Church no longer has the formal authority that it once had. Very few of the participants saw the church as an authority that had to be obeyed. What was once taken for granted—the moral authority of bishops and priests was openly questioned, resisted, and challenged. Not so long ago, priests would have walked the streets of Irish towns and cities, proudly wearing their clerical dress, assuming that passersby would greet them reverently. Now, as we have learned, Brian Doheny, the priest in this study, is afraid to wear his clerical dress when he goes to Dublin.

There was little or no evidence of any legalistic adherence to the church's teachings, rules, and regulations. Not only was there increasing variety in the ways of being Catholic but there also was evidence of a shift in the balance of power away from priests to the laity. Many of the participants pointed to how the clerical child sex abuse scandals had led them to see and understand the church differently. In many respects, it was the formal, authoritarian gap between parents and children, priests and the laity, that prevented the abuse that was pervasive, and in many ways obvious, from being seen and recognized.

One of the main findings of the study was how little not just the Catholic Church but religion in general was part of the cultural repertoires of the everyday lives of the people I interviewed. There were few indications that God was in their minds and hearts and on their lips, that religion provided them with either a model or explanation of life, or that it was a model for how they should live their lives. Very few respondents mentioned God or religion until we reached the end section of the interview when I asked them specific questions about their religious beliefs and practices. When I asked them how they decided what was right or wrong, very few mentioned religion or the teachings of the church or the Bible. When I asked those who had suffered a major illness, tragedy, or death, how they got through their ordeal, only a few mentioned religion. Being Catholic is, then, a cultural ingredient that many participants used to facilitate and create meaning with each other, to mark major life transitions, to celebrate, and to mourn. For many, being Catholic seems to be a vague, thin web of meaning within which other webs of meaning are spun: it was less of an ideological conviction and more of a learnt, habitual way of being in the world.

Although most of the people in this study had been brought up in a strong orthodox Catholic culture, many had become cultural Catholics. They identified themselves as Catholics, they sent their children to Catholic schools, and they attended Catholic rituals. For them, being Catholic was a tradition. It was part of who they are. It was part of their cultural inheritance. This identification and sense of belonging to a Catholic culture was reflected in the way they talked about money and being successful. Very few respondents indicated that they were oriented to making money, material success, or self-indulgence. Even though many of them were experiencing economic hardship, generally related to the onset of a major recession in the Irish economy, they insisted that money was not that important in their lives. Many used phrases such as "as long as I have enough to get by." Others suggested that they would like a little more, as if they were being polite when asked if they would like more food. However, the main theme to emerge was that family and health were more important than material success.

What we can see here, then, is that although many participants may not be strongly attached to the Catholic Church and its teachings, they employed a Catholic cultural strategy of denying the importance of money and success in their lives. In other words, the cultural repertoire that they used to create meaning was based around ways of being, strategies and values that emphasized bonding and belonging over money and success. In some respects, even though they may have striven to make money and be successful, they had to deny its importance. It was part of the cultural logic into which they had been socialized. In this sense, Catholic values still operate as a model on how to live life. There is an acceptance that striving to make more money and to be successful is not the best way to finding happiness.

The process of individualization revolves around people seeing and understanding themselves as discrete, free, independent individuals who are not bound by the family, community, and religion into which they were born. Instead of adopting the blueprints they inherited from their parents and teachers about the explanation of life and how to live a good life, they have increasingly become architects of their own lives, their own arbiters of what is right and wrong. Social life always involves a balance between "we" and "I," and over the last two generations there has been a shift away from the dominance of "we" to the dominance of "I." Individualization is about transforming inherited social identities and developing new personal ones.

The meanings of participants' lives revolved around events and experiences and the stories that they told about themselves. This is part and parcel of a shift from a culture of self-denial to one of self-expression and self-fulfillment. Nevertheless, there was little evidence of rampant rugged, individualism in which the individual pursuit of life, liberty, and happiness was paramount. There was, instead, plenty of evidence of participants balancing self-interest and self-realization with love, care, and concern for others.

We can see this process of individualization working in politics, not only in the decline in political activism, particularly trade unionism, but also in the decline in local voluntary organizations and social movements. Many participants admitted to being interested in politics but saw it more as a game in which they did not want to participate. It was something they watched from the sidelines. They followed the games and the players in the media. They had access to political cultural ingredients that could have been used to develop their repertoires and strategies, but the majority did not make use of this culture other than to be informed about what was happening in the world. There were only a handful of people who were, or had been, politically active either through their involvement in national politics, being members of trade unions, or actively involved in interest groups or social movements.

The few that were involved in party politics often saw it as part of a family cultural repertoire: it was as if it was an overcoat of privilege that fitted them comfortably, and that they felt obliged to wear. It may well be, then, that as with the decline in institutional religion, we are witnessing a decline in institutional party politics. It may well be that this reflects a shift toward more identity recognition, minority rights and issue-based politics such as campaigning for women's rights, gay rights, the environment, and so forth. However, this did not emerge strongly in the interviews. It is hard to know if we are witnessing a decline in participative democracy. Certainly, there was little evidence of participants being eager and willing to challenge and change the existing political and economic structures.

The interviews took place at the beginning of a very unsettled economic period in Ireland. Many of the participants expressed their fears and anxieties about the developing recession. And yet most of the participants seemed to live very settled lives. With some exceptions, there was little or no ideological fervor. It seemed as if the fears and anxieties about the possible loss of income, jobs, and houses were things that would be suffered and dealt with within existing strong webs of meaning.

But, we have seen, there was plenty of evidence to suggest that the level of interest and involvement in politics mirrored their interest in religion. There was a time and place to be political—mainly voting in elections— as much as there was a time and place to be religious. Many may have voted —in the same way that many went to Mass—but it seemed to mean little to them. It may well be that another reason why people are less politically concerned and active is that they are more concerned about sport. While both sport and politics dominate the media—with religion being increasingly confined to the personal and private sphere—for many of the participants it was the webs of meaning woven around sport that had more significance than either religion or politics. Sport can be seen as the new religion in terms of providing a sense of identity, bonding and belonging, of collective effervescence, and, in some respects, of models that interpret life in terms of effort, performance, and chance, of winning and losing and, generally, models for how people should live healthy and fit lives. However, there was a strong divide among the interviewees. For some sport was an integral part not just of their leisure lives, but of family and community life. It was a central element in their cultural repertoire. This was often the case even if they did not play or had never played. However, for many others, sport meant little or nothing. They neither followed, believed in, nor played but, as with atheists in religious culture, they have to live in cultural world increasingly dominated by sport.

The ways in which participants used culture, and the ingredients they used to talk about themselves, varied significantly. Some people made extensive use of a wide range of culture. They had extensive repertoires that they were able to make use of in spinning the webs of meaning in their lives. Others had quite a limited repertoire. It seemed as if while some liked and wanted to explore meaning, others were quite happy to take things as they were. They had a set of cultural strategies, ways of being and doing, and did not examine their lives in any great detail. They had a set of well-established beliefs and values that they used to spin their webs of meaning. Many of the participants said, after the interview, that they did not think much about the issues we discussed.

There was little evidence of religious or political fundamentalism. Indeed, there did not seem to be any major concern to discover *the* meaning of life. There was instead a sense that life revolved around a number of different meanings that were created and maintained among family, friends, and loved ones. Participants talked about the pleasures of "chilling out"' after a day's work, going on holidays, reading, sport, exercise, pets, gardening, and so forth. We could characterize this less as a search for the meaning of life and more as an "arts of existence." There was a concern for living a good, fulsome life, of feeling bonded and connected, and enjoying small pleasures. But there was also a concern for fulfilling responsibilities, of looking after and caring for others, particularly loved ones.

APPROXIMATE UNDERSTANDING

It would, then, be impossible to capture all the webs of meaning in contemporary Ireland. Any description, understanding, and explanation is necessarily limited. I have argued, however, that it is important to explore the webs of meaning that are at the core of people's lives. These form a hub from which all the other webs of meaning are spun. These are the ones that sustain other webs when they become frail and fragile and are, perhaps, in danger of collapsing. These are the webs that sustain an ongoing, shared sense and explanation of what life is about and the best ways to live a good life. They provide love, care, comfort, and consolation, particularly in times of trouble. They are webs that are based more on pure meaning, that is meanings that exist for the sake of bonding and belonging, as opposed to meaning that is oriented toward fulfilling other goals and interests.

But if we want to provide a rich, deep description and understanding of these webs of meaning we have to try to capture what they mean to the people who spin them. Although in everyday life we say to each other that we can put ourselves in other people's shoes," it is impossible to understand and appreciate the subjective meanings of each other's lives. We can, in effect, only develop an approximate understanding. We can only try to approach "the other," to get as near to them as possible. This is what we do in our own lives when we talk to those to whom we are close, with whom we have an intimate relationship. But even then we never really get to understand their subjective meanings. It might, then, seem pointless to try to and capture the subjective meaning of the webs of strangers. It might seem even more point-less to try and do so through an interview that generally lasted less than an hour. And yet, if we do not make some attempt to capture the subjective meanings of others, if we do not try to put ourselves in other people's shoes, if we do not try to discover their understandings, moods, and motivations, we can never develop an adequate understanding of cultural life.

Our everyday lives are bound up with stories that we tell each other. It is part of bonding and belonging. As with all the stories told about Ireland the world, there are some stories in our lives that are more significant than others. They describe defining moments. They are seen as a sign of the times. They seem to encapsulate the relationships between people. They become part of the strong webs of meaning in which we are suspended. There are other weak webs as well. Some of the webs that are spun early in the morning may have faded and disappeared by lunchtime. But there are others that last for days, some for a lifetime, and others for generations. The stories that people hear and read about others, through conversations and the media, become interwoven with their own stories. It is through this pro-cess of telling stories that people come to know and understand themselves and each other. There is not any one, true, universal meaning to life. There are many truths. Inasmuch as it is difficult to discover the meanings of our own lives, we can never discover the meanings of the lives of others. We can never get inside their minds and bodies and see and feel the world from their perspective. We can only approach them and develop an approximate understanding. But unless we try to understand them, we can never under-stand ourselves.

APPENDIX: THE STUDY

THIS IS A NONPARAMETRIC STUDY. I MAKE NO CLAIMS THAT THE HUNDRED people I interviewed are in any way a representative sample of the Republic of Ireland population. However, they are not completely unrepresentative. In some respects, I approached this as if I was a botanist who had come to Ireland to study the flora and, recognizing that it would be impossible to identify, describe, catalogue, and analyze all the plants on the island, decided that the best approach would be to try to find as many different ones as possible to give some overall picture and understanding of the enormous variety.

However, due to limited funding—with the exception of a small grant from University College Dublin to cover travel expenses and equipment the study was self-financed—I could not select people from all around the country: I had to confine myself to five areas. I decided that in each area, I would rely on a gatekeeper to find me twenty potential participants. In doing so, I asked them to try, as much as possible, to provide an even distribution of men and women, young and old, working and middle class, and, insofar as possible, members of different religious, ethnic, and racial minorities.

The gatekeepers were crucial to the success of the study. If I was going to question and probe people about the meanings of their life, and if they were going to share some of their more personal thoughts and reflections, it was crucial that they trusted me. To achieve this level of trust without them knowing me, I needed an intermediary, who knew me and was willing to vouch for me and to introduce me to his or her friends, neighbors, colleagues, and so forth. Three of the gatekeepers were community activists, one was a lecturer in a third-level college, and one was a primary school teacher.

As described below, each of the five areas in which I did the interviews was very different. Most of the participants lived in the area, but some just worked there and lived elsewhere.

MAYFARM

There are many old inner-city areas of Dublin that are similar to Mayfarm. They are wedged between the city center and the sprawling private and local authority housing developments that emerged on the outer rim of the city from the 1960s. Today it is a combination of narrow streets that lead off each other and onto bigger thoroughfares. Many of these streets are made up of solid, gray concrete local authority houses, most of which were built in the 1950s. These are mixed in with streets of older redbrick houses from the early 1990s. Many of these houses have been turned into bed-sits and small flats. In between these streets, there are a number of large, local authority flat complexes made up of individual buildings four or five stories high. Some of these complexes have been renovated in recent years but most still show signs of deprivation.

What has perhaps changed most in Mayfarm since the 1990s has been the increase in the number of immigrants into the area during the years of the Celtic Tiger: I interviewed two of them. Many of them are evident, not just because they speak differently, have different features and skin colors, but also because they dress differently. There are East Europeans, Africans and Asians, Pentacostalists, and Muslims, men and women in long bright-colored gowns and dresses. In this respect, Mayfarm has become very similar to many multicultural, inner-city areas in Europe.

GREYROCK

There are hundreds of towns and villages around the greater Dublin area that were transformed during the boom times of the Celtic Tiger. Up until the 1990s, Greyrock was a sleepy village of less than four hundred people. In the past, the daily lives of most people in the village revolved around interactions and exchanges with each other and the people from the surrounding rural area. The villagers were mainly members of established families that had lived in and around Greyrock for generations. They had a cognitive map that placed people in families, time, and place. There was a strong sense of social identity. Villagers were seen, and saw themselves and others, as being from a certain family from a particular townland.

The center of the village has not changed significantly. It is dominated by a long wide main street. For years before the new motorway was built, people used the road through the village as an alternate way of getting to and out of Dublin. It still gets a fair amount of cars, trucks, and buses passing through. But most of the traffic on the main street is local: people from the surrounding area and housing estates coming in to shop, or going to and coming from the local school, the GAA club, and the local parish churches.

What transformed Greyrock, and brought Angela Doyle and her fellow Dubliners to the village, was the availability of relatively cheap, houses with good gardens situated in well-designed housing estates with plenty of green spaces. It was this attraction that led the population to increase from 400 to 1,700 within 20 years.

CASTLEBAY

There are many areas like Castlebay in the west of Ireland. As in Greyrock, the village and surrounding area is dominated by the main county road that traverses the village. The surrounding network of roads is dotted with houses, some of them new and substantial, which were built during the boom days of the Celtic Tiger. Others are older and more modest. Some of the houses are part of small farms. But the soil is not great and most farming revolves around rearing some cattle and sheep. There is no local industry. There are very few substantial businesses. Most of the population who are employed work in the two large county towns, each of them about 20 kilometers from Castlebay.

Castlebay has a couple of small housing developments—but there was nothing like the expansion in Greyrock. The main road running through the village has its pubs, a supermarket, petrol station, a Chinese takeaway, and a few shops. My interviewees were scattered in the rural areas between Castlebay and Dromina, a smaller village down by the sea. The population of Castlebay is about two hundred and fifty; Dromina is about a hundred and fifty. There is a scattering of Europeans in the area, but most of the people were born and raised in the locality, are white, Catholic, and English speaking. In many respects, life in Castlebay today is somewhat similar to what life used to be like in Greyrock before it became a satellite town. For most people, it is a village through which travelers and commuters pass by, or stop off in, on their way to and from the county towns. For locals living in the surrounding area, it is the place they come to shop, pray, play, and share a drink in the local pub. However, unlike Greyrock, there is a stronger history of emigration. Whereas Greyrock was a place to which most of the population had migrated, Castlebay was a place from which many had migrated and returned. Many of my participants had spent time abroad or in other parts of Ireland.

HILLBROOK

There are many large county towns in Ireland like Hillbrook. These form the hub for the surrounding rural areas, small towns, and villages. In the past, Hillbrook was the place where farmers brought their cattle to the market, where major goods and services were available, and where people took the bus and train to and from Dublin. It is still dependent on providing services to farmers but, from the 1970s, it developed a number of small companies and manufacturing plants. During the Celtic Tiger years, Hillbrook mushroomed in size and population, but not to the same extent as Greyrock. There were more immigrants but lesser numbers commuting to Dublin to work. The long-term plan for Hillbrook in the Celtic Tiger years was that it would become a hub for smaller towns and villages in the surrounding area with industrial parks and housing estates to accommodate the workers. The reality, however, is that many of the parks and estates on the edge of Hillbrook remain half-built and derelict.

Hillbrook developed a bypass a number of years ago. Nevertheless the main street, particularly during the daytime, is choc-a-bloc with traffic. There are a couple of hotels and a few small supermarkets: the big chain supermarkets are on the outskirts of the town. The main street looks much the same as it did in the 1950s. My participants were a mixture of some who lived in and around the town and some who lived in the surrounding countryside.

FALDERRY

I had always intended to conduct interviews of respondents from a middle-class suburban area of Dublin, but it was the last area to be studied, and having completed the interviews in the other areas, I realized that I needed to include more young people. This was why I decided to conduct interviews in a third-level college. The interviews were mostly with students, but also included lecturers and administrative staff. Like many other third-level colleges, Falderry is a cosmopolitan, transitory place in which students are here today, gone tomorrow, and staff come from different parts of the world, mainly Ireland and Britain. As in most colleges, staff and students are bound together more by mutual interests rather than by any sense of being in a neighborhood.

THE SELECTION

As mentioned above, the objective in selecting hundred participants was to try and capture the social diversity of the Irish population. The social demographic profile of the participants can be seen in table A.1.

Table A.1   Social demographic profile of the participants

Gender	Age	Nationality	Occupation
Females (51)	18–30 (20)	Irish (91)	Nonskilled Manual (9)
Males (49)	31–39 (14)	Non-Irish (9)	Semiskilled (6)
	40–49 (28)		Skilled Manual (10)
	50–59 (23)		Routine Nonmanual (18)
	60–69 (8)		Supervisory/ Low-Managerial (17)
	71+ (7)		Prof./High Managerial (18)
			Artist/Musician (2)
			Farmers (3)
			Students (9)
			Unemployed/Homeworker (9)

THE INTERVIEWS

In the vast majority of cases, participants were given a briefing document and a copy of the topic guide in advance of our meeting. I conducted all the interviews personally. I wanted to get to know the participants so that I would remember them when describing and analyzing the interviews. I felt that one hundred was as much as I could manage on my own. The interviews lasted on average 50 minutes.

The interviews took place in a variety of settings, mostly in participants' homes or their place of work or education, but also in the gatekeepers' homes and their places of work. The interviews revolved around a schedule of topics and questions that I had devised in advance and which, for consistency and comparative purposes, I generally asked of each participant. However, the main task was to get the participant to talk freely about themselves. The questions were open-ended, and if participants became animated about a particular issue or topic, I let them elaborate. The interview began with questions about themselves, where they had grown up, with whom, their life story, reflections about their childhood, etc. It then moved on to the importance of family, the people to whom they were attached. This led into questions about work, money, ambition, and well-being. I then explored their sense of right and wrong, what they considered to be a good life, and how they dealt with loss and tragedy. The final part of the interview related to their religious beliefs and practices and, if relevant, their attachment to to the church or religious denomination to which they belonged.

I was tempted to use a grounded-theory approach as initially described and developed by Glaser and Strauss.[1] However, the goal of interviewing a large number of people with limited resources and being able to make comparisons between the participants meant that return interviews were not possible. Within the open-ended, flexible structure that I adopted, I was able to watch out for clues in what people said that helped reveal the issues, experiences, and relationships in their lives that were meaningful and important to them. Once all the interviews were transcribed edited, and cleaned, I began the task of making sense of them. I decided that rather than using a computer software package to aid in the description and analysis, it was crucial to spend as much time as possible reading and rereading the transcripts of each complete interview and to try, as much as possible, to relive the experience of the interview and to remember the character and personality of the participant.

There was a considerable variety in the willingness and ability of the participants to talk about themselves. The topic guide contained about sixty questions. However, in general, those who were older or less educated were more likely to give short staccato answers. This required me asking more answers.

Consider, for example, Eamon O'Loughlin. He is the late middle-aged, well-educated, high-ranking civil servant who works in the public sector and has a postgraduate degree. I asked him 87 questions, which included probes and clarifications. The transcript of his interview ran to 10,377 words. On the other hand, there were some people who were shy and reticent. For example, I asked Carol Kilfeather 319 questions, probes, and clarifications, and her transcript ran to only 5,224 words. Carol is a twenty-year-old woman who lives in the countryside near Hillbrook. She lives in a modest house just down the road from my gatekeeper's house. She and her family had known my gatekeeper and her family for years. The interview took place in my gatekeeper's living room.

Carol came across as a quiet reserved young woman. Her life seemed to revolve around her family, the family pets, and her friends. It was immediately obvious to me that Carol was a little awkward, embarrassed, and shy about the interview process and talking about herself. Although she had received the interview questions in advance, it seemed to me that she saw the process more as an ordeal that she was going through, perhaps to please my gatekeeper. She tended to give short, clipped answers to my questions as, for example, when I asked her who were the most important people in her life:

Carol: Friends.
Tom: You have lots of friends?
Carol: Yeah.
Tom: And they live around locally?
Carol: Yeah one lives beside me.
Tom: Oh great.
Carol: And then the rest live around town.

Tom: And would you go in and out often to town?
Carol: Yeah, nearly every day.
Tom: Everyday?
Carol: Well nearly every day, as much as I can.
Tom: You like it in there?
Carol: Yeah.
Tom: What do you like about it?
Carol: I just like going around with my friends.
Tom: Where would you meet? Would you meet anywhere?
Carol: Shopping center but on a Friday and Saturday night we go out.
Tom: Where would you go?
Carol: The pub and then nightclub.

No matter how much I tried, I had difficulty connecting with Carol. While she did answer all my questions, I felt it was an ordeal for her. I had hoped that when we came to talk about her friends that she might become more relaxed. Her life revolves around her family, her friends, and her pets. The family has two dogs and two cats and she has two rabbits. She says of the rabbits: "One of them is a bit boring but the other one follows me everywhere. If you give him to anybody else, he'll jump back over to my knee." She enjoys swimming and horse riding, but does not get many opportunities to go horse riding as the center is too far away.

But, then, as the interview developed, I wondered if something had happened recently in her life. When I asked her what she would feel lost without, she immediately responded by saying her car, "cause I can go wherever I want to." She added that she would also feel lost without her family, friends, and pets. She admitted, then, she gets depressed now and then but not as bad as it was two years before, "there's someone I knew died, and so." I asked her what had happened. It was a few years ago, when she was sixteen, the man for whom she worked took his own life. "I still don't understand why he did it because everything seemed great for him but it obviously wasn't...Yeah, anytime you'd see him he'd be laughing and joking and I'd seen him on Saturday before he died." For a long time she was not able to talk about it. "I just didn't want to get out of bed in the morning and didn't want to do anything and missed like two months of school."

In some respects, the meanings of Carol's life are simple and straightforward. She was born into a set of meanings that revolve around family, friends, pets, and work. She does not seem to question the meanings that she inherited. It is as if they have done her well and she is happy to recreate them. "If you have friends and family and enough money to get by and to go out with or anything. I wouldn't be bothered about fancy cars or holidays or anything. Just say to spend time with your family, friends, to get married."

It is as if she assumed that the meanings of life were the same for everyone and, for that reason, there is no need to question or critically reflect on what life is about. The meanings of life are beyond question, they go without saying. This taken-for-grantedness can be shattered, particularly in times of death, loss, and tragedy. This is what may have happened when her boss took his own life. She was like a fish out of water. She could not comprehend what had happened. It was beyond the realm of thought, talk, or critical reflection.

In some respects, Paddy Timmons is like Carol Kilfeather. He is twenty-five. He grew up with his parents and his younger brother in a small town. Both his parents were from the area and came from large families. So he grew up in a large extended family of aunts, uncles, and cousins. He went to the local Catholic secondary and then came up to Dublin to do his degree. His parents were both seventeen when he was born. They separated seven years ago. His father remarried last year. Paddy took two years out of college, most of which he spent working and traveling mainly in Europe. But he also spent time at home with his mother and brother. Since coming back to college, he spends most of the time with his flatmate—they share an apartment—but he goes home regularly, particularly at weekends. I asked him who were the most important people in his life:

> Today I think it is, it's my friends like. I think I have a really, really close relationship with four or five friends and we've kind of, as a group...been really close friends for a long time...kind of towards the end of secondary school, I think, I was friends with people in school but I wasn't friends with them outside of school and I had a couple of closer friends. I think people who have heard this before said that, you know...the friends you have around that age, the late teens...are kind of the friends that you almost...stick with....I think...myself and the four or five of us, there's a mixture of male and female now, were all kind of...on the fringes of other groups as such...we all feel that we are ourselves. I'm as open and honest with them as I would be with anybody. My parents, it's strange...I have a very good relationship with my parents but as I'm older it's becoming more clear how young they are...you know compared to some of my friends' parents you know, that they [his friends' parents] are of a different generation...I had my twenty-first before they'd become forty so...landmark things like that, they kind of come in strange order so I have a very...yeah it's a strange. It is a parental relationship but...since mid to late teens...there's not kind of an authoritarian theme there...we're so close now with our lives.

There are many differences between Carol Kilfeather and Paddy Timmons, but when it comes to self-talk—which is central to understanding and discovering the meaning of their lives—the most obvious difference is Carol's dependency on stimuli from me to talk, compared to Paddy's ability to allow one thought to stimulate another, giving rise to a constant flow of thoughts and ideas. However, he is also operating with a much more elaborate code of language when it comes to talking about friendship. He operates in a much richer understanding of friendship that comes from discussion and critical reflection about friendship. His close friends are both male and female (one of whom is his ex-girlfriend). He says that he would be "open with everything with them." He talked to his friends all through the time his parents were separating. Without prompting, he is able to distinguish the intimacy and sense of bonding and belonging that he has with his friends from that which he has with his parents. He is able to reflect critically about the difference between them. Paddy came to the interview with the necessary skills and strategies to talk about himself. It is a cultural game that he had played before. Unlike Carol Kilfeather, he is part of a community of discourse in which friendship is discussed at a more abstract general level.[2]

Paddy is generally more immersed in cultural self-expression. He plays music, does creative writing, and has an "incredible strong interest in sport." He hopes to do an MA in literature. He says that from a very young age, he had "a very keen mind," that he "wanted to know more, wanted more information." He has always had a passionate interest in reading. When he was in primary school, and when he moved up a class each year, he looked forward to the new material he would be reading.

While I may not have been able to tap into the areas of Carol's life that she may not feel confident to talk about, that she might chat more easily about with her friends, the other difference was that when it comes to talking about herself, Carol operates with a more restricted code of language than Paddy or Eamon O'Loughlin. And, yet, there is a great danger of thinking that life is more meaningful for those who critically reflect and talk about it more. In some respects, a Zen Buddhist master might have given similar responses as Carol. One of the changes that has taken place in Irish culture is the general move from a way of being in which self-talk was confined to the Catholic confessional to a more open, public form of confession among friends and family. However, while we should not surmise that anyone who did not go to Confession was less religious, so too we should not surmise that the lives of those who are not so willing or able to talk about themselves are somehow less meaningful. What it means is that the method of understanding the meaning of Carol's life—short, in-depth, semistructured personal interviews—is not as appropriate as it may be for others like Paddy Timmons.

In everyday life, then, we understand others and the meanings of their lives by the way they talk about themselves. But what they talk about, the stories about themselves, depends on the social context. There is a distinction between the way Carol and Paddy presented themselves and talked to me and the way they present themselves and talk to their friends. But in both contexts, for different reasons, they will highlight and emphasize some aspects of their lives and experiences and conceal and downplay others. In this sense, it is wrong to think that an interview ever captures any real self. The self that was presented to me was simply a different self, presented in a different context, for different purposes.

We can, then, understand what Carol and Paddy said in response to my questions as approximations to the self that they present to family and friends, recognizing at the same time that this self is not necessarily any more authentic than the ones they presented to me. There is a correspondence between the strategic way they presented themselves to me and the strategic way I presented myself to them. Inasmuch as they selected words as a means of presenting themselves, I have selected passages from what they said as a means of presenting them. So what we get is presentations of presentations of self.

But there is more. In presenting Carol, Paddy, and the other participants, I deliberately edited what they said, so that it would read more easily. There is a genre in reporting qualitative interviews that uses a variety of codes and icons to indicate pauses, silences, stresses in the way words are pronounced, and so forth. I could have tried to capture every "em," "ah," "sigh," correction, hesitation, and silence. I didn't and often, as was the case with Paddy Timmons, I have used ellipses and put words in brackets to explain the context of what was being said, in order to provide a better flow and make my sense of his meaning more obvious. My approach, then, is to accept that I present my participants as approximations, representations of representations. I therefore make no apology for editing what they said so that it is more coherent and easily read. I think of this as a form of cosmetics. I have painted over some of the cracks—the contradictions, repetitions, and hesitations in what they said—but I don't believe it significantly misrepresents them or what they said.

The meanings my participants give to their lives are shaped by the culture in which they grew up. They were immersed into a world of being, of saying and doing, which they made use of to create their own subjective meanings. The construction of a self, the representation of inherited social identities such as gender, family, religion, and class, the cultivation of personal identities through lifestyle and tastes, and the presentation, negotiation, and reflection on these with others, is central to the meanings of life. Every presentation of self, every engagement with other people in everyday life, every time we talk about themselves, we add to the story about ourselves. We have always had an interest in the lives of others. In reading about Carol and Paddy, in trying to understand the meanings of their lives, we can explore the meanings of our own lives.

One of the changes that has taken place in Irish culture is that people have become more accustomed not just to talking about themselves, but to the notion of talking about themselves to relative strangers either in a social or professional context. In effect, I was part of, and made use of, this cultural shift to get the participants to talk freely and openly about themselves. In some respects, I often felt I vacillated between being a counselor and an interviewer. I may have been asking questions and listening to the participants' answers for professional sociological reasons, but I was also interested in the meanings of my own life. This often led me to become more involved, more interested in, and more committed to the participants than might occur in other qualitative interviews. And yet, if we are to study the meaning of life through interviews, then it is necessary to be more involved than detached, to be more sensitive and engaged than distant and objective, and to be more caring and compassionate than merely interested.

TOPIC GUIDE

1. Information about the participant.
   (a) Would you like to tell me about yourself? Have you always lived in this area? Have you ever lived or worked abroad?
       Marital Status/Children/Spouse—partner
       Occupation
       Education
       Mother's and Father's occupations
       Siblings
   (b) What was your childhood like?
   (c) Growing up, what did you learn about what was important in life.

2. What is important in life?
   (a) Who are the most important people in your life?
       If family not mentioned: How important is family to you?
   (b) What gives you pleasure and satisfaction?
   (c) Do you have any hobbies, pastimes?
   (d) What would you feel lost without?
   (e) How important is work?
   (f) How important is money?
   (g) How important is success?

(h) How important is politics?

(i)   How important is sport?

(j)   How important is looking and feeling good?

(k) When do you feel calm and relaxed?

(l)   When do you feel stressed?

(m) What worries or anxieties do you have?

(n) What have been the major disappointments in your life?

(o) Are you an emotional person? When are you emotional? In what way?

3. What is the meaning of life?

(a) What does it mean to you to live a good life?

(b) What is your main source of deciding what is right and wrong, good and bad?

(c) Have you suffered any major tragedy, illness or loss? If so, how did you make sense of it? What did you do to help you get through the experience?

(d) Do you believe in God? Is this a personal God or some kind of life force? What does God mean to you? How important?

(d.1) How does belief in God influence your everyday life?

(d.2) How do you connect with the God or the Divine? Have you had an important religious experience?

(d.3) What is your way of being in touch with God, the supernatural?

(e) Would you say you are a spiritual person? What spiritual practices do you engage in?

(f) Do you pray? How often? How do you pray? To whom do you pray?

(g) Do you believe in magic, charms, and horoscopes?

(h) Are you a member of a church? Were you once? What changed? What has been the effect of the church on your life?

(h.1) How important is church membership to you?

(i)   Do you go to church? How often, what occasions? Why do you go? What do you like about going to church?
If Catholic:

(i.1) Do you believe in core Catholic beliefs about Jesus and Mary?

(i.2) Do you have a devotion to any saints?

(i.3) Do you have medals, statues, holy pictures?

(j)   What do you think happens when you die? Do you believe in life after death/ reincarnation?

(k) Do you believe in heaven and hell? Who gets into heaven? What is your conception of heaven?

(l) So, what for you is the meaning of life?

4. Three wishes: If you were granted three wishes, what would they be?

5. Finally, this conversation has been about what is important and meaningful in your life. Is there anything that you think I should have asked you, that I have left out, that you would like to add?

Notes

1 WEBS OF SIGNIFICANCE

1. All the participants, the people they mention, and the places in which they live, have been given pseudonyms.
2. This study pertains to the Republic of Ireland. It was limited to the Republic for practical (mainly financial) and cultural reasons. There are many similarities between the culture of Northern Ireland and the Republic, but the main difference, particularly in relation to culture, is the dominance of the Catholic Church in the Republic, and that for much of the twentieth century over 90 percent of the population identified themselves as Roman Catholics.
3. This concept of people being suspended in webs of meaning, which they spin afresh themselves in their daily lives, comes from Clifford Geertz, "Thick Description: Toward an Interpretive Theory of Culture," in Clifford Geertz, *The Interpretation of Cultures* (New York: Basic, 1973), 5.
4. For a description and analysis of how Irish culture is a mix of local, national, and global cultural elements, see Tom Inglis, *Global Ireland: Same Difference* (New York: Routledge, 2008).
5. As Swidler notes: "People vary greatly in *how much* culture they apply to their own lives. Some people draw on a wide range of cultural precepts, psychological theories, personal incident, and anecdote, while others move within narrow confines, using one or two formulas or phrases again and again." Ann Swidler, *Talk of Love: How Culture Matters* (Chicago: Chicago University Press, 2001), 46 (emphasis in original).
6. See Swidler, *Talk of Love,* 24–40.
7. "If anthropological interpretation is constructing a reading of what happens, then to divorce it from what happens—from what, in this time or that place, specific people say, what they do, what is done to them, from the whole vast business of the world—is to divorce it from its applications and render it vacant." Geertz, "Thick Description," 18.
8. For an analysis and critique of the different theories and methods used in Irish Studies, see Tom Inglis, "Are the Irish Different? Theories and Methods in Irish Studies," *The Irish Review,* 46 (2013), 41–51.
9. There have been many anthropological studies that have provided rich thick descriptions of Irish culture during the twentieth century; see

Conrad Arensberg and Solon Kimball, *Family and Community in Ireland* (Cambridge: Harvard University Press, 1968 [1948]); and Hugh Brody *Inniskillane: Change and Decline in the West of Ireland* (Harmondsworth: Penguin, 1974). For an overview of these and many other important anthropological studies that have described and analyzed Irish culture, and the meanings of people's lives, see Thomas Wilson and Hastings Donnan, *The Anthropology of Ireland* (Oxford: Berg, 2006).

10. For a more detailed description of these changes, see Anne Byrne, Ricca Edmondson, and Tony Varley, "Introduction of the Third Edition: Arensberg and Kimball and Anthropological Research in Ireland," in Conrad Arensberg and Solon Kimball, *Family and Community in Ireland*, (Ennis [Co. Clare]: CLASP Press, 2001), v–vi.

11. This notion of culture, particularly religion, providing a model, or explanation, of life, as well as a model for how to live life, comes from Clifford Geertz, "Religion as a Cultural System," *The Interpretation of Cultures* 93.

12. See Diarmaid Ferriter, *Occasions of Sin: Sex and Society in Modern Ireland* (London: Profile, 2009); Tom Inglis, *Lessons in Irish Sexuality* (Dublin: University College Dublin Press, 1998); Inglis, *Moral Monopoly: The Rise and Fall of the Catholic Church in Ireland* (Dublin: University College Dublin Press, 1998), 129–177; Inglis, "Origins and Legacies of Irish Prudery: Sexuality and Social Control in Modern Ireland," *Eire–Ireland*, 40.3 and 4 (2005), 9–37.

13. The shift from external to more internalized forms of self-restraint is central to Elias's theory of the civilizing process, but it can also be linked to Foucault's argument that within modernity there was a shift from physical to more subtle forms of discipline and punishment. See Norbert Elias, *The Civilizing Process: Sociogenetic and Psychogenetic Investigations* (Oxford: Blackwell, 2000); Michel Foucault, *Discipline and Punish: The Birth of the Prison* (New York: Vintage, 1979).

14. See Tom Inglis, "From Self-Denial to Self-Indulgence: The Clash of Cultures in Contemporary Ireland," *The Irish Review*, 34.2 (2006), 34–43; Inglis, "Pleasure Pursuits," in *Ireland Unbound: a Turn of the Century Chronicle*, ed. M. Corcoran and M. Peillon (Dublin: Institute of Public Administration, 2002), 25–35.

15. See Tom Inglis, "The Global and the Local: Mapping Changes in Irish Childhood," *Éire-Ireland*, 46. 3 and 4 (2005), 63–83.

16. See, Pat O'Connor, *Emerging Voices: Women in Contemporary Irish Society* (Dublin: IPA, 1998), 81–108; Betty Hilliard, "The Catholic Church and Married Women's Sexuality: Habitus Change in Late 20th Century Ireland," *Irish Journal of Sociology*, 12.2 (2003), 28–49; Hilliard, "Changing Gender Roles in Intimate Relationships," in *Irish Social and Political Attitudes* ed. J. Garry, N. Hardiman, and D. Payne (Liverpool: Liverpool University Press, 2006), 33–42; Inglis, *Moral Monopoly*, 178–200.

17. In 1971, only 8 percent of married women were in the labor force. By 2006, this had increased to 52 percent. See Betty Hilliard, "Family," in *Contemporary Ireland: A Sociological Map*, ed. S. O'Sullivan (Dublin:

University College Dublin Press, 2007), 90; Pat O'Connor, *Emerging Voices: Women in Contemporary Irish Society* (Dublin: Institute of Public Administration, 1998), 193. Finola Kennedy, *Cottage to Crèche: Family Change in Ireland* (Dublin: Institute of Public Administration, 2001), 63.

18. See, D. Hervieu-Léger, "Individualism, the Validation of Faith, and the Social Nature of Religion in Modernity," in *The Blackwell Companion to Sociology of Religion*, ed. R. Fenn (Oxford: Blackwell, 2003), 161–175.

19. Tom Inglis, "Individualisation and Secularisation in Catholic Ireland," in *Contemporary Ireland: A Sociological Map*, ed. S. O'Sullivan (Dublin: University College Dublin Press, 2007), 67–82.

20. Susie Donnelly and Tom Inglis, "The Media and the Catholic Church in Ireland: Reporting Clerical Child Sexual Abuse," *Journal of Contemporary Religion*, 25.1 (2010), 1–19.

21. Inglis, *Moral Monopoly*, 203–243.

22. Danièle Hervieu-Léger, *Religion as a Chain of Memory* (Cambridge: Polity Press, 2000); Tom Inglis, "Catholic Identity in Contemporary Ireland: Belief and Belonging to Tradition," *Journal of Contemporary Religion*, 22.2 (2007), 205–220.

23. See Inglis, "From Self-Denial to Self-Indulgence."

24. Wouters defines informalization as a process in which "more and more of the dominant modes of social conduct, symbolizing institutionalized power relationships, come to be ignored and attacked, with the result that the standards of social conduct change towards greater leniency, variety and differentiation. At the same time this signifies a shift in power relationships between social superiors and subordinates in favour of the latter." Cas Wouters, "Formalization and Informalization: Changing Tension Balances in Civilizing Processes," *Theory, Culture & Society*, 3.2 (1986), 1. See also Wouters, *Informalization: Manners & Emotions since 1890* (London: Sage, 2007).

25. Ulrich Beck and Elisabeth Beck-Gernsheim, *Individualization: Institutional Individualism and Its Social and Political Consequences* (London: Sage, 2002); Beck and Beck-Gernsheim, The *Normal Chaos of Love* (Cambridge: Polity, 1995); Anthony Giddens, *Modernity and Self-Identity* (Cambridge: Polity Press, 1991), 189–201. Bauman summarized it: "In a nutshell, 'individualization' consists in transforming human 'identity' from a 'given' into a 'task.'" Zygmunt Bauman, "Individually, Together," in *Individualization*, Beck and Bech-Gernsheim, xv.

26. Elliot and Lemert have characterized rugged individualism as necessary to survive challenges, risks, and pitfalls of contemporary life in Western society. See Anthony Elliot and Charles Lemert, *The New Individualism: The Emotional Costs of Globalization* (London: Routledge, 2009), 185–196.

27. Peter Berger, *The Sacred Canopy* (Garden City, NY: Doubleday, 1967).

28. This is an adaptation of Kluckohn and Murray's original description of how human beings are similar, yet different. See Clyde Kluckhohn and Henry A. Murray (eds.), *Personality in Nature, Society and Culture* (New York: Knopf, 1948), 35.

2 CULTURE AS MEANING

1. The notion of other people being the mirrors through which we come to
   know and understand ourselves and develop a sense of self comes from
   Cooley's concept of the looking-glass self. See Charles H. Cooley, *Human
   Nature and the Social Order* (Piscataway, NJ: Transaction, 1992 [1902]),
   150–151.
2. "Telling stories is as basic to human beings as eating. More so, in fact, for
   while food makes us live, stories are what make our lives worth living.
   They are what make our condition human." Richard Kearney, *On Stories*
   (London: Routledge, 2002), 3.
3. "The story or stories of myself that I tell, that I hear others tell of me, that
   I am unable or unwilling to tell, are not independent of the self that I am:
   they are constitutive of *me*. This is a central claim of the cultural psychology
   of selfhood." Ciarán Benson, *The Cultural Psychology of Self: Place, Morality
   and Art in Human Worlds* (London: Routledge, 2001), 45 (emphasis in
   original).
4. The blowing of a kiss has, then, concrete specific meaning for Angela,
   Martin, and the children, but can also be understood as an ideal type of
   action, belonging to a range of gestures of love and affection. See Max Weber,
   Economy and Society, ed. Claus Wittich and Guenther Roth (Berkeley:
   University of California Press, 1978), 4.
5. This is what Weber meant by social action, Weber, *Economy and Society*,
   22–23. As Schutz points out, what made Weber unique was his interpretive method (*Verstehen*), which placed the search for meaning at the center
   of sociological understanding and reduced all kinds of social relationships
   and structures to the most elementary forms of individual behavior. Alfred
   Schutz, *The Phenomenology of the Social World* (London: Heinemann,
   1972), 8.
6. Weber was not interested in "irrational, affectually determined elements of
   behaviour" that "cannot be related to an intended purpose." Actions, for
   Weber, are devoid of meaning if they are only a stimulus and cannot be
   related to means or ends; see Weber, *Economy and Society*, 6–7. The problem,
   however, is that it is hard to identify the intended purpose of such actions
   as lighting candles. The only way to get to the logic of "prophetic, mystic or
   affectual modes of action" is through theoretical concepts that are adequate
   at the level of meaning, that is, they themselves are rational and consistent,
   see Weber, *Economy and Society*, 17, 20.
7. The understanding of the meaning of action cannot be achieved through
   direct observation or interpretation. For Weber, we arrive at explanatory
   understanding when we explain or understand the motive behind the action.
   Weber, *Economy and Society*, 8–9.
8. Sayer points out that modernist thinkers, including Weber, tend to divorce
   reason from emotion. This leads to emotion being seen as a threat to reason. He argues, however, that emotions are a key part of practical reason.
   He argues that instead of looking for rational explanations and motives

for action, practical reason derives from a concern for others and a moral concern for what we should do and how we should live our lives. Andrew Sayer, *Why Things Matter to People: Social Science, Values and Ethical Life* (Cambridge: Cambridge University Press, 2011), 36–41, 61–63.

9. Schutz argues that much of what happens in the common sense world of everyday life revolves around distinguishing what is individual or different from what is typical or similar. Alfred Schutz, *Collected Papers 1: The Problem of Social Reality 1*, ed. Maurice Natanson (The Hague: Martinus Nijoff, 1967), 8–9.

10. One of the key struggles in sociology is to find a way of balancing subjectivism, that is, how Angela sees, reads, and understands her world, with objectivism, that is, the external, preexisting world into which she has been born. A phenomenologist like Schutz recognizes the objective side, but emphasizes the subjective. (Note: while he uses "man," we could easily substitute "Angela.")

> Man finds himself at any moment in his daily life in a biographically determined situation, that is, in a physical and socio-cultural environment as defined by him, within which he has his position, not merely his position in terms of physical space and outer time or his status and role within the social system but his moral and ideological position. To say that this definition of the situation is biographically determined is to say that it has its history; it is the sedimentation of all man's previous experiences, organized in the habitual possessions of his stock of knowledge at hand, and as such his unique possession, given to him and him alone. (Schutz, *Collected Papers*, 9).

The problem is how can other people, particularly sociologists, ever access the way the individual views the world? This is the major difficulty that Talcott Parsons had with Schutz's phenomenological methodology. Parsons argued that there was no point in trying to get at subjective experience and meaning. It could not be achieved and therefore it could not be the starting point for developing an analytical realist explanation of social life. In a long correspondence with Schutz, Parsons concluded that there were irrevocable differences in their epistemology:

> We may now come to the question of the objective and subjective points of view. I really think that I have finally succeeded in straightening out the differences between us on this question. I think what you mean essentially is an ontological reality, what a concrete real actor "really" experiences. I think I have legitimate reasons to be sceptical that by your analysis or by any others available it is possible to arrive at anything approaching a definitive description of such a reality. I am afraid I must confess to being sceptical of phenomenological analysis. (Richard Grathoff (ed.), *The Theory of Social Action: The Correspondence of Alfred Schutz and Talcott Parsons* [Bloomington: Indiana University Press, 1978], 89–90)

11. "Sharing a community of time…implies that each partner participates in the on-rolling life of the other, can grasp in a vivid present the other's thoughts as they are built up step by step." Schutz, *Collected Papers*, 16.

12. Schutz extends this natural attitude or shared common sense view of the world to include what is right and wrong, the good life, and "the many recipes for handling things and men in order to come to terms with typified situations." Schutz, *Collected Papers*, 13.

13. Schutz, *Collected Papers*, 26. As Schutz points out, Weber does not consider how meaning is produced and modified through interaction with others. And while he distinguishes between the subjective, intended meaning of action and the way it is objectively understood, he pays little attention to the way the observer modifies meaning through his conceptual and theoretical framework. Schutz, *Phenomenology of the Social World*, 8. It might also be added that, as in the case of interviewing, that the observer is not detached but involved in the production of the meaning that he is trying to capture and the subjective and intended meaning that is produced for him.

14. As Schutz points out, "The everyday actor has, in principle, only a partial knowledge of the world of his daily life, which he only partially understands. His propositions thus have but a small range of applicability, namely within the concrete situation. They are not formed with the aim of being valid for the broadest possible sector of the empirical world, a principle common to all scientific thought." See, Grathoff, *The Theory of Social Action*, 27.

15. This is the difference between first- and second-order constructs. When it comes to understanding meaning, the sociologist is dealing with constructions of constructions. Schutz, *Collected Papers*, 59.

16. Schutz, *Collected Papers*, 41.

17. Schutz refers to this as the postulate of adequacy:

> Each term in a scientific model of human action must be constructed in a such way that a human act performed within the life-world of the individual actor in the way indicated by the typical construct would be understandable for the actor himself as well as for his fellow-men in terms of common-sense interpretation of everyday life. (Schutz, *Collected Papers*, 44)

This is one of the more problematic positions of Schutz's theory. It would be better if he had included "all things being equal." While I might try to write an explanation of Angela's actions in a way that she could understand, it is not and cannot be a determining influence or a principle of what defines an adequate explanation. To insist that she could would blur the distinction between common sense and scientific understanding. However, it could be argued that the notion of adequacy assumes that Angela would understand my explanation if she had an adequate understanding of sociology. This is where Schutz departs from Weber. When Weber refers to meaning, it is not so much that such meaning "really exists" and can be accessed, but rather that the concept of subjective, intended, or purposeful meaning, "is capable of providing a logical framework within which scientifically important observations can be made. The test of the validity of the observations is not whether their object is immediately clear in common sense, but whether the results of these technical observations can be satisfactorily organized and related to those of others in a systematic body of knowledge." Weber, *Economy and Society*, 58. However, any construction that I make of Angela's life is just that, a construction, one that, despite its theoretical congruity, does not have any more validity than not just other scientific constructions but also Angela's own construction.

18. Schutz would have perhaps argued that whatever way I construct Angela, whatever questions I asked, whatever way I present her responses, whatever theories and concepts I use to interpret her responses, has the effect of creating a puppet that only moves according to my manipulations of her. He argued that the way a social scientist constructs someone like Angela necessarily makes her into a puppet. "The puppet exists and acts merely by the grace of the scientist; it cannot act otherwise than according to the purpose which the scientist's wisdom has determined it to carry out. Nevertheless, it is supposed to act as if it were not determined but could determine itself." Schutz, *Collected Papers*, 47.

19. Weber defined culture as "a finite segment of the meaningless infinity of the world process, a segment on which *human beings* confer meaning and significance." Max Weber, "Objectivity in Social Science and Social Policy" in *The Methodology of the Social Sciences*, ed. E. Shills and H. Finch (New York: Free Press, 1949), 49.

20. This is an adaptation of Geertz's famous definition of culture as "an historically transmitted pattern of meanings embodied in symbols, a system of inherited conceptions expressed in symbolic forms by means of which men communicate, perpetuate, and develop their knowledge about and attitudes toward life." See Clifford Geertz, "Religion as a Cultural System" in *Interpretation of Cultures* (New York: Basic Books, 1973), 89. The notion of culture being "taken for granted" comes from Bourdieu and his concept of habitus. See Pierre Bourdieu, *Outline of a Theory of Practice* (Cambridge: Cambridge University Press, 1977), 165–167.

21. See Ann Swidler, *Talk of Love: How Culture Matters* (Chicago, IL: Chicago University Press, 2001); Swidler, "Culture in Action: Symbols and Strategies," *American Sociological Review*, 51.2 (1986), 273–286.

22. As mentioned earlier, the ability to see, understand, and relate to other people, generally, as holders of positions and roles, rather than as specific individuals becomes the basis not just of participating in wider social networks but of social scientific thought as well. The notion of "generalized other" comes from Mead. He argued that in the beginning children play games of specific others as when they play nurses and doctors, mummies and daddies, and so forth. They then move on to play board games in which they learn to play with or against other general players. The role becomes generalized. This is what happens in organizational and social life. We learn to deal with people in terms of their roles and positions rather than as specific people.

See George Herbert Mead, *Mind, Self and Society* (Chicago, IL: Chicago University Press, 1967 [1934]), 155.

23. Robert Wuthnow, *Meaning and Moral Order: Explorations in Cultural Analysis* (Berkeley: University of California Press, 1987); Roger M. Keesing "Theories of Culture," *Annual Review of Anthropology*, 3 (1974), 73–97.

24. See Geertz, *The Interpretation of Cultures*, 89.

25. Geertz, *The Interpretation of Cultures*, 89.

26. Swidler, *Talk of Love*, 20–21.

27. For a discussion of the difference in beliefs and values in settled and unsettled times, see Swidler, "Culture in Action," 278–282; Swidler, *Talk of Love*, 89–107. However, although Irish society was very settled in the 1980s and 1990s, there was a major ideological conflict about what constitutes a good life during the constitutional referenda on abortion and divorce.

28. This is an adaptation of Weber's famous description of ideas operating as "switchmen" that send the way human beings fulfill basic interests down different tracks. Max Weber, "The Social Psychology of the World Religions," in *From Max Weber*, ed. Hans Gerth and C. Wright Mills (New York: Oxford University Press, 1946), 280.

29. In contrast to Weber who emphasized the importance of rational ideas as the driving force behind cultural change—the rationalization of ideas about God and salvation within Calvinism being a good example—Swidler follows Geertz and stresses that culture revolves less around forming goals and objectives and more around generating moods and feelings that create a general ethos or way of being. This comes close to Bourdieu's concept of habitus that creates flexible, dynamic, and transposable dispositions about life that revolve around "a feel for the game." See, Swidler, *Talk of Love*, 79; Bourdieu, *Logic of Practice*, 66.

30. There has been a tendency in the structure/agency debate in sociology, to move away from an analytical perspective that sees structures and institutions having a real independent, constraining influence on behavior and seeing institutions, such as the Catholic Church, simply in terms of what people do within them. Collins argues that since culture, the economy, states, organizations, and classes do not act, any causal explanation in sociology has to start with the empirical world and the real live actions of individuals. "The structures never *do* anything: it is only persons in real situations who act. It is on the micro level that we must show the emerging processes, both those that cause structural change and those that are responsible for maintaining and reproducing the structures from one occasion to another (that is to say, the "glue" that holds structures together)," Randall Collins, "Interaction Ritual Chains, Power and Property," in *The Micro-Macro Link*, ed. J. Alexander, B. Giesen, R. Münch, and N. Smelser (Berkeley: University of California Press, 1987), 195 (emphasis in the original). However, it is not just that concepts such as church, state, media, market, capitalism, and so forth are an essential part of developing a sociological explanation of life, that they are deemed to have an external reality that shapes and constrains what people do and say, but insofar as people use these concepts

in their everyday communication, sociology imitates life. Individual actors, like Angela Doyle, see and explain social life in terms of "the state," "the Church," and the "the media," that is, as "obdurate structures with their own reality" and other areas as organized more by the independent actions of individuals. See Swidler, *Talk of Love*, 130.

31. Swidler links the difference in the extent to which people use culture to Basil Bernstein's concepts of "restricted" and "elaborated" codes. Bernstein found that working-class children tend to speak in concrete terms because they take for granted that other people see and read the world the same way as them. However, he found that middle-class children tended to be more explicit and abstract in their language that enabled them to relate to wider audiences who might not share their assumptions and opinions. See Swidler, *Talk of Love*, 52; Basil Bernstein, *Class, Codes and Control: Theoretical Studies Towards a Sociology of Language* (London: Routledge & Kegan Paul, 1971). As Swidler suggests, people like Angela "use culture primarily to defend a stable orientation to the world rather than interrogating experience in light of cultural aspirations or searching for new cultural possibilities to interpret their experience." Swidler, *Talk of Love*, 55–56.

32. This resembles Levi-Strauss's concept of "bricoleur." As opposed to the scientist who develops consistent theories, the "bricoleur" creates meaning more like an artist by bringing together cultural elements into a mosaic that is constantly being added to and subtracted from. See Claude Levi-Strauss, *The Savage Mind* (London: Weidenfeld and Nicolson, 1966), 20–22.

33. See Swidler, *Talk of Love*, 73–75.

34. Swidler, *Talk of Love*, 78–84.

35. Joas has developed an alternative understanding of action that gives as much primacy to the body as to the mind:

> According to this alternative view, goal-setting does not take place by an act of the intellect *prior* to the actual action, but is instead the result of reflection on aspirations and tendencies that are pre-reflective and have *already always* been operative. In this act of reflection, we thematize aspirations which are normally at work without our being actively aware of them. But where are these aspirations located? They are located in our bodies. It is the body's capabilities, habits, and ways of relating to the environment which form the background to all conscious goal-setting, in other words, our intentionality. (Hans Joas, *The Creativity of Action* [Chicago, IL: University of Chicago Press, 1996], 158)

36. Swidler argues that institutional demands give coherence to individuals' lives in two ways: first, by filtering out and rationalizing away experiences that do not fit with the institution and, second, by providing the basis for a shared culture. Swidler, *Talk of Love*, 176.

37. For a rich, thick description of the strategies of attaining honor and avoiding shame in gift-giving relations, see Bourdieu, *Outline of a Theory of Practice*, 4–8. See also, Theodore Caplow, "Rule Enforcement without Visible Means:

Christmas Gift Giving in Middletown," *American Journal of Sociology*, 89.6 (1984), 1306–1323.

38. The concept of cultural codes helps overcome the notion of cultures or cultural systems being unified, rigid, and regimented. The notion of codes emphasizes that cultures are continually changing. Codes are used in innovative ways by individuals seeking to attain position, honor, and respect. They are open to local variation and, therefore, have multiple nuanced interpretations. See, Swidler, *Talk of Love*, 194.

39. Much of Bourdieu's work can be seen as an attempt to overcome the divide between structure and agency. There are two key strategies in this attempt. First, instead of seeing culture as epiphenomenal or secondary to economic and political forces (as much structural Marxism had done) it is seen as part and parcel of the reproduction of power. Second, Bourdieu sees habitus—the inherited, embodied, predisposed, flexible, and dynamic ways of seeing, understanding, and being in the world—as the link between social structures and individual agency. As Swartz notes:

> The term "disposition" is key for Bourdieu, since it suggests two essential components he wishes to convey with the idea of habitus: *structure* and *propensity*. Habitus results from early socialization experiences in which external structures are internalized. As a result, internalized dispositions of broad parameters and boundaries of what is possible or unlikely for a particular group in a stratified world develop through socialization. Thus, on the one hand, habitus sets structural limits for action. On the other hand, habitus generates perceptions, aspirations, and practices that correspond to the structuring properties of earlier socialization. (Swartz, *Culture and Power*, 103)

40. The concept of interests and the ways in which they are fulfilled is enormously complex and has been subject to much sociological investigation. Unlike Weber who saw human interests as given and universal—and how they are fulfilled as subject to the cultural ideas of the time and place—Bourdieu argues that interests are variable and that someone like Angela has as many interests as the fields in which she is struggling for position. The logic of Bourdieu's position would suggest that creating and maintaining meaning is done for symbolic profit. Bourdieu would suggest that everything that Angela does, all her practices, is directed toward material or symbolic rewards. For him, then, marriage is seen less about love, care, and bonding and more "as a social strategy defined by its position in a system of strategies oriented towards the maximizing of material and symbolic profit." Bourdieu, *The Logic of Practice*, 16.

41. Although Bourdieu sees action as always interested, it is not always conscious and intentional, let alone rational and calculated. In this utilitarian view of action, people like Angela Doyle may always act in her own interest, but she has numerous interests from maintaining her material benefits and social position, to being liked and loved. As he notes: "The most profitable

strategies are usually those produced, on the hither side of all calculation and in the illusion of the most 'authentic' sincerity." Bourdieu, *Outline of a Theory of Practice*, 214.

42. As Bourdieu argues, "personal style... is never more than a *deviation* in relation to the *style* of a period or class so that it relates back to the common style not only by its conformity... but also by the difference." Bourdieu, *Outline of a Theory of Practice*, 105 (emphasis in original).

43. For Bourdieu, charisma is not just a form of traditional authority associated with precapitalist societies. It is, rather, closely linked to the idea of the gifted individual who, because of his or her "natural" talents, is successful in whatever field he or she operates in. But symbolic capital is also accrued by being honorable and respectable, and in much of his work Bourdieu saw this as particularly crucial in terms of knowing the habitus of each field and doing the right thing at the right time in relation to the right person. This is particularly seen in the gift relationship and knowing what to give to whom, when, where, and how. See Bourdieu, *Outline of a Theory of Practice*, 5–6; Swartz, *Culture and Power*, 91.

44. As Bourdieu points out, social capital is a "capital of social connections, honorability and respectability" and, as such, can be converted into economic, political, and social advantages. Bourdieu's theoretical and empirical investigations about social capital—and how it can be accumulate and traded—are few. In general, he suggests that it is easier to accumulate social capital through economic and cultural capital than vice versa. But he recognizes that some positions, goods, and services are more dependent on social capital. Bourdieu, "Forms of Capital," 252. Although he made an analytical distinction between social and symbolic capital, Bourdieu recognized that they were inextricably linked. "It goes without saying that social capital is so totally governed by the logic of knowledge and acknowledgement that it always functions as symbolic capital." Bourdieu, "Forms of Capital," 257.

45. Following Swidler, we can say that shared meaning is more taken for granted when lives are settled: meaning is seen as common sense or traditional. In times of social upheaval, "established cultural ends are jettisoned with apparent ease" and replaced with ideologies, "explicit, articulated, highly organized meaning systems (both political and religious)." See Swidler, "Culture in Action," 278.

46. The distinction between front- and backstage regions of meaning making comes from Goffman. He saw front-stage regions as places where some presentations of self were accentuated and others repressed. He saw backstage regions as places where the suppressed presentations are subverted, challenged, and contradicted. The individual "can relax: he can drop his front, forgo speaking his lines, and step out of character." Goffman, *Presentation of Self*, 115. Probably the best description of a backstage region for Goffman was the kitchen in a café, restaurant, or hotel where waiters subvert their accentuated front-stage role of waiter by saying and doing things, for example, cursing and laughing, that would undermine their status if done out

front. I see backstage regions of meaning as places where there is comfort
and consolation from having engaged the slings and arrows of public or
organizational life and the taken-for-granted meanings of that life can be
questioned and challenged.

47. For a discussion of the difference between rationality and practical reason in
everyday life, see Sayer, *Why Things Matter to People*, 59–97.

48. Christopher Lasch, *Haven in a Heartless World: The Family Besieged* (New
York: Basic Books, 1977), 111–133.

49. In this sense, social life is about means and ends. We can see values as ultimate
ends, ideals to which people strive, often set within religious and ethical discourses. In any situation, individuals are constrained in fulfilling these values by the means that are available to them. However, in between means and
values, individuals' actions are guided by specific norms, protocols, codes,
and the specific context in which they find themselves. See Talcott Parsons,
Societies, Evolutionary and Comparative Perspectives (London: Prentice-Hall,
1966); Parsons, *The Structure of Social Action* (New York: Free Press, 1949),
44, 732.

50. Swidler, *Talk of Love*, 86, 106.

51. Swidler emphasizes that indifference and skepticism are pervasive in cultural life, and that we cannot describe culture by describing people's beliefs.
We have to know when and how they are used. But we also have to know
what they disbelieve "since they are touched by a great deal of culture they
ultimately reject." Swidler, *Talk of Love*, 16.

52. For a good description and analysis of the conflicts, misunderstandings, and
deceptions in culture, see Geertz, *Interpretation of Cultures*, 3–30.

53. Erving Goffman's great achievement was the meticulous, detailed descriptions and analyses of the way meaning is negotiated and maintained in
social interactions. The way people create and sustain meaning in different contexts was a constant theme in his work. See Erving Goffman,
Frame Analysis: An Essay on the Organization of Experience (Boston, MA:
Northeastern University Press, 1986), 1–16.

54. See Erving Goffman, *The Presentation of Self in Everyday Life* (London:
Penguin 1990); Goffman, *Strategic Interaction* (Philadelphia: University of
Pennsylvania Press, 1969).

55. "Society is organized on the principle that any individual who possesses
certain social characteristics has a moral right to expect that others will
value and treat him in an appropriate way. Connected with this principle
is a second, namely that an individual who implicitly or explicitly signifies
that he has certain social characteristics ought in fact to be what he claims
to be." Goffman, *The Presentation of Self*, 24.

56. The reason why social interaction is orderly is because it is based on
"shared cognitive presuppositions, if not normative ones, and self-sustained
restraints." Gofffman, "The Interaction Order," *American Sociological
Review* 48.1 (1983), 5.

57. Goffman, "Interaction Order," 14.

58. However, as Goffman points out, people may go along with the social conventions that enable interaction to take place even though they may not believe in them and may try to resist or subvert them, Goffman "Interaction Order," 5. Swidler analyzes the importance of codes in everyday cultural life and, similarly, argues that there are many codes in everyday life, such as celebrating Mother's Day, which we are constrained to follow even if we disagree with them. Swidler, *Talk of Love*, 162–169. And what makes interaction all the more complicated is that the codes of being mannerly and polite vary across contexts and are subject to long-term processes of change. See Norbert Elias, *The Civilizing Process: Sociogenetic and Psychogenetic Investigations* (Revised ed.), (Oxford: Blackwell, 2000); Cas Wouters, *Informalization: Manners and Emotions since 1890* (London: Sage, 2007).

59. Berger and Luckmann point out, "*All* social reality is precarious. *All* societies are constructions in the face of chaos. The constant possibility of anomic terror is actualized whenever the legitimations that obscure the precariousness are threatened or collapse." Peter Berger and Thomas Luckmann, *The Social Construction of Reality: A Treatise in the Sociology of Knowledge* (New York: Anchor Books, 1967), 103 (emphasis in original).

60. Geertz saw religion as the key component of culture. His definition of religion is so broad it could be taken as a further explication of culture: "(1) a system of symbols which acts to (2) establish powerful, pervasive, and long-lasting moods and motivations in men by (3) formulating conceptions of a general order of existence and (4) clothing these conceptions with such an aura of factuality that (5) the moods and motivations seem uniquely realistic." Geertz, *Interpretation of Cultures*, 90. In some respects, Geertz's definition of religion seems more appropriate for a more tight-knit religious group. The problem, in contemporary Ireland and in more secular and cosmopolitan societies, is to identify the symbols that establish long-lasting moods and motivations, create a shared conception of a general order of existence, and provide a model of how to live life.

61. The problem with Bourdieu's concept of habitus is, first, that it generally pertains to power and to social fields—thereby denying any whole culture —and, second, that it does not capture how culture is used in specific contexts. For a more detailed analysis of Bourdieu's concept of culture and, in particular, of how habitus works, see Jeffrey Alexander, "The Reality of Reduction: The Failed Synthesis of Pierre Bourdieu," in *Fin de Siècle Social Theory: Relativism, Reduction, and the Problem of Reason* (London: Verso, 1995), 128–217.

62. Bourdieu argues that it is this continual critical self-reflection that attempts to respond to the perceived needs and interests of the participant that makes a mockery of the "the positivist dream of an epistemological state of pure innocence" that is often taken for granted in social survey research. However, it may well be that positivist approaches are more useful and appropriate in gathering facts and information and less appropriate in attempts to understand meaning. Pierre Bourdieu, "Understanding," *Theory, Culture & Society*, 13.2 (1996), 18.

63. Bourdieu describes active and methodological listening as "the display of total attention to the person questioned, submission to the singularity of her own life history—which may lead, by a kind of more or less controlled imitation, to adopting her language and espousing her views, feelings and thoughts—with methodological construction, founded on the knowledge of objective conditions common to an entire social category." Bourdieu "Understanding," 19.

64. This raises issues of "pre-understanding" and how my unannounced assumptions and prejudices about Angela Doyle's "natural attitude" (her dispositions, orientations, and prejudices) necessarily distort and undermine the interview process. The only way to overcome "pre-understanding" is through rigorous critical self-reflection before, during, and after the interview. See Lawrence C. Watson, "Understanding a Life History as a Subjective Document: Hermeneutical and Phenomenological Perspectives," *Ethos* 4.1 (1976), 103.

65. Bourdieu considers this problem many times in his different studies. See, for example, Pierre Bourdieu, *Pascallian Meditations* (Cambridge: Polity Press, 2000), 49–92; Pierre Bourdieu, *The Logic of Practice* (Cambridge: Polity Press, 1990), 30–51.

66. "Narratives, like memoirs, are constructed ways of making sense of a life. People tell stories and/or write memoirs to say something about who they are as individuals and the combination of personal experiences and social/cultural contexts that shaped their identities. Our stories root us, give us identity and grounding, and a guideline for action." Lynn Davidman, "The Personal, the Sociological, and the Intersection of the Two," *Qualitative Sociology* 20.4 (1997), 512. For my own narrative, see Tom Inglis, *Making Love: A Memoir* (Dublin: New Island, 2012). As Benson points out, all autobiographies are constructions, made with the tools and ingredients that culture provides. The stories that are told depend on the skills and motivations of the storyteller. "Personal narratives depend on the person's skill in using these tools and their abilities to innovate and invent new narrative tools thereby enabling new experiences of hearing and reading. These expressions of self also depend on the reasons why the person feels they want their story told and on the particular circumstances giving rise to those reasons." Benson, *The Cultural Psychology of Self*, 48. We tell stories about ourselves every day, but often the main stories that emerge are when we are more critically reflective about ourselves, as happens in turbulent times or, as I would argue, when being asked by an interviewer. As much as there are some stories of the self that are more important than others, there are some stories in a cultural history that become more important than others. This brings us back to Geertz's story of the sheep raid in Morocco and why it was still being told over fifty years later. Geertz, *The Interpretation of Cultures*, 8–9. For a discussion of what stories have been told about modern Ireland, see Tom Inglis, *Truth, Power and Lies: Irish Society and the Case of the Kerry Babies* (Dublin: University College Dublin Press, 2003), 1–16.

67. Elias writes about this in a journal article:

> The way in which individual members of a group experience what-
> ever affects their senses, the meaning it has for them, depends on the
> standard forms of dealing with, and of thinking and speaking about,
> these phenomena which have gradually evolved in their society. Thus,
> although the degree of attachment shown in one's encounter with
> natural forces may vary from individual to individual and from situ-
> ation to situation, the concepts themselves, which, in societies like
> ours, all individuals use in thinking, speaking and acting, concepts
> like "lightning," "tree," or "wolf" not less than "electricity," "organ-
> ism," "cause-and-effect," or "nature," in the sense in which they are
> used today, represent a relatively high degree of detachment; so does
> the socially induced experience of nature as 'landscape' or as "beauti-
> ful." (Norbert Elias, "Problems of Involvement and Detachment,"
> *The British Journal of Sociology* 7.3 (1956), 227–228)

68. As Parsons put it in his letter to Schutz: "I think that most of our self-knowl-
edge is derived from our knowledge of our interrelations with other actors.
But I see no reason to believe that the knowledge acquired by self-reflection
is any closer to ontological reality than the knowledge acquired by observation of the action of others." See, Grathoff, *The Theory of Social Action,* 89.

69. The task then in understanding cultural life, as Geertz reminds us, is to
produce a rich, thick description of everyday life that captures the subjective meanings, moods and motivations of actors. The more interpretation
becomes divorced from what happens in time and this place, from what
people do and say, the more it becomes abstract and vacant. "A good interpretation of anything—a poem, a person, a history, a ritual, an institution,
a society—takes us into the heart of that of which it is the interpretation".
See Geertz, *The Interpretation of Cultures,* 18.

70. As Alexander notes, description is rich when it is "analytically informed and
culturally contextualised." To achieve this rich description it is necessary
to capture the "convictions, feelings, ethics, dramas, and patterned texts
of meaning that give life to society." The interpretation of these convictions, feelings, and meanings is "central for the human sciences because the
inner life is pivotal for social action and collective subjectivity alike." Jeffrey
Alexander, "Clifford Geertz and the Strong Program: The Human Sciences
and Cultural Sociology," *Cultural Sociology* 2.2 (2008), 159–160.

3   PLACE, FAMILY, AND IDENTITY

1. For an analysis of how meaning becomes structured in place and objects in
space, particularly in houses and domestic spaces, and how these structured
spaces reproduce social relations and symbolic domination, see P. Bourdieu,
"The Kabyle House or the World Reversed," in *The Logic of Practice*
(Cambridge: Polity Press, 1990), 271–283.

2. In some respects, the way in which inanimate objects become sacred is similar to the way in which Durkheim describes the nature of *churingas* in totemic religions. The *churinga* embodied the sacredness of the tribe. They were often pieces of wood or stone, in a variety of forms, all engraved with the totem of the tribe. People who did not belong to the tribe, or had not been initiated into the religious life of the tribe, often women and children, were not able to touch or even see the *churinga*. See Emile Durkheim, *The Elementary Forms of the Religious Life* (London: George Allen & Unwin, 1976), 119–120.

3. See John McGahern, *Memoir* (London: Faber and Faber, 2005).

4. In his study of Inveresk, a small fishing village (pop. 450), Peace showed that while there was a strong sense of community, of bonding and belonging, there was also strong sense of villagers belonging to different domains. There were the farmers and others who lived outside the village, there were those that lived in the main village, and there were those that lived down in the port and were involved in fishing. Within these domains, there were distinctions not only between pubs and shops, but also between which villagers went to which pubs and on what occasion and for what reasons. Interaction between the villagers revolved around knowing who was talking to whom and about whom. Each social engagement was in terms of who belonged to what family and from which domain. "The first consideration, essentially, is that the individual's identity is on the whole inseparable from the family into which he or she was born." This identity then determined not just what to say, "but also precisely *how* to say it, and exactly *who* to say it to." Adrian Peace, *A World of Fine Difference: The Social Architecture of a Modern Irish Village* (Dublin: University College Dublin Press, 2001), 21–22, 43, 73. As Peace notes: "This is not simply a matter of understanding the specifics of what others like oneself are saying, but also of experiencing the unrivalled sense of taking one's proper place in the world, of being amongst those with whom one has most affinity," 47.

5. See Tom Inglis, *Global Ireland: Same Difference* (New York: Routledge, 2008).

6. This is a regular theme in many studies of globalization. For Giddens, "the primacy of place in pre-modern settings has been largely destroyed by disembedding and time-space distantciation," Anthony Giddens, *The Consequences of Modernity* (Cambridge: Polity, 1997), 108. Baumann argues that since distances no longer mean anything, localities lose their meanings. Zygmunt Bauman, *Globalization: The Human Consequences* (Cambridge: Polity, 1998), 9. For a description of globalized, mobile lives, see Anthony Elliot and John Urry, *Mobile Lives* (London: Routledge, 2010). Elliot and Urry argue that "the lifestyles of globals is cemented in various new mobile strategies, which range from *detached engagement* to *distance from neighbourhood* to the *chronic mapping of escape routes*," 22. The ability to live such mobile lives depends on people's emotional capacities to maintain and negotiate both their public, personal, and family lives while

moving back and forth between jobs and residences. However, as Loyal
points out, although the number of international migrants in the world
has increased to close to 200 million, this only represents 3 percent of
the world's population. See Steven Loyal, *Understanding Immigration in
Ireland: State, Capital and Labour in a Global Age* (Manchester: Manchester
University Press, 2011), 20.

7. Victor Roudometof, "Transnationalism, Cosmopolitanism and
Glocalization," *Current Sociology,* 53 (2005), 113–135: Florian Pichler
"'Down-to-Earth' Cosmopolitanism: Subjective and Objective Measurements
of Cosmopolitanism in Survey Research," *Current Sociology* 57 (2009),
704–732; Anna Olofsson, and Susanna Öhman, "Cosmopolitans and Locals:
An Empirical Investigation of Transnationalism," *Current Sociology* 55 (2007),
877–895.

8. Crowley provides a detailed description and analysis of home and place in
contemporary Ireland. Ethel Crowley, *Your Place or Mine? Community and
Belonging in Twenty-First Century Ireland* (Dublin: Orpen Press, 2013).
See also, Crowley, "Feeling at Home in Contemporary Ireland," in *Are the
Irish Different?* ed. T. Inglis (Manchester: Manchester University Press,
2104) (forthcoming).

9. Savage and his colleagues use Simmel's phrase of "come today, stay tomorrow" to describe how, even in an increasingly mobile world, the local is not
pitted against the global. They argue that there are new cosmopolitan forms
of "elective belonging." Some "blow-ins" become more attached to and
involved in neighborhoods than those who grew up in them. Residential
areas, they suggest, have "become sites for new kinds of solidarities among
people who chose to live in particular places, and whose deep concern about
where they live is unlikely to be overlain with extraneous concerns arising
from knowledge of others who have historically lived in the place." Mike
Savage, Gaynor Bagnall, and Brian Longhurst, *Globalization & Belonging*
(London: Sage, 2005), 53.

10. Attachments to place vary across time and space. People may be attached to
the local place in which they are living as well as to the place in which they
grew up, to other places in which they lived, and to wider sense of place such
as county or nation. A study of local and national belonging in Ireland in
2003 found that more than eight in ten Irish people felt close to the village,
suburban area, town, or city in which they lived, but close to nine in ten
respondents said they felt close to their county and to Ireland. However,
attachment to place has to be put within the context of other attachments
and belongings. When respondents were asked about their social identities,
the following were seen as the most important, their family (35 percent),
nationality (16 percent), and occupation (14 percent). Only 4 percent ranked
the part of the country in which they lived as their most important identity. Nevertheless, when respondents were asked to nominate their second
and third most important identities, the place where they lived increased in
importance: 9 percent ranked it second and 17 percent ranked it third. Most

significant, perhaps, was that taking into consideration first, second, and third rankings, the identity with the part of the country in which people lived ranked ahead of religion, gender, and age group. See Tom Inglis and Susie Donnelly, "Local and National Belonging in a Globalised World," *Irish Journal of Sociology* 19.2 (2011), 132–134.

11. Central Statistics Office, *This Is Ireland: Highlights from Census 2011*, Part 1 (Dublin: Government Publications, 2012), p. 25.

12. In their analysis of the 2006 Census data, Peter Lunn and Tony Fahey found that the majority of cohabiting couples married within five years of the birth of their first child. *Households and Family Structures in Ireland: A Detailed Statistical Analysis of Census 2006* (Dublin: ESRI, 2011), p. 114.

13. The 2011 Census revealed that the number of people divorced more than doubled between 2002 and 2011, from approximately 35,000 to 88,000, an increase of 150 percent. The number of divorced people is, in comparison with other Western societies, relatively low and may be related to the late introduction of divorce in 1996 and, therefore, the absence of a divorce culture. The number of separated people (116,000) is higher, but this is only up 17,000 from 2002—a 17 percent increase. The comparatively low level of increase in separated people may be because more people are getting divorced. But divorce and separation has also led to an increase in the number of people remarrying. While the number of divorced more than doubled in the ten-year period 2002–12, so too did the number of people who remarried after the ending of their first marriage: up from 21,000 to 43,000. Again this could be related to the emergence of a new culture of couples being able to separate, divorce, and remarry.

14. Tony Fahey, Patricia Keilty, and Ela Polek, *Family Relationships and Family Well-Being: A Study of the Families of Nine Year Olds in Ireland* (Dublin: UCD and the Family Support Agency, 2013), p. 80.

15. See P. Bourdieu, "On the Family as a Realized Category," *Theory, Culture & Society*, 13.3 (1996), p. 20.

16. Family is seen as "the sets of practices which deal in some way with ideas of parenthood, kinship and marriage and the expectations and obligations which are associated with these practices." David Morgan, *Family Connections: An Introduction to Family Studies* (Cambridge: Polity Press, 1996), p. 11.

17. Smart has argued that families should be conceptualized as hosts of collective memories. They share stories about the past, often recorded in photographs. Memories, Smart argues, are closely allied to individual biographies and how individuals create a sense of self as the move in and out of the family. Moving beyond a narrow notion of family practices in the present, she thinks it is better to think of families and family members as being embedded in dense networks of historical and contemporary connections. Family members operate across time and space with a sense of being connected to previous generations as well as those presently elsewhere. Carol Smart, *Personal Life: New Directions in Sociological Thinking* (Cambridge: Polity, 2007), p. 27.

18. For a more detailed analysis of emotions in family life, see Tom Inglis, *Love* (London: Routledge, 2013), pp. 46–58.

19. A study of Irish adults in 2001 found that three in ten women and one in four men reported some level of sexual abuse in childhood. Among the women surveyed, one in five reported some kind of physical contact sexual abuse: one in twenty reported that the abuse involved penetrative sex. Among men, one in six reported contact physical abuse in childhood. The SAVI Report: "Sexual Abuse and Violence in Ireland. Executive Summary," (Dublin: Royal College of Surgeons in Ireland, 2002). The family is often a place of gender domination. As many feminists have pointed out, family work, like most care work, is mainly undertaken by women and, therefore while the family may be a site of love and care, it is, often at one and the same time, a site of symbolic domination and, often, of neglect, abuse, and violence.

4   MONEY AND SUCCESS

1. In her analysis of how culture shapes action, Swidler refers to codes, contexts, and institutions. She sees codes as semiotic structures of meaning that evolve among people in specific contexts and uses the examples of gift-giving and card-sending. The codes and the ways in which they are used will vary according to the specific context. As well as codes and contexts, culture is also shaped by institutions, which she sees as shared narratives, practices, and capacities that enable people to employ different strategies. See Ann Swidler, *Talk of Love: How Culture Matters* (Chicago, IL: Chicago University Press, 2001), 160–185. However, I think, following Bourdieu, it is important to see people as operating in social fields in which there are dominant and subordinate positions as people struggle to attain different forms of capital and to legitimate their positions. See Pierre Bourdieu and Loïc Wacquant, *An Invitation to Reflexive Sociology* (Chicago, IL: Chicago University Press, 1992), 94–115. But where I differ from both Swidler and Bourdieu is that while people are rational, instrumental, and strategic in their struggle for capital, they have to be emotional and reasonable in their struggle to bond and belong and to love and care for each other.

2. The question as to whether there is an overall culture of meaning, and how this shapes actions in specific contexts, is a core issue in cultural sociology. There are those who argue that culture is shared and coherent and others who argue that it is continually renegotiated and inconsistent. See Swidler, *Talk of Love*, 179–189.

3. Bourdieu sees the field of power as the struggle between the value and distribution of economic capital (income, wealth, and property) and the value and distribution of cultural capital (knowledge, education, and culture). See Bourdieu and Wacquant, *An Invitation to Reflexive Sociology*, 76; David Swartz, *Culture & Power: The Sociology of Pierre Bourdieu* (Chicago, IL: Chicago University Press, 1997), 136–142.

4. For Bourdieu, meaning is conflated with habitus. But the problem with his conception of habitus, as Alexander points out, is that it is a structural reduction, a structure that reproduces domination. It does not allow for independence of language, symbols, and meaning and of individuals continually recreating and sustaining meaning. See Jeffrey Alexander, *Fin de Siècle Social Theory: Relativism, Reduction, and the Problem of Reason* (London: Verso, 1995), 136–149.

5. The relation between economic and religious interests was central not just to Weber's sociology of religion, it was also central to his conception of culture. He saw religion as providing fundamental views about the purpose, ends, and means of life and that this shaped people's actions. When one understood the logic of the Protestant ethic, one could explain the economic behavior of Calvanists and, therefore, why modern capitalism emerged when it did. See Max Weber, *The Protestant Ethic and the Spirit of Capitalism* (New York: Scribner's Sons, 1958), esp. 232.

6. For a more detailed discussion of the relationship between culture and action, see A. Swidler, "Culture in Action: Symbols and Strategies," *American Sociological Review* 51 (1986), 273–286; Stephen Vaisey, "Motivation and Justification: A Dual-Process Model of Culture in Action," *American Journal of Sociology* 114 (2009), 1675–1715; Vaisey, "Socrates, Skinner and Aristotle: Three Ways of Thinking about Culture in Action," *Sociological Forum* 23 (2008), 603–613; Swidler, "Comment on Stephen Vaisey's 'Socrates, Skinner and Aristotle: Three Ways of Thinking about Culture in Action,'" *Sociological Forum* 23 (2008), 614–618.

7. Again, this is derived from Geertz's definition of religion. See Clifford Geertz, *The Interpretation of Cultures* (New York: Basic Books, 1973), 90.

8. http://www.oecdbetterlifeindex.org/countries/ireland/ (Accessed June 11, 2013).

9. Habitus is central to Bourdieu's way of reading, understanding, and investigating the social world. It focuses attention on the embodied dispositions, ways of thinking and being, into which people are socialized. These dispositions become almost automatic, taken-for-granted, second-nature ways of being. For Bourdieu, all forms of identity, personal meaning, subjectivity, and sense of self are structured within habitus. "To speak of habitus is to assert that the individual, and even the personal, the subjective, is social, collective. Habitus is socialized subjectivity." Bourdieu and Wacquant, *An Invitation to Reflexive Sociology*, 126. It is within habitus that individuals are socialized into their identities and their social relations with others. See, Craig Calhoun, "Social Theory and the Politics of Identity," in *Social Theory and the Politics of Identity*, ed. Craig Calhoun (Oxford: Blackwell, 1994), 11; James Bohman, "Practical Reason and Cultural Constraint: Agency in Bourdieu's Theory of Practice," in *Bourdieu: A Critical Reader*, ed. R. Schusterman (Oxford: Blackwell, 1999), 132. We can take it from this that any sense of identity is derived within "the limits of the system of categories he (the individual) owes to his upbringing and training." Bourdieu and Wacquant, *An Invitation to Reflexive Sociology*, 126. Identity can be seen

as an arbitrarily constructed story that one tells about oneself to create an ongoing sense of coherence and logic about oneself, the events and experiences that constitute one's life. Pierre Bourdieu, "The Biographical Illusion," in *Identity: A Reader*, ed. P. Du Gay, J. Evans, and P. Redman (London: Sage, 2000), 298. Identity, then, from a Bourdieusian perspective, is the socially structured story that constitutes oneself as constant, intelligible, and responsible. "The social world, which tends to identify normality with identity understood as the constancy to oneself of a responsible being that is predictable, or at least intelligible, in the way of a well-constructed history (as opposed to a history of an idiot), has available all sorts of institutions of integration and unification of the self." Bourdieu, "The Biographical Illusion," 299. However, rather than seeing Mark as "an arbitrarily constructed story," it would be better to see him as a bricoleur of meaning, someone who uses the cultural ingredients into which he was socialized to create an ongoing, durable, but transposable sense of self that enables him to create and sustain meaning with his customers as well as his loved ones.

10. In this sense, Mark's identity emerges from his cultural repertoire and his specific capacities that have become embodied in particular strategies that he has adopted and adapted over the years and which he employs in various different contexts, in the shop, at home, and elsewhere. Swidler refers to this as an identity model of how culture works. "The fundamental notion is that people develop lines of action based on who they think they are. This is true in two senses. First, as I have been saying, actors' capacities shape the lines of action that they find possible and promising. The second sense in which mine is an identity-based model is that a great deal of culture operates by attaching meanings to the self." Swidler, *Talk of Love*, 87.

11. In his study of world religions, Demerath distinguished cultural Catholics as those who were not really believers, and while they attended church sporadically they had a good deal of contempt for some of the church officials and policies. But they still saw Catholicism as part of their national and family cultural heritage. See N. Jay Demerath III, *Crossing the Gods: World Religions and Worldly Politics* (New Brunswick, NJ: Rutgers University Press, 2001), 43. For a description of Irish Cultural Catholics and how they differ from other types, see Tom Inglis, "Catholic Identity in Contemporary Ireland: Belief and Belonging to Tradition," *Journal of Contemporary Religion* 22.3 (2007), 205–220. We will return to this in chapter 8.

12. http://www.oecdbetterlifeindex.org/countries/ireland/ (Accessed June 11, 2013).

13. Kathleen Lynch and Judy Walsh, "Love, Care and Solidarity: What Is and Is Not Commodifiable," in *Affective Equality: Love, Care and Injustice*, ed. Kathleen Lynch, John Baker, and Maureen Lyons (London: Palgrave Macmillan, 2009), 31–53.

14. In his study of working-class schoolchildren back in the 1970s, Paul Willis found that there some pupils opted out of the formal school culture that was oriented to educational success and, instead, focused on trying to avoid confrontation with the formal requirements and have a good time. Later, they

took a similar attitude to work: it was more about maintaining relationships, being able to get on with colleagues, than about personal success. See Paul Willis, *Learning to Labour* (Farnborough: Saxon House, 1977), 22–49.

15. Analyzing the ways in which culture operated in and through social class was a major feature of Bourdieu's work. Class position is structured through a habitus that structures the way people see and understand themselves within the class structure. For Bourdieu, what are objective social structural realities become internalized as subjective dispositions. "The categories of perception of the social world are, as regards their most essential features, the product of the internalization, the incorporation, of the objective structures of social space. Consequently, they incline agents to accept the social world as it is, to take it for granted, rather than to rebel against it, to counterpose to it different, even antagonistic, possibles. The sense of one's place, as a sense of what one can or cannot 'permit oneself,' implies a tacit acceptance of one's place, a sense of limits ('that's not for the likes of us,' etc.), or, which amounts to the same thing, a sense of distances, to be marked and kept, respected or expected," Pierre Bourdieu, "Social Space and the Genesis of Groups," *Theory and Society* 14.6 (1985), 728.

5   POLITICS

1. On the distinction between political and social revolutions, see Theda Skocpol, *States and Social Revolutions: A Comparative Analysis of France, Russia and China* (Cambridge: Cambridge University Press, 1979).

2. Alexander sees the civil sphere as the public space beyond power and self-interest. "Feelings for others matter, and they are structured by the boundaries of solidarity. How solidarity is structured, how far it extends, what it's composed of—these are critical issues for every social order, and especially for orders that aim at the good life." Jeffrey Alexander, *The Civil Sphere* (Oxford: Oxford University Press, 2006), 3.

3. As discussed in chapter 2, there is, of course, a gap between this structural realist analysis of the webs in which people are suspended and the description and explanation they give for what is important and meaningful in their lives. Much of the explanation that I have developed here derives from a reading of Bourdieu. See Pierre Bourdieu, *On the State: Lectures at the College de France 1989–1992* (Cambridge: Polity Press, 2014). Pierre Bourdieu and Löic Wacquant, *The Purpose of Reflexive Sociology* (Chicago, IL: Chicago University Press, 1992), 104–115. In many respects, the reluctance and inability of the state to deal with the market, banks, and bondholders is in stark contrast to its willingness and ability to resist and challenge the power of the Catholic Church in relation to sexuality, health, and education, and to set up tribunals to investigate clerical child sex abuse and to send members of the clergy and religious orders to prison.

4. Much of contemporary Western philosophy is concerned about what constitutes and how to form a good society. The problem, of course, is

transcending the gap between theorizing what constitutes a good society and how to get there and translating these ideas into policies and practices that animate and lead to engagement in participative democracy. See Maeve Cooke, *The Good Society* (Cambridge: MIT Press, 2006).

5. The classical discussion of the role of the public sphere in democratic societies and within the public sphere, the role of the media is Jürgen Habermas, *The Structural Transformation of the Public Sphere* (Cambridge: Polity Press, 1992). See also Craig Calhoun (ed.), *Habermas and the Public Sphere.* (Cambridge: MIT Press, 1992); Jean Cohen and Andrew Arato, *Civil Society and Political Theory* (Cambridge: MIT Press, 1992).

6. Obviously there have been times in Irish history, such as during the War of Independence and the subsequent Civil War, when political debate and activity permeated everyday life. The importance of politics increases in unsettled times, particularly during conflicts, rebellions, wars, and revolutions. Sewell, for example, has done extensive studies of the different types of political activity in France, and the differences they made in the eighteenth and nineteenth centuries. See William H. Sewell "Ideologies and Social Revolutions: Reflections on the French Case," *Journal of Modern History* 57 (1985), 57–85; Sewell, "Collective Violence and Collective Loyalties in France: Why the French Revolution Made a Difference," *Politics and Society* 18.4 (1990), 527–552. Swidler argues that political culture, like culture generally, becomes more significant in unsettled times, Ann Swidler, *Talk of Love: How Culture Matters* (Chicago, IL: Chicago University Press, 2001), 89–107.

7. See Pipa Norris (ed.), *Critical Citizens: Global Support for Democratic Government* (Oxford: Oxford University Press, 1999); Mattei Dogan and Ali Kazancigil, "The Pendulum between Theory and Substance: Testing the Concepts of Legitimacy and Trust," in *Comparing Nations,* ed. Mattei Dogan (Oxford: Blackwell, 1994), 296–313. In their analysis of trends in seventeen different democracies, using data from various World Values Surveys, Newton and Norris found that confidence in public institutions declined in the 1980s and 1990s: confidence in parliament declined from 48 to 43 percent. The decline in confidence in parliament in Ireland was from 52 to 50 percent. While there was no significant difference between men and women, the young, the unemployed, working-class respondents, and those without third-level education all indicated less interest or involvement in politics. See, Kenneth Newton and Pippa Norris, "Confidence in Public Institutions: Faith, Culture or Performance?" American Political Science Association Conference, Atlanta, 1999.

8. Tony Fahey, Bernadette Hayes, and Richard Sinnott, *Conflict and Consensus: a Study of Values and Attitudes in the Republic of Ireland and Northern Ireland* (Dublin: Institute of Public Administration, 2005), 185–21. However, when asked, in the same year, if they were satisfied with the way democracy was developing in Ireland, 64 percent said that they were either rather or very satisfied. However, only 56 percent voted in the 2011 presidential election, while 58 percent voted in the 2009 European Parliament elections.

9. Source International Institute for Democracy and Electoral Assistance (International IDEA): www.idea.int (Accessed October 18, 2012).
10. For Bourdieu, participation in every social field is premised on self-interest. Like every other social field, the political field has its own *illusio*, that is a belief in and acceptance that the game is worth playing. Everyone in the political field, whether traditional activists or radicals and intellectuals, has embodied the political habitus. All of them know the rules of engagement and pursue position and rewards. See Bourdieu and Wacquant, *Invitation to Reflexive Sociology*, 117.
11. It is the embodiment of the habitus and the engagement in the *illusio* that enables political activists to develop appropriate and successful strategies of action. See Swidler, *Talk of Love*, 78–84.
12. Sarah Jane Delaney, Richard Sinnott, and Niall O'Reilly, "The Extent of Clientelism in Irish Politics: Evidence from Classifying Dáil Questions on Local-National Dimension," AICS: Proceedings of 21st Irish Conference on Artificial Intelligence and Cognitive Science, 2010; Elaine Byrne, *Political Corruption in Ireland 1922–2010* (Manchester: Manchester University Press, 2012).
13. In concluding her historical study of political corruption in Ireland, Elaine Byrne refers to the existence of a "homogenic political culture" in which there was an expectation of "reciprocal control." This, combined with a lack of regulation, stigma, and sanctions, gave rise to social values that were more orientated to religious and nationalistic attachments than to "a sense of state." Byrne, *Political Corruption*, 208–239.
14. Swidler, *Talk of Love*, 99.
15. For more detail about these debates see, Peter Mair, *Ruling the Void: The Hollowing-Out of Western Democracy* (London: Pluto Press, 2013); David Farrell, "'Stripped down' or Reconfigured Democracy," *West European Politics* 37.2 (2014), 439–455; Craig Calhoun, *Social Theory and the Politics of Identity* (Oxford: Blackwell, 1994); Michael Saward, *The Representative Claim* (Oxford: Oxford University Press, 2010); Russell Dalton, *The Good Citizen: How a Younger Generation is Reshaping American Politics,* 2nd ed. (Washington, DC: Congressional Quarterly Press, 2009).

6 SPORT

1. See Norbert Elias and Eric Dunning, *Quest for Excitement: Sport and Leisure in the Civilizing Process*, (Oxford: Basil Blackwell, 1986): Eric Dunning, *Sport Matters: Sociological Studies of Sport, Violence and Civilisation* (London: Routledge, 1999).
2. Eileen Kennedy and Laura Hills, *Sport, Media and Society* (New York: Berg, 2009), 1.
3. As Van Krieken argues, this is partly because the absence of a language barrier enables them to cross national boundaries. See Robert Van Kreiken, *Celebrity Society* (London: Routledge, 2012), 51.

4. Mike Cronin, "Beyond Sectarianism: Sport and Irish Culture," in *Ireland: Beyond Boundaries*, ed. L. Harte and Y. Whelan (London: Pluto Press, 2007), 215–237; John Hargreaves, *Sport, Power and Culture* (Oxford: Polity, 1986), 57–113.

5. See Mike Cronin, *Sport and Nationalism in Ireland: Gaelic Games, Soccer and Irish Identity since 1884* (Dublin: Four Courts Press, 1999).

6. See Paul Darby, *Gaelic Games, Nationalism and the Irish Diaspora in the United States* (Dublin: University College Dublin Press, 2009); Tom Humphries, *Green Fields: Gaelic Sport in Ireland* (London: Weidenfeld & Nicolson, 1996).

7. Pete Lunn and Richard Layte, *The Irish Sports Monitor*, Third Annual Report. Dublin: The Economic and Social Research Institute, 2009, 12, 46, 52, 40. Of the main sports, leaving aside walking, jogging, cycling and dancing, swimming was the most popular (7.2 percent) followed by soccer (5.6 percent), golf (4.6 percent), Gaelic football (2.6 percent), hurling (1.4 percent), and rugby (0.9 percent). Lunn and Layte, *Sports Monitor*, 23. One of the problems in measuring the level of participation in sport is how to distinguish it from fitness and exercise. When is going for a run, walking, or cycling a sport? A survey in 2003 found that 78 percent of respondents engaged in physical activities to some degree, but only about 40 percent did so regularly enough to correspond to the minimum standards of physical activity recommended by the World Health Organisation. Recreational walking was by far the most popular form of leisure-time physical activity: 60 percent of adults had taken a walk in the four weeks prior to the survey. See Liam Delaney and Tony Fahey, *Social and Economic Value of Sport in Ireland* (Dublin: Economic and Social Research Institute, 2005), 16, 23.

8. Delaney and Fahey, *Social and Economic Value of Sport*, 48.

9. Delaney and Fahey, *Social and Economic Value of Sport*, 23, 27, 4.

10. Dunning, *Sport Matters*, 1.

11. Delaney and Fahey argue that it is, after war, the strongest form of collective identification, Delaney and Fahey, *Social and Economic Value of Sport*, 4.

12. In his classic analysis of social capital, Putnam argued that the decline in collective sports (he focused on bowling leagues in the United States) led to a decline in social capital. Putnam linked this to the arrival of the mass media and the commodification of sport. Robert Putnam, *Bowling Alone: The Collapse and Revival of American Community* (New York: Simon & Schuster, 2000). However, research suggests that the social bonding of sport is not even or homogeneous. Membership of sports clubs is higher among younger people—particularly men—and those with better educational backgrounds and higher occupational groups. Women, unskilled workers, the unemployed, and older people are not as much involved in sporting clubs; see Delaney and Fahey, *Social and Economic Value of Sport in Ireland*, 2–3.

13. This is adapted from Durkheim's definition. See Emile Durkheim, *The Elementary Forms of the Religious Life* (London: George Allen & Unwin, 1976 [1915]), 47.

14. See Clifford Geertz, *The Interpretation of Cultures* (New York: Basic Books, 1973), 93.

15. See Elias and Dunning, *Quest for Excitement*, 222. There is also an argument that sport is a legacy of religious ritual, and that the origins of many modern-day sport are to be found in the practices associated with fertility festivals. See Susan Birrell, "Sport as Ritual: Interpretations from Durkheim to Goffman," *Social Forces* 60.2 (1981), 354; Dunning, *Sport Matters*, 7.

16. Durkheim, *The Elementary Forms*, 215, 319.

17. Birrell, "Sport as Ritual," 374.

18. Birrell, "Sport as Ritual," 374.

19. Carl Stempel "Adult Participation Sports as Cultural Capital: A Test of Bourdieu's Theory of the Field of Sports," *International Review for the Sociology of Sport* 40.4 (2005), 411–432.

20. This is derived from Durkheim, see *The Elementary Forms*. Cronin suggests that sports identities are evanescent and ephemeral and that it only comes into play as part of an occasional thrill or transitory spectacle. "The displays of emotion and excitement that accompany such occasions assist in the temporary articulation of national and local identities, but do not provide definition in themselves. When the game or tournament ends, other factors replace or supplement sport in sustaining and defining identities." See Cronin, "Beyond Sectarianism," 217. But this leads to a misunderstanding about the nature of personal identities and how they are relational and linked to maps of meaning. People might not consider themselves to be Irish or Catholic except when abroad, watching sport, or going to Mass, but these can become very strong identities built on bonds of belonging that have been developed over long periods of time.

21. Hans Joas, *The Creativity of Action* (Chicago, IL: Chicago University Press, 1996); Ann Swidler, *Talk of Love: How Culture Matters* (Chicago, IL: Chicago University Press, 2001), 71–88.

7   RELIGION

1. This is adapted from Geertz. See Clifford Geertz, *The Interpretation of Cultures* (New York: Basic Books, 1973), 90.

2. For a more detailed description and analysis of these changes, see Tom Inglis, *Moral Monopoly: The Rise and Fall of the Catholic Church in Modern Ireland*, 2nd ed. (Dublin: University College Dublin Press, 1998), 159–242.

3. Susie Donnelly and Tom Inglis, "The Media and the Catholic Church in Ireland: Reporting Clerical Child Sexual Abuse," *Journal of Contemporary Religion* 25.1 (2010), 1–19.

4. See Tom Inglis "Irish Civil Society: From Church to Media Domination," in *Religion and Politics: East-West Contrasts from Contemporary Europe*, ed. T. Inglis, R. Mazanek, and Z. Mach (Dublin: University College Dublin Press, 2000), 49–67.

5. See Tom Inglis, *Global Ireland: Same Difference* (New York: Routledge, 2008), 13–35.

6. In the twenty years between 1991 and 2011, there was a steady rise in the number of atheists and agnostics—up from 1,143 to 8,569. However, the most dramatic increase was among those with no religion up from 66,270 in 1991 to 269,811 in 2011, a 400 percent increase. However, "no religion" cannot be interpreted as necessarily being atheist or agnostic. It may also include people who may have religious beliefs but do not belong to a religion or church. Central Statistics Office, "Profile 7: Religion, Ethnicity and Irish Travellers," Dublin, 2012, 42–48.

7. The International Social Survey Programme (2008) conducted a study of religious belief and practice in forty-two different countries. For details of the study, see www.issp.org; M. Nic Ghiolla Phádraig, "Religion in Ireland: Preliminary Analysis," *Social Studies* 5.2 (1976), 113–180. It is hard to decipher from the 2008 survey data to what extent Irish Catholics believe in a personal God who can and does directly intervene in their lives. Seven-in-ten believed that God concerns himself with human beings. A similar proportion believed in miracles. However, less than four in ten (37 percent) linked the meaning of life to God's existence. There was some evidence to suggest that many Irish Catholics do not depend on the church or see its prayers and rituals as a means of reaching out to God. Six in ten agreed that they had their own way of connecting with God. However, despite an increase in the level of doubt about God, there appears to have been an increase in belief in life after death. In 1973/74, 36 percent of Catholics were "very sure" that there is life after death, and 29 percent were "pretty sure." In 2008, 43 percent said that they "definitely" believed and 39 percent said they "probably" believed in an afterlife. There was an indication that there had been little change in the level of belief in Hell. This distancing from orthodox, institutional religious practice and an increase in religious individualism is also indicated in the number of Irish Catholics who have supernatural beliefs that are at variance with church teaching. As the International Social Survey Project (ISSP) survey was conducted in over forty different countries, Irish respondents, like all other respondents, were asked about other supernatural beliefs. Again there is a difficulty in interpreting how these beliefs link in with traditional Catholic beliefs. More than a third (38 percent) of the Irish Catholic respondents said they definitely or probably believed in the supernatural powers of deceased ancestors. Three in ten believed in reincarnation and almost a quarter (24 percent) believed in Nirvana.

8. Tom Inglis, "Catholic Identity in Contemporary Ireland: Belief and Belonging to Tradition," *Journal of Contemporary Religion*, 22.2 (2007), 205–220.

9. M. Nic Ghiolla Phádraig, "The Power of the Catholic Church in the Republic of Ireland," in *Irish Society: Sociological Perspectives*, ed. P. Clancy, S, Drudy, K. Lynch, and L. O'Dowd (Dublin: Institute of Public Administration, 1995), 597.

10. The analytic distinction between ideal types of orthodox, cultural, creative, and disenchanted Catholics is developed in Inglis, "Catholic Identity."

11. For a description of hell-fire sermons, see Lawrence J. Taylor, "The Mission: An Anthropological View of an Irish Religious Occasion," in *Ireland from Below: Social Change and Local Communities*, ed. T. Wilson and C. Curtin (Galway: Galway University Press, 1989), 1–22.

12. For a more detailed discussion of magic and Catholicism based on the findings of this study, see Tom Inglis, "Religion, Magic and Practical Reason: Meaning and Everyday Life in Contemporary Ireland," in *Religion and Science as Forms of Life*, ed. C. Salazar and J. Bestard (New York: Berghahn, 2015), 188–206.

13. See Marie Keenan, *Child Sexual Abuse and the Catholic Church* (New York: Oxford University Press, 2011); Donnelly and Inglis, "Media and the Catholic Church."

14. Tom Inglis, *Moral Monopoly*, 30–36. In 2013, the archbishop of Dublin argued that Ireland had become a post-Catholic society and that while this was strongly linked to the scandals, the authority of the church had been on the wane for some considerable time previous to that. Diarmuid Martin, "Catholic Ireland: Past, Present and Future," *The Furrow* 64.6 (2013), 323.

15. For a contrast between American and Irish Catholics, see Michele Dillon, "The Difference between Irish and American Catholicism," in *Are the Irish Different?* ed. Tom Inglis (Manchester: Manchester University Press, 2014), 110–20.

16. The concept of believing without belonging, particularly adhering to Christian beliefs without going to church, was devised by Davie, see Grace Davie, *Religion in Britain Since 1945: Believing without Belonging* (Oxford: Blackwell, 2000). However, there has been considerable debate about the connection between levels of belief and levels of practice. See David Voas and Alasdair Crockett, "Religion in Britain: Neither Believing nor Belonging," *Sociology* 39.1 (2005), 11–28; Crockett and Voas, "Generations of Decline: Religious Change in 20th Century Britain," *Journal for the Scientific Study of Religion* 45.4 (2006), 567–584; Robin Gill, C. Kirk Hadaway, and Penny Long Marler, "Is Religious Belief Declining in Britain?" *Journal for the Scientific Study of Religion* 37.3 (1998), 507–516.

17. The 2008 ISSP study, referred to above, found that 11 percent of Irish Catholics believed in the supernatural powers of deceased ancestors. A similar proportion believed in reincarnation. It is difficult to decipher how deeply these beliefs are held.

18. See Hubert Knoblauch, "Europe and Invisible Religion," *Social Compass* 50 (2003), 264–274; Thomas Luckmann, "Transformations of Religion and Morality in Modern Europe," *Social Compass* 50 (2003), 275–285; Rodney Stark, Eva Hamberg, and Alan Miller, "Exploring Spirituality in America, Sweden and Japan," *Journal of Contemporary Religion* 20 (2005), 3–23.

19. As Taylor characterizes it, Ireland has moved "from a society where belief in God is unchallenged and indeed, unproblematic, to one in which it is understood to be one option among others, and frequently not the easiest to embrace." Charles Taylor, *A Secular Age* (Cambridge, MA: Harvard University Press, 2007), 3.

20. See, Taylor, *A Secular Age,* 171–196. Indeed, in some respects the pendulum has swung the other way. In the West, there are new secular voices that claim that God is not only irrelevant, but also irrational and socially dangerous. See Christopher Hitchens, *God Is Not Great: How Religion Poisons Everything* (New York: Warner Twelve, 2007); Richard Dawkins, *The God Delusion* (London: Black Swan). However, these are a small minority. There is plenty of evidence to show that, even in the West, God has not gone away. See Peter Berger, "The Desecularization of the World: A Global Overview," in *The Desecularization of the World: Resurgent Religion and World Politics,* ed. P. Berger (Grand Rapids, MI: William B. Eerdamns, 1999), 1–18. But the point that Taylor makes, which has been substantiated by the findings of this study, is that God and religious beliefs and practices are no longer the basis for common action.

21. Danièle Hervieu-Léger, "Individualism, the Validation of Faith, and the Social Nature of Religion in Modernity," in *The Blackwell Companion to Sociology,* ed. R. K. Fenn (Oxford: Blackwell, 2003), 161–175; Hervieu-Léger, *Religion as a Chain of Memory* (Cambridge: Polity Press, 2000), 65–100.

8 LOVE

1. For a more detailed discussion of love as the new religion, see, Ulrich Beck and Elisabeth Beck-Gernsheim, *The Normal Chaos of Love* (Cambridge: Polity, 1995), 168–201. However, their description and analysis concentrates more on romantic love and does not deal with the decline of religion in people's lives.

2. For a discussion of the work-love balance, see Tom Inglis, *Love* (London: Routledge, 2013), 48–50.

3. For a discussion of the ingredients of love, see Thomas Scheff, *What's Love Got to Do with It? Emotions and Relationships in Popular Songs* (Boulder, CO: Paradigm Books, 2011), 26–35; Ellen Berscheid, "Love in the Fourth Dimension," *Annual Review of Psychology* 61 (2011), 1–25.

4. See Inglis, *Love,* 46–58.

5. See Niklas Luhmann, *Love as Passion: The Codification of Intimacy* (Cambridge: Polity Press, 1986); Eva Illouz, *Consuming the Romantic Utopia: Love and the Cultural Contradictions of Capitalism* (Berkeley: University of California Press, 1997).

6. For a description and analysis of the differences between romantic, or "movie" love, and real, adult, practical love, see Ann Swidler, *Talk of Love: How Culture Matters* (Chicago, IL: Chicago University Press, 2003), 111–134.

7. For a description and analysis of the impact of globalization on love and intimacy and the emergence of "world families," see Ulrich Beck and Elisabeth Beck-Gernsheim, *Distant Love* (Cambridge: Polity, 2014).

8. For a discussion of infatuation as a dimension of unconnected love, see Scheff, *What's Love Got to Do with It?* 114–116.

9. This exemplifies the complex connection between meaning and action that was discussed in chapter 2.
10. See Swidler, *Talk of Love*, 4–40, 71–88.
11. Weber's concept of life chances is mixed up with his concepts of lifestyles and life conduct. See Thomas Abel and William Cockerman, "Lifestyle or Lebensfhührung? Critical Remarks on the Mistranslation of Weber's 'Class, Status, Party,'" *The Sociological Quarterly* 34.3 (1993), 551–556. He undoubtedly linked life chances to class situation, that is, the "shared typical probability of procuring goods, gaining a position in life, and finding inner satisfaction." Max Weber, *Economy and Society*, ed. Guenther Roth and Claus Wittich (Berkeley: University of California Press, 1978), 302. In other words, the ability of people to fulfill their needs, interests, and pleasures depends primarily on their wealth, their skills, and other cultural assets, which, for Weber, meant their social class or market position. Following Darhendorf, it is probably best to see Weber's notion of life chances as the likelihood of the occurrence of certain events, that is, satisfying one's interests, being dependent on a number of different economic, social, and cultural conditions, including income, property, norms, rights, power of command, and so forth. What is important, however, is that for Weber, life chances are not the attributes of individuals, but rather that individuals have life chances and their lives are about how they respond to these chances. See Ralf Dahrendorf, *Life Chances* (Chicago, IL: Chicago University Press, 1979), 29.
12. Weber emphasized the crucial role new ideas have in changing the direction of how people live their lives and fulfill their interests. He argued that while human interests are almost universally similar, the way in which these interests were fulfilled depended on ideas, and that new ideas and beliefs about life could switch the ways in which people fulfilled these interests. "Not ideas, but material and ideal interests directly govern men's conduct. Yet very frequently the 'world' images that have been created by 'ideas' have, like switchmen, determined the tracks along which action has been pushed by the dynamic of interest." Max Weber, "The Social Psychology of the World Religions," *From Max Weber: Essays in Sociology*, ed. H. H. Gerth and C. Wright Mills (New York: Oxford University Press, 1946), 280.
13. See Pat O'Connor, *Friendships between Women: A Critical Review* (Hemel Hempstead: Harvester Wheatsheaf, 1992); Lynn Jamieson, *Intimacy: Personal Relations in Modern Societies* (Cambridge: Polity, 1988).
14. Swidler, *Talk of Love*, 87.
15. Swidler, *Talk of Love*, 136–146.
16. It may well be, of course, that there were such calculations by others and that they were part of their motivations, but they were not revealed or presented in the interview.
17. Parsons developed a detailed analytical model of love in which he made distinctions between universal and particular love and, within these, between specific and diffuse. When love is universal it can be diffuse, such as the love of God or mankind, or it can be specific such as the love of fellow

Christians, soccer, or dogs. One the other hand, when it is particular and specific it can be the affection for a particular soccer team (as long as one has no instrumental interest through betting or having to pay in). Finally, affection can be particular and diffuse as in the ideal type of romantic love when a range of "cathectic-expressive" interests are realized through a love object. Talcott Parsons, *The Social System* (New York: The Free Press, 1951), 86–87.

18. The question, of course, is to what extent a deep, passionate, loving relation between two people enables or disables a more generalized love, care, and concern for others, see Inglis, *Love*, 102–108.

19. Alexa Albert and Kris Bulcroft, "Pets, Families and the Life Course," *Journal of Marriage and the Family* 50 (1988), 543–552; Erika Friedman and Sue Thomas, "Health Benefits of Pets for Families," *Marriage & Family Review* 8.3/4 (1985), 191–203.

20. Pat Sable, "Pets, Attachment, and Well-Being across the Life Cycle," *Social Work* 40.3 (1995), 334–341.

21. Clifford Geertz, "Religion as a Cultural System," in *Interpretation of Cultures* (New York: Basic Books, 1973), 89.

APPENDIX

1. Barney Glaser and Anselm Strauss, *The Discovery of Grounded Theory* (New York: Aldine 1967); Anselm Strauss and Juliet Corbin, *Basics of Qualitative Research: Grounded Theory Procedures and* Technique, 2nd ed. (London: Sage, 1998). Fowler points out the Bourdieu's method comes very close to the grounded-theory approach. Boudieu insisted that the researcher should never raise questions that do not come from the respondent her/himself. The aim of the researcher is to listen and develop a knowledge of the respondent's worldview, frameworks of thought, assumptions, and hopes. Bridget Fowler, "An Introduction to Pierre Bourdieu's 'Understanding,'" *Theory, Culture & Society* 13.2 (1996), 12.

2. Paddy Timmons has developed "richer cultural understanding" of friendship. He is integrated into "a wider community of discourse." He is practiced at formulating his understanding of friendship and he has developed an elaborate code of words and expressions for doing so. See Ann Swidler, *Talk of Love: How Culture Matters* (Chicago, IL: University of Chicago Press, 2001), 52.

INDEX

INDEX

241

class. *See* social class

colleagues. *See* workmates

Collins, Randal
micro-sociology, 214n30

community, 9–10, 13, 57

confession, 12, 125, 147, 151, 201

Confirmation, 2, 5, 11

consumer capitalist society, xiv, 6, 13–14, 66, 71, 85, 107, 157

context of action. *See* action

Cooke, Maeve
the good society, 228n4

Cooley, Charles, H.
looking glass self, 210

counselling, 55, 61, 75

craic, 33, 57, 69, 70, 73–4, 98–9, 100, 119, 129

Cronin, Mike
sport and identity, 231n20

Crowley, Ethel, 223n8

cultural
actor, 15, 17–18, 24, 27, 32, 181, 212n13, 212n17
capital (*see* capital)
codes, 27, 33–4, 65, 183, 202, 216n38, 219n58, 225n1
contexts, 13, 32–4, 65, 178, 218n53, 219n61, 225n1, 225n2, 227n10
entrepreneur, 98
frames, 6
ingredients, 6, 13, 26, 32, 34, 37, 39, 123, 139, 156, 160, 164, 167, 182–4, 187, 191
products, 7
repertoire(s), xiv, 6, 56, 7, 84, 98, 103, 107, 120, 160, 167, 184, 188–9, 191, 201, 227n10
resources, 31, 126, 130
skills, 25, 27
strategies, 2, 9, 11, 24, 26–9, 32, 36, 45, 56, 71, 84, 92, 94, 110, 118, 130, 160–1, 164, 167, 173, 184, 190–1, 215n36, 216n41, 225n1, 227n10, 230n11

style, 6, 25, 36, 56, 65, 68, 71, 160, 167, 184, 217n42

culture
as blueprint, 22
as bricolage, 24
as coherent, 225n1
contradictory, 6, 34, 123, 130, 143, 148, 184–5
definition, 213n19, 213n20
as diversified and contested, 22, 56
of drugs, 55–7
as embodied, 13–15, 26, 47, 62, 90, 101, 141, 146, 156, 213n20, 216n39, 222n2, 226m9, 227n10, 230n10
and emotions and moods, 23–4, 38
frames of thought, 6, 130, 184
and gift-giving, 27, 29, 45, 118, 214n29, 215n37
and goals, 19, 23–8, 183, 192
as habitual, 10, 26, 56, 188
inconsistent, 6, 185, 225n1
indifference, 218n51
influence of institutions, 215n36
Irish, 6–7, 8–14, 22, 32, 59–60, 120–1, 167, 184, 187, 201, 203, 207n4, 207n9
local, 20, 42–4, 56, 113–14, 182
making use of, 6, 15, 24, 38, 77–8, 81, 84, 97, 182, 184–5, 207, 215n31
national, 182, 184
as open, 6
and power, 28–30, 66–7
as a reservoir, 25
as second nature, 14, 22, 44, 139, 226n9
settled and unsettled, 10, 23, 32, 89, 98, 190, 214n27, 217n45, 229n6
as shaped, 37, 225n1
shaping interests, 23
as shared, 8, 20, 34, 57, 212n12, 215n36, 214n45, 218n56, 219n60, 225n2
skeptical beliefs, 32, 101–4, 131–2, 185, 218n51

methodology—*Continued*
 phenomenological approach, 211n10
 positivistic approaches to research,
  219n61
  social demographic profile, 197
 validity and reliability, 7
micro-macro levels of analysis, xiii, 37
miracles. *See* religion
miscarriage, 5
mobile lives, 42–3, 222n6
money
 and church, 5
 importance of, 70, 72–3, 76, 189
 interest in, 29
 unimportance of, 72, 77
 worries, 3, 73
moods and motivations, 17, 19, 39, 89,
  123, 124, 182
 in Irish culture, 219n60
Morgan, David
 definition of family, 224n16
mother(s)
 and Catholic culture, 9, 11, 12, 13,
  27, 48–51, 53, 60, 80, 112, 163,
  165, 174, 177
 conception as good, 11
 and daughter differences, 13–14
 devotion to, 48, 50–2
 stay at home, 2, 80
Muslim. *See* religion

natural science
 difference from social science, 20–1
neighborhood. *See* place
neighbors, 14, 17, 48, 172, 183

objectivity, xii, 20, 36
 and understanding, 21–2
 and validity, 22
OECD (Organisation for Economic
  Co-operation and
  Development), 67, 76
Our Lady. *See* religion

Parsons, Talcott
 action as value-driven, 218n49

analytic model of love, 236n17
epistemology, 211n10
 and Schutz, 211n10
 understanding reality, 221n67
participants. *See* methodology
Peace, Adrian
 domains of belonging, 222n4
pets, 52–3, 69, 129, 174–7, 199
phenomenological understanding,
  211n10
photographs, 8
 and family, 41, 45, 224n17
place, xiv
 attachment to, 185, 223n10
 "blow-ins," 43
 as community, 57
 as domains, 222n4
 "elective belonging," 223n9
 embodied memory, 41
 and family, 43
 flat complexes, 49
 as home, 223n8
 homesickness, 48
 and identity, 43
 local, 42, 182
 as meaningful space, 41, 57
 structured relations within, 42
 and time, 42
 traditional communities, 42
plausibility structure. *See* culture
pleasure(s), 12–13, 22, 26–7, 45, 74,
  84, 124, 164, 191
 of sport, 107, 111, 114, 117, 119, 121
politics, xiv, 3, 113, 190
 alternative form of religion, 97–8
 civil society, 97
 clientalist approach, 93, 98
 community activists, 101, 113
 conviction, 102
 and corruption, 230n13
 democracy (attitudes to), 229n7
 environmental, 97–8
 and family, 92–4
 field of, 65–6, 92
 game of, xiv, 94, 98–9, 103, 105
 gay and lesbian, 96

250   **I N D E X**

generalized other, 21, 213n22
knowledge of the world, 212n14
logic of practice, 21–2
making actors in puppets, 213n18
meaning, 38–9
and methodological
listening, 220n63
phenomenological
approach, 211n10
postulate of adequacy, 21, 212n17
and reality, 221n68
researching, 219n62
and science, 212n14
and self-presentation, 202
sociological approach, 7–8, 20–1,
38–9
typifications, 21
use of analytical concepts, 214n30,
221n67
validity of interpretation, 7, 212n17
unemployment
stress of, 79

Weber, Max
conception of culture, 226n5
definition of culture, 213n19
human interests, 216n40
ideal types of action, 210
ideas as switchmen, 214n28,
216n40, 236n12
interpretation of action, 212n17
irrational action, 210n6
life chances, 236n11
motives for action, 210n7
webs of meaning, 6, 10, 65, 121,
182–3, 191
basis of, 18
changes in structure, 156
complexity, 6, 20, 33
conflicting demands, 66–7
context, 65, 183
core, 186, 191
emotional, 55–9
families, 44–5, 54, 55–9, 61–2,
167, 171

flexible, transposable and
adaptable, 13
fragility of, 18, 155, 170
image of, 181, 183
interweaving, 33, 172
life chances, 170
memory, 47
moving in and between, 183
occupations, 66
place, 41, 43, 47, 69
politics, 87, 185
power relations, 66, 87
reconstruction, 56, 170
religious, 123, 130
shops, 69
skilfully constructed, 183
social fields, 65, 67, 183
social order, 33, 181
socialization into, 23
sport, 121
strong and weak, xiv, 30–2, 156,
183, 186
structural realist analyses, 228n3
and structural transformations, 186
studying, 38
variety, 20
work, 74
see also meaning
Willis Paul
schooling, 227n14
women
emancipation of, 11
less dependent on church, 9, 11
married in labor force, 208n17
see also mothers
work life, 67, 75, 84
enjoyment of, 68–73, 78, 81, 84, 96
working class life, 56, 79, 114
see also culture, social class
work-life balance, 67–8, 70
symbiotic relationship, 71
workmates, 48–9, 75, 112
Wouters, Cas
informalization, 209n24

youth projects, 56–7